CHRISTMAS
ON THE
AMERICAN FRONTIER

Christmas
on the
American Frontier
1800-1900

By

JOHN E. BAUR

ILLUSTRATED BY CHARLES McLAUGHLIN

THE CAXTON PRINTERS, LTD.
CALDWELL, IDAHO
1961

Republished by Omnigraphics ● Penobscot Building ● Detroit ● 1993

© 1961 BY
THE CAXTON PRINTERS, LTD.
CALDWELL, IDAHO

Library of Congress Cataloging-in-Publication Data

Baur, John E.
Christmas on the American frontier, 1800–1900 / by John E. Baur.
  p. cm.
Includes bibliographical references and index.
Originally published: Caldwell, Idaho : Caxton Printers, 1961.
ISBN 1-55888-171-9 (lib. bdg. : alk. paper)
1. Christmas—West (U.S.)—History. I. Title.
GT4986.W47B38   1993
394.2'663'0978—dc20   93-8918
                                                          CIP

This book is printed on acid free paper meeting the ANSI Z39.48 Standard. The infinity symbol that appears above indicates that the paper in this book meets that standard.

Printed in the United States of America

For
John W. and LaRee Caughey
whose Western Christmas cards inspired this
volume and whose basic Christianity is revealed
in a thousand ways

A Few Words of Appreciation

LIKE Christmas shopping at its best, the research on this book was much more a labor of love than a duty-bound chore, but also similar to the hectic holiday season rush, much footwork was involved. The kindness and help of friendly folk in various libraries made lighter the wear and tear on both shank's mare and a pair of myopic eyes. I am especially grateful to the staffs of the Los Angeles Public Library, the Los Angeles County Museum, the library of the University of California at Los Angeles and that of the University of Southern California, the Henry E. Huntington Library, the Bancroft Library at the University of California, Berkeley, the California State Library in Sacramento, the Pasadena Public Library, and the New York Public Library.

Among the individuals not officially connected with the institutions mentioned above, I owe a great deal to the friendship and generosity of Dr. and Mrs. John W. Caughey who gave so much time and consideration to suggesting changes in the manuscript. In a similar vein, my parents, Edward S. and Mary Louise Baur, read and criticized the potential book, and along with my aunt, Ellen E. Ries, gave that motive power invaluable for any historical or literary pursuit—more encouragement than at the time of endeavor seemed deserved.

Dr. Charles McLaughlin of the Division of Science, Los Angeles County Museum, ably illustrated this book, and he deserves abundant thanks for bringing to life pictorially the events and individuals so long gone. I also want to thank Mr. Robert C. Clark, another of my colleagues at the Los Angeles County Museum, where he is Staff Artist, for his work and advice on the original layout of two of Dr. McLaughlin's pen-and-ink pictures. The imagination and accuracy of these two have enhanced the volume considerably.

Quotations from eyewitnesses to important events are, of course, another form of illustration, and many of these have been used in this book. They appear through the kindness and courtesy of the following publishers, whose permission to use appropriate excerpts I deeply appreciate.

Biobooks: Ida Pfeiffer. *A Lady's Visit to California, 1853*, republished in 1950, p. 68.

Bobbs-Merrill Company, Inc.: Homer W. Wheeler. *Buffalo Days: Forty Years in the Old West*, 1925, p. 326.

California Historical Society: Charles L. Camp. *James Clyman: American Frontiersman*, 1928, p. 239.

University of California Press: Herbert Eugene Bolton. *Fray Juan Crespi, Missionary, Explorer on the Pacific Coast, 1769-1774*, 1927, pp. 258-59; *Diary of Nelson Kingsley*, ed. Frederick J. Teggart ("Publications of the Academy of Pacific Coast History," Vol. III, No. 3), 1914, p. 163; and William H. Brewer, *Up and Down California in 1860-1864*, ed. Francis P. Farquhar, 1949, pp. 20 and 359.

Society of California Pioneers *Quarterly:* Anson S. Blake. "An

Early Day California Letter from Charles T. Blake," VII (March, 1930), p. 25; and William Wellington White, "An Autobiography," IV (December, 1927), p. 211.

The Arthur H. Clark Company granted permission to quote from five of its publications; acknowledgement is given in the text at the end of each excerpt.

Colorado Historical Society: E. Shelton. "The Religious Side of Pioneering in Routt County," *Colorado Magazine*, VII (November, 1930), pp. 237-38.

Columbia University Press: J. Goldsborough Bruff. *Gold Rush: The Journals, Drawings, and Other Papers of J. Goldsborough Bruff*, ed. Georgia Willis Read and Ruth Gaines, 1944, II, pp. 673-75.

Denver Public Library: *Zebulon Pike's Arkansaw Journal*, eds. Stephen Harding Hart and Archer Butler Hulbert, 1932, I, pp. 146-47; and *Where Rolls the Oregon*, ed. Archer Butler Hulbert, 1933, pp. 212-13.

Edward Eberstadt and Sons: *The Journals and Letters of Major John Owen*, eds. Seymour Dunbar and Paul C. Phillips, 1927, I, p. 90.

Harper and Brothers: Elizabeth B. Custer. *Tenting on the Plains; or, General Custer in Kansas and Texas*, 1915, p. 155.

Houghton Mifflin Company: *The Journals of Lewis and Clark*, ed. Bernard De Voto, 1953, pp. 74, 294-95; and *A Yankee Trader in the Gold Rush: The Letters of Franklin A. Buck*, comp. Katherine A. White, 1930, p. 210.

Hudson's Bay Company Record Society: *Peter Skene Ogden's Snake Country Journals, 1824-25 and 1825-26*, ed. E. E. Rich, 1950, p. 7.

Kansas Historical Society: "German-Russian Settlements in Ellis County," *Collections*, XI (1909-10), p. 518; and "A Southerner's Viewpoint of the Kansas Situation, 1856-1857," ed. William Stanley Hoole, *Kansas Historical Quarterly*, III (May, 1934), p. 153.

Alfred A. Knopf, Inc.: Louise Amelia Knapp Smith Clappe. *The Shirley Letters from the California Mines, 1851-1852*, ed. Carl I. Wheat, 1949, pp. 51-52 and 103-4.

Ladies Home Journal: William R. Lighton. "Christmas When

the West Was Young," XXX (December, 1913), pp. 12 and 64; and Francis E. Leupp, "How the Indians Spend Christmas," XXIV (December, 1906), p. 18.

Lakeside Press: Charles Larpenteur. *Forty Years a Fur Trader on the Upper Missouri,* ed. Milo Milton Quaife, 1933, pp. 135-36.

Minnesota Historical Society: *Military Life in Dakota: The Journal of Philippe Régis de Trobriand,* ed. Lucile M. Kane, 1951, p. 194.

Missouri Historical Society: Alfred S. Waugh. *Travels in Search of the Elephant,* ed. John Francis McDermott, 1951, p. 77.

Montana State University Press: David Thompson. *David Thompson's Journals Relating to Montana and Adjacent Regions, 1808-1812,* ed. M. Catherine White, 1950, pp. 74 and 190.

New Mexico Historical Review: "Notes and Documents: Letters of Rev. Jacob Mills Ashley, 1887-1888" XXIV (April, 1949), p. 158.

University of New Mexico Press: George C. Sibley. *The Road to Santa Fe,* ed. Kate L. Gregg, 1952, p. 134.

North Dakota Historical Society: "The Diary of Surgeon Washington Matthews," ed. Ray H. Mattison, *North Dakota History,* XXI (January, 1954), pp. 28-29.

University of Oklahoma Press: *A Pathfinder in the Southwest: The Itinerary of Lieutenant A. W. Whipple,* ed. Grant Foreman, 1941, page 171; and *William Bollaert's Texas,* ed. W. Eugene Hollon and Ruth Lapham Butler, 1956, p. 293.

The Old West Publishing Company: Warren S. Ferris. *Life in the Rocky Mountains,* ed. Paul C. Phillips, 1940, p. 238.

Oregon Historical Society: *Journal of a Trapper: Nine Years in the Rocky Mountains, 1834-1843,* 1950, pp. 114-15.

University of Pennsylvania Press: Garret W. Low. *Gold Rush By Sea,* ed. Kenneth Haney, 1941, p. 17.

Riverside Press: *The Diary of a Forty-Niner,* ed. Chauncey L. Canfield, 1928, pp. 127-28.

Charles Scribner's Sons: Hudson Stuck. *Ten Thousand Miles With a Dog Sled*, 1914. p. 189.

Smithsonian Institution: Rudolph Friederich Kurz. *Journal . . . During the Years 1846 to 1852*, trans. Myrtis Jarrell and ed. J. N. B. Hewitt ("Bureau of American Ethnology Publications," Bulletin 115.), 1937, p. 250.

South Dakota Historical Society: Joy Keve Hauk. "The Story of Gus and Jessie McGaa Craven," in *Collections*, XXVII, 1954, p. 539.

Southwestern Historical Quarterly; Texas State Historical Association: William A. McClintock. "Journal of a Trip Through Texas and Northern Mexico in 1846-1847," XXXIV (January, 1931), p. 249; Harriet Smither, ed. "Diary of Adolphus Sterne," XXXV (July, 1931), p. 80; and R. L. Biesele, "Prince Solms's Trip to Texas, 1844-1845," XL (July, 1936), p. 20.

Mr. Walter G. Staley of Mexico, Missouri: Ulla Staley Fawkes. *The Journal of Walter Griffith Pigman*, 1942, p. 49.

University of Texas Press: *Gustav Dresel's Houston Journal: Adventures in North America and Texas, 1837-1841*, trans. Max Freund, 1954, pp. 41 and 90.

Utah State Historical Society: "The Diary of Lorenzo Dow Young," *Utah Historical Quarterly*, XIV (1946), p. 164; "The Journal of Robert S. Bliss," ed. Mary J. Clawson, *Utah Historical Quarterly*, IV (1931), pp. 127-28; "Journal of Thomas H. Haskell," ed. Juanita Brooks, *Utah Historical Quarterly*, XII (1944), p. 88; and also "Journal of Captain Albert Tracy, 1858-1860," *Utah Historical Quarterly*, XIII (1945), pp. 79-80.

Harr Wagner Publishing Company: Herbert Bashford and Harr Wagner. *A Man Unafraid: The Story of John C. Frémont*, 1927, p. 200.

University of Washington Press: John Boit. *A New Log of the Columbia*, ed. Edmond S. Meany, 1921, p. 20; Clarence B. Bagley, "Journal of Occurrences at Nisqually House, 1833," *Washington Historical Quarterly*, VI (October, 1915), p. 273; and "Diary of Colonel and Mrs. I. N. Ebey," ed. Victor J. Farrar, *Washington Historical Quarterly*, VIII, 1917, p. 58.

Wetzel Publishing Company: David L. Spotts. *Campaigning with Custer*, ed. E. A. Brininstool, 1928, p. 88.

World Book Company: William Francis Hooker. *The Bullwhacker: Adventures of a Frontier Freighter*, 1924, p. 117.

Mr. Lyle H. Wright, Huntington Library, San Marino, California: *John Udell Journal: Kept During a Trip Across the Plains*, ed. Lyle H. Wright. Los Angeles: N. A. Kovach, 1946, pp. 62-63.

Yale University Press: Chester S. Lyman. *Around the Horn to the Sandwich Islands and California, 1845-1850*, ed. Frederick J. Teggart, 1924, p. 287.

Finally, a word of thanks to those not named who gave a boost to the author's morale along the paths of research and writing. Any errors in this book are the author's, and he hopes they are few so that he may warrant the efforts expended by the above mentioned.

                                                  J. E. B.

Foreword

THE STORY of Christmas on the frontier should be interesting and important to us all, for most will agree that the first Christmas was the greatest frontier in history. The shepherds and the Wise Men were trail-blazing pioneers in the wilderness that was the ancient pagan world. Throughout America's westward movement, too, the spiritual factor was always important, from Columbus, who was named for Christopher (the Christ-bearer) and his first New World settlement, Navidad (the Nativity), to the latest missionary in our Alaskan outposts.

Christmas was always the greatest day on the trans-Mississippi frontier. If no other season was celebrated, at least Christmas was, with long-hoarded delicacies and almost-forgotten joviality. Some pioneers, dogged by misfortune and the vital need of reaching a goal, geographic or otherwise, might fail to commemorate the prime day of their patriotism, the Fourth of July, though such was a rare oversight. But these same men would certainly pause on the trail for a brief Yuletide respite. In that short period, the hopes and best deeds of frontiersmen were often summed up. Christmas might sometimes be a rowdy celebration, but its spiritual nature penetrated beneath the rough bark of these rugged men. Even strangers to formal religion felt the season's mood. Women and children were rare in the first days of the West, and yet Christmas was kept. This is good evidence that Christmas is not reserved for children alone, though a childlike spirit is always indispensable for keeping the Day of Days.

This book does not deal with more than a small fraction of early Western Yuletide celebrations, or does it attempt to cover geographically each minor section of the Old West. Its purpose is not to be exhaustive but to preserve the flavor of a great Western holiday and to show today's Americans something of the spirit of yesterday's pioneers.

Although you may be opening these pages any day of the year, the fact that you have stopped to read them is evidence enough that the spirit of Christmas is in your heart, too. Therefore, whatever the season, a very merry Christmas!

J. E. B.

Table of Contents

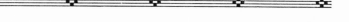

List of Illustrations

CHRISTMAS
ON THE
AMERICAN FRONTIER

CHAPTER I

Transplanting the European Christmas

THERE IS an old couplet which goes, "There are nine and ninety ways to write a song, and every single one of them is good." The same could be said of celebrating Christmas. Each of the North American colonies marked the season in a different way, and each way fitted the needs, spiritual and social, of the first Americans. These patterns were old when they were imported by the settlers, and during the first century or so in the New World they changed but slowly from their European origins.

It may be hard for today's Americans to believe, but the Pilgrims at Plymouth thought Christmas had been much too worldly a holiday in England. Hard drinking and loudly expressed merriment seemed a sacrilege to their severe sect. They frowned on even the most innocent pleasures. Besides, the Puritans of New England had a rival in the Anglicans, members of the established Church of England, whose jurisdiction they had at last escaped by coming to America. To the Anglicans, Christmas was the greatest of holidays. This fact by itself lowered it in the eyes of those who scorned elaborate religious trappings.

Thus it was natural for the Pilgrim Fathers to disregard the twenty-fifth of December at Plymouth in 1620 by working as if it were any other day. Indirectly, though, they marked the day by beginning their first public building. They had landed just four days earlier and could not have lost any time in idleness. Yet even somber Plymouth on a dark and blustery December day was not all heavy with profound contemplation and backbreaking labor. There was one dissenter, one rebel for the sake of merriment. This was Captain Christopher Jones of the *Mayflower,* who had a different outlook on Christmas. He opened a barrel of beer for the occasion, and, it is written, most of the Pilgrims eventually shared it with him.

Still, Christmas was a poor winter orphan throughout most of pioneer New England in the seventeenth century. In 1659 the General Court of Massachusetts enacted a fine of five shillings for the observance of the holiday, and this law was not repealed until 1681, although some broader-minded folk, of a temperament like that of Captain Jones, broke it and played ball and pitched the bar to make the season a little merry.

Oppositely inclined, the Dutch who settled New Amsterdam believed in a jolly holiday. For them Christmas was a double celebration, because this was the day on which a large party of immigrants had arrived from Holland. Thus it was commemorated as "Landing Day." The Christmas of 1625 was observed in new-born New Amsterdam with the old Dutch customs of ice skating, the drinking of punch, and the lighting of the Yule log. Already something new had been added by the adaptable Hollanders;

they dined on turkey, recently brought down by their blunderbusses.

In the Netherlands before they had crossed the ocean, the Dutch burghers had celebrated St. Nicholas Day on December 6, when presents were given to children in memory of good St. Niklaas. Later a contraction of his name would give rise to our own "Santa Claus." After the British captured New Netherland from the Dutch in 1664, the influx of English settlers, mostly Anglicans, gradually influenced the Netherlanders to move their holiday to December 25. Whatever the day on which they celebrated, these people instinctively knew how to keep Christmas gay and light, yet profound in its role as a family institution. Great visitors around each others' firesides, these hard-working merchants, sailors, and farmers must have made a scene resembling those cheerful domestic groups painted by the Dutch masters of the same period.

Farther south, Virginians, under Anglican influence and generally more worldly in their outlook toward holidays than the New Englanders or the Quakers, enjoyed the season in the manner that the Pilgrims so decried.

The Yule log, traditional midwinter ritual followed by the pagan Druids of ancient Britain, was dragged by household slaves into the great hall of every Virginia and Carolina mansion. Virginia, at its first and finest colonial flowering in Williamsburg, the capital, probably celebrated Christmas in a more magnificent and patrician way than any other

American colony. Here, where there was wealth and leisure enough for elegance and the courtly manner which must accompany it, the air of eighteenth-century English aristocracy was imported to Tidewater North America.

On Christmas morning one might expect a large and early breakfast, followed by a fox hunt, indulged in by the gentlemen in powdered wigs, gold lace, and scarlet waistcoats. The crisp and bracing air and the exercise produced an appetite fit for the pleasures of the table which awaited.

Christmas dinner was fashionably early at half past three in the afternoon. And it was a wondrous meal! A background of centuries of good eating and a rich folklore of Anglo-Saxon recipes had become the English heritage of this first frontier. Food was abundant and always varied. Not far from the plantation wild geese abounded. As each large estate used a river for transportation, fish were always nearby, and up that same stream came vessels laden with spices from the Indies, East and West, and familiar foodstuffs from Old England. In came dish after dish, and finally the plum pudding and the mince pie arrived. In later years a wild stranger from the New World, roast turkey, graced the long and well-attended table. Hot toddies were drunk, with rounds of toasts: to the ladies, to the flourishing tobacco plantations, and, with an optimistic touch, to the coming year and all its promises.

Men may change their dress and their tools to fit more appropriately a new land, and adopt fresh jargons to explain their new livelihoods, but last of all do they modify their religion and the ancient ways of keeping its great days. And so it was that the Virginia Christmas, not only in foodstuffs but even in decorations, was Merry England on the Potomac or the James. Here one might see again garlands of English ivy and the holly wreath, which is said to stand for the crown of thorns, its berries for drops of blood. Ever since the Druids had considered it sacred, the English had honored the mistletoe, and we shall never know how many maidens on both sides of the water were wooed and won under its unobtrusive blossoms.

Once they had rested awhile after the hearty adventures of an overly rich dinner, Englishmen of Britain as well as those of the colonies loved their Christmas-time games. Today they seem rather naive pastimes, including as they did such children's diversions as blindman's buff and hunt the slipper, but even sophisticated Virginians sometimes unbent to engage in them. Present giving, however, was not as extensive a custom as it has since become. Usually only sweethearts and children were remembered with special gifts. Yet hospitality was expansive. Even the slaves of the plantation received particular treats. On Christmas Day they eagerly awaited methiglar, a concoction of fermented honey, spices, and water, which the master supplied in abundance.

In the Middle colonies Puritans were rare and Christmas was well kept by Anglicans, Lutherans, and others. Where those of English ancestry or birth dwelt, the season was observed much as it was in Virginia, except on a more modest scale. By 1700 German dissenters from the established church of their rulers had begun to arrive in America seeking religious freedom. They settled for the most part in Pennsylvania and in the great Valley of Virginia. It was they who brought the German Christmas to the colonies, importing the tradition of the Christmas tree, the first of which was supposedly set up and decorated by Martin Luther two centuries earlier. Trees, of course, had been thought to be endowed with spirits by the pagans of ancient Germany, and so the traditional use of foliage in Christian rites was a very old one. Americans received the Christmas-tree custom directly from German immigrants and not from England, where the tree was not introduced until Prince Albert of Saxe-Coburg-Gotha, consort of Queen Victoria, brought it in 1840.

The Germans, to whom Christianity without Christmas and family life without Yuletide were unthinkable, made much of singing and of the giving of presents. For them the *Kristkindlein,* or Christ Child, arrived on Christmas Eve, with presents for the children, and He had no trouble whatever in finding them far across the water in the forested farmlands of Pennsylvania.

As the eighteenth century progressed, the New Englanders came to look much more kindly upon Christmas. Some account for this change of heart by referring to the German settlers, who wholeheartedly gave themselves to the celebration. More likely

Yuletide Sport in New Amsterdam

the Yankees were won over by the fact of the American Revolution. Now their would-be oppressors in church and state menaced no longer, so there was no point in opposing Christmas as a symbol of rejected English ways. Yet, for many years to come, on the typical New England Christmas Day stores remained open and workers had no holiday.

These were the ways of Christmas keeping when America was changed from an ill-assorted collection of thirteen colonies along the Atlantic into a new nation, vibrant with optimism and looking westward toward the Pacific. The English colonies in 1776 still had not adopted the German Christmas tree, or would they for another seventy years. The Dutch, meanwhile, had accepted December 25 as their holiday, but kept their old ways of celebrating it. Yet, wherever there was Christmas, the holiday had two facets, just as it had had in the Old World—the sociable and the spiritual. Of all the ways of observing Christmas, singing seems to have been the bridge between the two roles of the festival and of the two natures of man. Christmas carols had in some cases already crossed the sea. "Adeste Fideles" was centuries old, the Welsh "Deck the Halls with Boughs of Holly" had been naturalized by the English, and France's "Cantique de Noel" was an integral part of the Latins' holiday, but on the whole simple hymns of everyday use were more often heard on this day. It would take more years of Americanizing before the German and the Dutch, the English and the French songs of holiness and happiness would be translated and naturalized as indispensable parts of the American Yuletide.

While the progressing eighteenth century was seeing a gradual reconciliation between Yankee and Yuletide, the frontier was moving from Tidewater to Piedmont, the foothill area close to the mighty Appalachian range. Christmas moved with it. Of course the luxuries of Old England did not reach most of the rugged but humble pioneers of these new western outposts, yet the Yule log and the Christmas candle and other venerable customs of the season were remembered. About the time of our Declaration of Independence, the first settlers beyond the mountains moved into the rich river valleys of what are now the states of Kentucky and Tennessee. There Christmas was observed in log cabin and stockade. The holiday at Boonesborough resembled Christmas at Williamsburg, although the luxuries of fine porcelains, cultured music, and polished manners were absent. In 1775, due to the fears of an attack by the Shawnee, on whose hunting grounds they had trespassed, the holiday at Boone's settlement was "one of grief, anxiety, and tears."

All this area west of the high mountains, from the plains beside the Great Lakes to the warm shores of the Gulf of Mexico, was rich hunting land, where "turkey shoots" soon became traditional preludes to the wonderful holiday season. Every frontiersman, by necessity a crack shot, liked to use the long-anticipated community get-togethers as an opportunity to show his marksmanship, and a turkey shoot provided for both this and the holiday meal. About this time, too, a new Southern custom, that of shooting off firearms at Christmas, began to appear. It would be carried to later frontiers settled by Southerners.

First of all, however, the new West would have to be won against both Indian and British soldier, and so it is not strange that on several Christmases Americans were fighting for their virgin land. Many Americans of today know that it was on Christmas of 1776 that Washington made his famous crossing of the Delaware for a surprise attack on the celebrating British and Hessian forces at Trenton. The Redcoats, both the English-born and the hired Germans, were keeping the day in the traditional manner, and of course they expected their cold and ragged adversaries to be doing the same. But Washington's army, worn by a hard year and with few victories to its record, set forth to give its commander a Christmas present rarer than any others that he might have received. In doing so the men gave themselves a place in history and the gift a soldier most requires, morale.

Two years later in the Old Northwest, George Rogers Clark achieved another victory of the Christmas season, this time over the British outposts in that still largely unsettled country. It was Clark that winter who won much of the present Middle West for the new United States.

America was at war again in 1814, and Christmas of that year found Andrew Jackson holding the approaches to New Orleans and thus the key to the Mississippi Valley. He had less than three thousand troops, some small gunboats, and a few scattered garrisons against a British fleet of fifty men-of-war, mounting over a thousand guns and carrying twenty thousand men. Their commander, Sir Alexander Cochrane, boasted that he would eat his Christmas dinner—good old English goose, no doubt—in New Orleans. Usually ready for an apt reply, Jackson said, "Perhaps so, but I shall have the honor of presiding." Cochrane did not come that day, and Jackson's men were busy throwing up earth fortifications against an unwelcome Christmas visit. A few days later, on January 8, Jackson did have the honor of presiding at the routing of the badly beaten enemy forces on the plains of Chalmette, near New Orleans. The war had already ended, but American prestige was upheld and the West was never again threatened, much less invaded, by British armed might. The treaty which ended the War of 1812, interestingly enough, had been signed on Christmas Eve, 1814, at Ghent, Belgium.

A typical Christmas in the Old Northwest which Clark had won, and of the Mississippi Valley which Jackson's victory had made safe, was described by an Englishman, Richard Flower, who spent the holiday season of 1820 at Albion, Illinois. There in the prairie wilderness this Hertfordshire-born Briton and thirty-one companions enjoyed the festive symbol of the new land, turkey, not to mention their more conventional English dishes—mutton, roast beef, plum

pudding, and mince pie. It may seem unbelievable
to our ears tuned to the fiscal sounds of an age of
inflation, but turkeys could then be had four for
a dollar.

In this pioneer party, as in almost any like group
of that time and region, good musicians and singers
were discovered on the spur of the moment, and
the young people took advantage of the season and
local talent to dance, while "the whole party was
innocently cheerful and happy during the evening."

On the banks of the Ohio, just the Christmas before, another diarist wrote of humbler fare: "I went
one mile and a half, to borrow, from Mrs. Delight
Williams, six tumblers, for the use of our coming
Christmas party. This step was necessary, or our
friends, the Dons of the settlement, must drink out
of tin cups or pots."* Tin and woodenware might
have been all right for 364 days of the year, but
Christmas, glamorized in the Old World, remained
special on this and every other frontier.

---

* Reprinted by permission of the publishers, The Arthur H. Clark Company, from *Faux's Journal, 1818-1820* ("Early Western Travels Series," ed.
Reuben Gold Thwaites, Vol. XI), Cleveland, 1905, p. 300.

CHAPTER II

Noel

UNTIL AFTER the Declaration of Independence, Americans had as neighbors people who for the most part differed culturally from themselves a great deal in small particulars, but very little indeed in fundamentals. The Indians were a special exception. The French were another. The latter had not been far away from the English colonies, as many a pioneer had learned when he took up his musket to fight them in Canada or in the coveted Ohio country. As the manpower of an overseas empire, the French Americans ceased to exist when the French king lost his New World possessions in 1763, but as human beings, individuals with a rich culture, Frenchmen they remained.

Now, as Americans crossed the mountains, moved into the Great Lakes plains and down toward the rich expanses of land along the Gulf Coast, they met many French settlers and came in contact with their customs, already long established. In this way Americans learned to know the French Christmas, *Noel*.

The French of the Great Lakes region were traditionally fur trappers, hardy settlers and traders who had a particular bent for the wilderness, who got along well with the Indians and became an integral part of the landscape. Yet they clung to their French ways. Characteristic of these people when they came under American rule were the inhabitants of Mackinac Island, a rugged dot of land strategically placed between two equally rugged peninsulas of richly forested Michigan. At holiday time the islanders forgot their isolation and prepared for great days. They met in each others' houses, read prayers, chanted psalms, and repeated the litany of the saints. Unanimously they were Roman Catholic and French-speaking. On Christmas Eve as the magic of the season captured them, they all sang and read aloud until midnight.

Then followed a *reveillon,* as they called it, a midnight treat partaken of by every islander. This was the first important feast of the season and no pains would be spared in preparing it. At an open fire, from which rose tantalizingly delicious odors, all the cooking was done, and the result was an unforgettable meal. It began with roast pig, goose, chicken pie, a round of beef, and *pattes d'ours,* which we would literally translate as "bear paws." This delicacy of chopped meat, prepared in a crust, was so named because of its odd shape, which reminded the French pioneers of the shuffling forest enemy most of them had seen and feared. Then followed sausage, headcheese, souse, fruit, cakes, and various preserves made from berries gathered on Mackinac. It should not be concluded that every celebrant ate all these meaty delicacies. No one was required even to sample each of them unless he so chose, but most, accustomed to cuisine without the added taste which Frenchmen love, took full advantage of this wonderful adventure in gorging, and came away from the festive table only after many helpings.

Quietly, Christmas followed the evening of dining and was a simple holy day of great beauty. Not unlike the Puritans of New England, the French Canadians of the Great Lakes country soberly observed the Nativity. Children were kept home and away from play until nightfall, but then at last they had their chance for fun and could rush out across the snow and wish their young friends a merry Christmas. Prayer and song greeted the evening. Although the music probably was no artistic triumph, the homely sentiment expressed was wholehearted and the harmony entirely spontaneous.

Present giving among the French had to wait until New Year's Day. On the previous evening fishermen passed from house to house in grotesque dress, just as their ancestors had for generations on the Bay of Biscay, singing and dancing as they went. Invariably they were received by their neighbors with little gifts.

American officials sent into the wilderness which was Wisconsin of the 1820's soon caught the spirit of French-Canadian Christmas making at Green Bay. Here were two utterly different peoples meeting in a new country, both a little concerned about what the other would think of them. The Americans wanted to establish good relations with the foreign-speaking trappers and fishermen, and what could bring mutual understanding more swiftly than a holiday ball? The *habitants,* as the French called themselves, could not turn down a frolic, and so it was that the dance held in 1824 was characteristic. Colonel McNeil, of the American post there, extended an invitation to the entire population of Green Bay, including French, half-breeds, Indians, and Americans. As a result the meeting hall was filled. At this grand get-together all sorts of apparel could be seen. Here was the finest Parisian dress brought in by ship, birchbark canoe, and pack animal. Next to it a son of the forest wore his buckskin coat, pants, and beaded moccasins, adapted directly from the Indians. As various was the menu, marvelously enriched with rare dishes, mostly of game. These included the finest cuts of venison, bear meat, and porcupine, a dozen varieties of geese, duck, fish, with the so-called king of fish, the sturgeon, heading the bill of fare. At six o'clock the guests rose happily from the table and indulged in some strenuous dancing. Although the revelry was both animated and prolonged, not ending until morning, the guests retired in both good order and good humor. This unaffected hospitality and the resulting good will among men had transformed one isolated outpost from a center of painful solitude and endless sameness into a scene of happiness. The mere twenty-four hours of Christmas Day could not encompass the results, which would be felt for weeks to come.

Elsewhere, French Americans were using their rare ability to combine the devout and the jolly in making

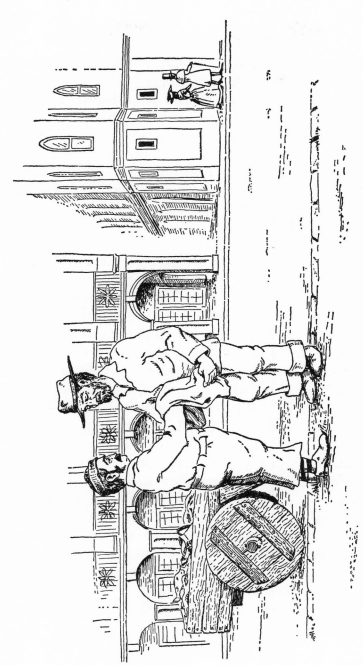

The Creole Nöel Was also Market Day

Christmas memorable, thereby improving life itself. When Louisiana had been founded early in the eighteenth century under the fleur-de-lis banner of Louis XIV, the French Christmas had already been celebrated at least once on the Gulf Coast. In 1686, Robert, Sieur de La Salle, earlier the explorer of the Mississippi Valley, was now lost on the Texas shore. In the midst of his desperate search for the great river, La Salle commemorated *Noel* with special prayers; Mass was celebrated. Again in 1718 the holiday was kept by the founder of New Orleans, the young nobleman, Sieur de Bienville, on the lowlands of Louisiana. With the opening of the nineteenth century, when Louisiana was added to the American Union, the typical prayer, song, and feasting of the Creoles had long since become set tradition. Here among the New World's sights and sounds a combination of medieval Gallic faith and magnificent mysticism mingled with Negro cultural elements imported from Africa in the crowded slave ship.

When, in 1803, American soldiers and government officials arrived in New Orleans to bring the institutions of the United States to the vast area between the Mississippi and the Rockies, they discovered a society far different from what they had known on the Atlantic coast or in the Ohio Valley. At the historic Place d'Armes, later renamed Jackson Square, they saw the spired Cathedral of St. Louis, the newly built Cabildo, with its ornate facade, and, nearby, the open-air markets up from the riverbank. In the square, or *plaza*, as the Spanish who had owned Louisiana for forty years called it, all gathered for the holidays. And here a holiday was a glamorized market day. Negro slaves, colored freedmen, mulattoes, and Natchez Indians came to trade. Filtering through the growing crowd were French Canadians, come down river with their thick, glossy furs to sell. There were Germans, too, and Frenchmen from Paris, chattering alongside the Spaniards fresh from Madrid or Mexico City. One might even encounter on this sunny occasion a peddler from far-off Provence, who, instead of carrying a pack, as a Yankee tinker might, had his many-hued goods spread out in a coffin-shaped cart which he wheeled before him. Some of these energetic tradesmen sold cakes, others "fresh" milk, and there were the equally vivid coffeewomen with their singular hawkers' cries which identified them unmistakably to the trained Creole ear as the shouts sounded throughout the little city of barely ten thousand inhabitants.

Like Christmas among the French Canadians, the Creole *Noel* was a sacred festival. The devout women of the community always led in the religious proceedings. In the Latin tradition, their lives were hedged in by age-old duties, a cloistered atmosphere, and public opinion. Yet they could excel in their world of domestic achievement, symbolized so well by the beloved Christmastide activities. On Christmas Eve the matriarch was in her glory; the family gathered at the fireside, not unlike those domestic congregations of chilly Michigan and Wisconsin, but here in the land of bayous and plantations the sun was warm and life was pleasant all winter. Visitors could look beyond the hearth to glimpse red peppers and oranges ripening in the patio.

The *reveillons* of New Orleans symbolized the wanderings of the Three Wise Men. While younger children were put to bed with whispered tales of the good "Papa Noel," parents rushed to prepare for the day ahead, but such plans did not involve presents, only small decorated cakes and candy. As elsewhere among the French, gift day was *le jour de l'an*—New Year's. A midnight Christmas mass followed the tucking in of the youngsters. Still later that night, Creole ladies engaged in their favorite pastime, dancing. They sang song after song, as if the whole past year had been soundless and no note would trill forth again for another twelvemonth. And they danced the latest steps from Europe as well as the beloved traditional ones. Of course there were games to be played, well-loved ones which they or their family had known in pre-Revolutionary France. Then at last the bell at St. Louis Cathedral rang the hour and festivities ended.

The week between Christmas and New Year's was marked by seven golden days of visiting and an equal amount of kissing, which also might be worth as much as bullion, depending, of course, upon whom one kissed.

Among these Latins, children were inevitably and badly spoiled by their numerous aunts, uncles, cousins, and other relatives, arrived in the family household to bind old ties of love and blood. Thus it is doubtful if the youngsters could be considered un-derprivileged for having missed knowing Santa Claus or never having gazed upon glittering Christmas trees, strings of mistletoe, and garlands of holly.

A Louisiana Christmas was never solely the white man's holiday. It was everybody's special occasion, a sort of birthday, since life in a sense seemed to be-gin anew. Although each shared in it according to his station, at least in that uncomplicated era, every-one did share. It was a long-awaited celebration for the slaves, too. Mrs. Mary S. Helm, who visited New Orleans on Christmas Day, 1828, tells us about the Negroes in their Sunday finery, freed by tradition to do as they pleased until January 1:

I never at one time had seen so many nice dresses, and was told they were the cast-off dresses of their owners of the pre-vious year, and that quite a rivalry existed as to whose slaves should be best dressed during the Christmas holidays. The men equalled, if they did not excel the women, in their shining broad-cloth and stovepipe hats, and as I listened to their pleasant salu-tations and jovial conversation, I changed my opinion in regard to the condition of the down-trodden slave. It all seemed like a fairy dream to me, being surrounded by this strange race in a country where all nature was clothed in summer attire—roses everywhere, with an endless variety of other flowers, and fruits brought from a tropical climate and seen now for the first time.

It was natural for visitors to notice the beautiful, and, as casual onlookers, to overlook the worst fea-tures of slavery, especially at Christmas, when, indeed, even the humblest was happy.

Here, then, was a significant pattern in the huge, rugged tapestry which was still the incomplete fabric of life in the Great West. French technology and political forms would never make much progress west of Louisiana, but the cultural institutions of the French, their social patterns, would be found clear to the Pacific in the days to come. For French trappers and hunters would carry their customs with them to Indians and American pioneers alike, and one of the traditions which Westerners might encounter in some unmapped valley was *Noel*. Of all the patterns for celebrating Christmas that Europeans offered them, the Indians of the Far West probably took best and easiest to the French. It is not difficult to see why.

Just across the river on which stood New Orleans was a vast territory two thousand miles broad, yet untouched in 1800 by any but the explorers and settlers of another Latin nation, Spain. These trail blazers, too, had already added their characteristic Christmas to Western culture.

CHAPTER III

Spanish and Pueblo Navidad

SPAIN, WHICH discovered and first explored the New World, brought its Christmas, *Navidad*, to what would later be the American Southwest. Through the rich mountains and valleys of many-hued New Mexico and the semiarid distances of Texas passed the Spanish soldiers and padres of the sixteenth century. "Glory, gold, and Gospel," the trinity of exploration and conquest for the sovereigns of Spain, caused the transplanting of Latin civilization and Roman Catholicism to the trans-Mississippi West. Dreams of fabulous realms of gold, the mythical Seven Cities of Cibola, and wealth of a hoped-for Quivira, an Eldorado on the Great Plains, stimulated explorations by Francisco de Coronado and his followers in the 1540's. Long before English colonists had established themselves on the Atlantic coast Spain had given up all delusions of rich cities and golden mines in the Southwest. Glory seemed an empty phrase when its realization at best could only be indirect, through paper claims on maps and proclamations. Yet, only two years after John Smith celebrated the first Virginia Christmas on the banks of the James, Spain had founded Santa Fe and established a foothold which would make New Mexico to this day largely Spanish in culture. Indeed, it is the only state that is officially bilingual.

New Mexico had important Indian settlements, far more advanced than any explorers had found elsewhere in what is today the United States. New Mexico remained the farthest frontier of Old Mexico until Texas was finally settled in the early eighteenth century as a strategic foothold against French encroachment westward from Louisiana. There was no gold, and on this isolated bastion of scattered native settlements, as century succeeded century, glory still seemed tawdry. But there was still the Gospel, and this shone out, often triumphantly, as New Mexico's Pueblo Indians and other tribes were slowly converted by the zealous clergy, ceaselessly working to build missions, baptize pagans, and bring a bit of Europe to this nearly forgotten corner of the New World.

The missionaries and the conquistadores imported the first Christmas customs of Castile, Leon, Aragon, and Navarre. There were plays, feasts, and sacred songs to introduce on these strange new mountains and plains. A modern folklorist of the Southwest, Ina Sizer Cassidy, says that the Christmas customs of New Mexico are more varied and rich than those of perhaps any other state. Certainly no other region offers so interesting a series of traditional events, from Christmas Day, given over almost entirely to religious services, to Twelfth-night, when gifts were exchanged.

Gradually the older Spanish traditions were modified by the addition of Indian customs, ingeniously joined to the Christian practices. At the same time local foods and materials supplemented the delectable medley of tastes, views, and noises of the European Christmastide. One practice was to set up *farolitos,* or little torches, and to burn *luminarias.* Children came forth, carrying bags and singing, *"Oremos, oremos, angelitos semos. Del cielo venemos, á pedir oremos; sí no nos dan, puertas y ventanas quebramos."* In other words, "Gifts, gifts, we are little angels. We came from heaven to ask for gifts. If you do not give to us, we will break doors and windows." This was a sort of Spanish-American trick or treat. There was no trick, however, for every New Mexican housewife prepared a supply of *buñuelos,* or fritters, *bizcochitos,* or sweet biscuits, and cookies, pies, candies, and choice fruits. On their way home the well-stuffed children looked for *bandidos* and *abuelos* who might be roving the streets to rob them of their easily won goodies. *Abuelos* were bogeymen who were supposed to get them if they had not been good boys and girls before Christmas.

Everyone attended Midnight Mass on Christmas Eve. There, gifts and money were presented at the altar, ablaze with hundreds of candles. This was the famous *misa de gallo,* or Mass of the Cock. An altar was especially decorated, and a creche stood before it with the figures of Mary and Joseph, the shepherds, an ox, and the faithful little donkey. At midnight the Rosary was sung, and the ceremony was only completed at dawn. Thus it was called a rooster's mass, for it ended with the cock's first crowing.

Christmas morning was merry. A hearty breakfast of meat and frijoles welcomed the new day, and neighbors were greeted by the family at this joyful meal. A little later, young and old went to see the *Matachines* perform in their beautiful dance drama, a fusion of an old Spanish morality play and an Indian dance. Probably *Los Pastores* was also enacted. This latter drama had been handed down from father to son, and thus each family had its own version with slight variations from the general theme.

Today there are numerous New Mexican interpretations of *Los Pastores,* with typical Indian characters added, plus a nearly all-wise padre. With the mid-twentieth century the drama is slowly dying out, although the *luminarias* and *farolitos* have even survived television. The *farolitos* are popular with all New Mexicans, including the "Anglos," for the lights seem appropriate as outdoor decorations similar to the lighted shrubbery of other states. On Christmas Eve sacks of apples, nuts, and candy are suspended, but the children do not sing songs when they pick up these treats, or do they break windows if nothing is given.

Christmas was not limited to those of Spanish blood. Of all the religious days and all the Christian services, Christmas was the most inspiring to the Indians. The Pueblos, who had centuries before built their multi-unit adobes resembling today's apartment houses, had long lived a sedentary life.

Like their Spanish coreligionists, the Pueblos of the eighteenth century and later celebrated Midnight Mass. After this rite the men adjourned to the sacred council room, the kiva. Special persons performed their ancient ritual dance in the plaza of the village. This ceremony continued through Christmas Day. It was usually a buffalo dance, a rhythmic ritual of prayer and thanksgiving for the year just past. At San Felipe Pueblo there is still celebrated at Midnight Mass a dance of about fifty Indians dressed as animals—bison, mountain sheep, deer, or antelope. They enter the mission and perform a dance for about fifteen minutes in appreciation to God for their simple livelihood. The dance is appropriately energetic, stepped to the beat of a cottonwood drum. Then the performers return to the kiva for their prayers.

Living their religion, the Pueblos acted out these special Christmas dances. Since they believed it irreverent to sit in the presence of God, at San Felipe even today, despite the cold floor, the church is crowded with kneeling people. Others stand against the walls. There are no seats. During the buffalo dance, the oldest of the Rio Grande dramas, the deep voices of the chanting men are heard. Ceremonial dances of both men and women are superb and dignified. They maintain absolute rhythm of their bodies in accord with the drums. Usually the women wear long black dresses, knee-length white leggings, and many silver necklaces, rings, and bracelets set with turquoise.

At Isleta Pueblo, near Albuquerque, the drum sounds from the underground kiva. Today, a tiny Christmas tree has been added to the altar of the church, but all still kneel there, too, on the cold floor. Dancers weave their intricate patterns up and down the aisles and gradually dance out of the church. It is Christmas Eve, and man's eternal faith has made his motions as beautiful as the Southwestern sky above the ancient plaza.

Today, as they have for centuries, the inhabitants of Isleta light lanterns and put them on the roofs of their houses. They also set bonfires in the plaza, one in their churchyard, another on the outskirts of the little town, and finally, one on the farther side of the drainage canal. Thus, quite appropriately, the season of Yuletide is called by them "Night fire." On Christmas Day the roofs of many Mexican houses on the road between Isleta and Albuquerque have paper bags set out containing offerings to Jesus.

In Isleta itself, a notable Christmas dance takes place. The Black Eyes, a group of Indian dancers, walk to the very center of their crowded church where a space has been cleared by six men, each wearing a red blanket and holding aloft a candle. A dab of white paint sets off their cheeks. Near the church entrance stands a choir of half a dozen men and the drummer. From that point twelve dancers start their steps toward the altar, dancing in single file, men and women alternating. Then they turn and dance back to the choir and repeat the procession. Finally, men and women separate and stand opposite each other, and this leads to a forward-bending dance step. In changing their position, the men shake their rattles. After this quadrille-like figure, the dancers go individually, first the men, then the women, to the place where the figures of the Mother and Child have been placed near the altar rail, and each kneels in turn and the men remove the *bandas* from their heads and pray.

On Christmas Day itself they dance once more, this time in the plaza. Their makeup and costume remain the same, but now the dancers are given bags of meal, poultry, calico, buckskin, belts, beads, and jewelry by their admiring relatives.

On Christmas Eve at Acoma, historic stronghold discovered by Coronado, the Indians bring their small clay figures of horses, cattle, and sheep and place them in the church in baskets or bowls. These are then put on the floor and the Indians pray to God and St. Stephen. A cross is within the bowl for God. By this ceremony the Pueblos hope to win the multiplication of their animals and crops in the year ahead. The figures are kept inside the church for four days and then deposited in the fields beneath cedar bushes. During these next four days there is much dancing. A buffalo, an eagle, and a Comanche dance are especially popular. The natives wear no masks, for these are not to be mystical steps, but are danced for pure pleasure.

Although these ceremonies were carefully prepared for long in advance, the Spaniards and Indians of the Southwest did not leave us such awe-inspired

documents describing with exactness the scenes of
their ceremonies as did the first Anglo-Americans to
witness them. With the development of the dramatic
Santa Fe trade between the American outposts in
Missouri and the capital of New Mexico from 1821
to the 1840's, English Americans came into contact
with the Spanish West. Their large wagons, carrying loads of two to three tons, were pulled by six
yoke of oxen. The huge wagon trains which set
out in May from the Missouri River usually arrived
at Santa Fe in July or August. Their supplies included drygoods, hardware, and "Yankee notions."
For these almost unheard-of luxuries, the unsophisticated citizens of New Mexico traded silver, woolens,
and mules. This northern possession of Old Mexico
was virtually isolated from the new republic set up
to the south.

The dark-eyed Spaniards of New World birth and
the Indians (who by now had become shepherds and
farmers) might be impressed by Anglo-American
goods, but as the exchange in material things was
great, so was that in cultural affairs. The rough
frontiersmen, months removed from even the simple
village life of western Missouri, were fascinated by
the sample of Latin civilization they had encountered.
Although most of them saw only the dusty, narrow
streets and mud-colored one-story adobe houses, a
few were privileged to view the fine furniture, Oriental rugs, and shy señoritas within. Among those
gringos who stayed the winter in Santa Fe, a few
fortunates became acquainted with a new kind of

Christmas. One Santa Fe trader, George Champlin Sibley, noted that on Christmas Eve of 1825 a fandango lasted all night at Santa Fe, while in other buildings citizens prayed. The next day, he briefly, and not quite accurately, remarked that Christmas was "kept by the People pretty much as with us. Fine day."

In 1846, with the outbreak of the Mexican War, more Americans than ever trudged into Santa Fe. These were soldiers, sent west from Fort Leavenworth by President James K. Polk to occupy New Mexico and then to move on to conquer California. The victory of this Army of the West under Stephen Watts Kearny had been a bloodless one. Santa Fe was occupied on August 18, 1846, and Old Glory was raised over the historic Palace of the Governors, used by New Mexico's Spanish and Mexican executives since the seventeenth century. Without a battle, and with the people seemingly satisfied with the new regime, boredom prevailed after the newness of the occupation wore off. Christmas must have been especially welcome that momentous year. James W. Abert, an American officer of the Topographical Engineers, describes the day:

We endeavored to make our time pass as pleasantly as possible. During the day Captain Fischer's company of Germans paraded in the plaza; they were in excellent discipline and excellent order, and have worthily been dignified by the soubriquet of the "star company." They are regarded with pride by all Americans and with awe by the Mexicans.

The next day his admiration was swiftly transferred

to the native culture rather than the recent Germanic imports. The newly appointed military governor gave the soldiery a dinner at the Palace:

> We had all the luxuries of an eastern table, and delightful champagne in the greatest abundance. Indeed, we concluded it was better to revel in the halls of the Armijos [Manuel Armijo was the last Mexican governor; he had fled before the American advance rather than fight] than to revel in the halls of the Montezumas [Mexico, where other Americans were then meeting much greater resistance], for the latter were poor uncivilized Indians, while the former may, perhaps, boast to be of the blood of the Hidalgos of Castile and Arragon.

The United States Army soon discovered that New Mexico could be not entirely hospitable, for Governor Charles Bent and some twenty other Americans were killed in an uprising. On the whole, however, life was both pleasant and interesting, and disturbances were of brief duration.

New Mexico, on the main southwestern trail to the Pacific, welcomed California gold seekers and army contingents in the early fifties. Surgeon P. G. S. Ten Broeck, U.S.A., was in Laguna, a pueblo on the Rio Puerco, forty miles west of Albuquerque. He recorded in detail what he saw at a church service there at Christmas, 1851. The building was large, of stone, and surmounted by a wooden cross. The long, narrow walls were whitewashed. Three arches above the church contained many-sized bells, which were tolled by Indians standing on the roof and pulling long cords attached to the clappers. Early that morning the Indians began to ring these bells.

After breakfast, Ten Broeck found in the church the Indian men in their best blankets, buckskin breeches, and moccasins, while the women were adorned with their gayest *tilmas*. Many women wore red cloth blankets thrown over an ordinary colored *tilma*. Candles were lighted at the altar, within the limits of which were two old men performing "some kind of mystic ceremony" which puzzled the surgeon. About the same time the Indian governor of the Pueblo of Laguna and the "city fathers" made speeches, and then the congregation dispersed. As Ten Broeck tells it:

As they passed out I noticed that a great many of them carried in their hands little baskets containing images, some of sheep and goats, others of horses, cows, and other domestic animals, and others, again, of deer and beasts of the chase, quite ingeniously wrought in mud or dough. Inquiring the reason for this, I was told that it was their custom from time immemorial that those who had been successful with herds, in agriculture, in the chase, or any other way, carry images (each of that in which he had been blessed during the past year) to the altar, there to lay them at the feet of the Great Spirit.

To Ten Broeck, the most curious and interesting part of the whole Christmas service was the "orchestra":

Just over the entrance door there was a small gallery, and no sooner had the Mexican commenced his rosary than there issued from this a sound like the warbling of a multitude of birds, and it was kept up until he had ceased. There it went, through the whole house, bounding from side to side, echoing from the very rafters—fine, tiny warblings, and deep-toned, thrilling sounds. The note of the wood-thrush and the trillings of the Canary bird, were particularly distinct.

To find out what had caused this effect, he went up to the gallery, and:

I there found fifteen or twenty young boys lying down upon the floor, each with a small basin two thirds full of water in front of him, and one or more short reeds perforated and split in a peculiar manner. Placing one end in the water, and blowing through the other, they imitated the notes of different birds most wonderfully. It was a curious sight; and taken altogether, the quaintly painted church, the altar with its lighted candles and singular inmates, the kneeling Indians in their picturesque garbs, and, above all, the sounds sent down by the bird orchestra, formed a scene not easily forgotten. I believe I was more pleased with this simple and natural music than I have ever been with the swelling organs and opera-singers who adorn the galleries of our churches at home.

This was not all. At four o'clock in the afternoon a party of seven Indian men and many women appeared in the courtyard of the church and began to dance. They had a tombé, used by the Indians at their festivals. This drum was made of a hollow log, about thirty inches long and fifteen inches in diameter. A dried hide from which the hair had been removed was stretched over either end. To one side a short pole was lashed to support the instrument when it was played. A drumstick produced a dull roar, heard at a considerable distance. Elderly men accompanied the dancers and sang in accompaniment to the drum. Dressed in their best attire, both men and women wore large sashes and eagle and turkey feathers in their hair and down their backs. From the waist of each hung the skin of a silver-gray fox. The men's legs were naked from the knee down and painted red. The women's hair was combed over their faces. The ceremony which Ten Broeck described was similar to the one at San Felipe today. The men at Laguna in 1851 carried gourds filled with pebbles, which helped them keep time. Said Ten Broeck, "They dance a kind of hopstep, and the figure is something like the countermarch, the couple leading up toward the church, and then turning, filed back again."

While Ten Broeck had looked with wonder and considerable admiration upon these traditional rites with their splendor of color and rhythm, the simplicity of the faith illustrated, and the talent of nearly everyone involved, his fellow countryman, John Udell, who visited Albuquerque seven years later, was outraged. He s.'id:

Last night and to-da. the Mexicans (Catholics) made themselves very ridiculous in he eyes of us Americans, in their attempts to celebrate the Birth of Christ. At night they claimed to have the Child (Jesus) born in their large Church. They presented the images of the Virgin Mary, the Apostles and many others, to a very large audience of spectators, and passed the ceremonies of having the Babe born in the presence of all, and had persons to talk and act the part of those who are recorded in Scriptures in relation to it. After the ceremony is over, all pay adoration and reverence to these images. To American Christians, it was considered most blasphemous mockery.

Udell had missed the allegory which made Christ and His coming real to these simple people of deep faith.

Another American, a man of God who was in New Mexico a generation later, presents a far more sympathetic account. The Reverend Jacob Mills Ashley found that for nine nights before Christmas the natives built holiday fires in front of most of the houses in their town, just as they do today, and each night a procession of women marched along the street, their leaders carrying an image called *Niño Dios,* the God Child. As they moved they sang of Mary and asked piteously for lodging for her Child. On Christmas Eve the procession, still mostly of women carrying lanterns, came up the street. The Christ Child was lying in a cradle with an arch of imitation flowers over it. As the procession stopped, a woman brought out hot coals on a shovel and knelt before the image, offering incense to it, and then returned to her house. Next, the procession came to a door and chanted an appeal for lodging for the Newborn King. An interior response told them that there was no room. This same performance was repeated at several doors until at last admission was granted, and the Babe was placed on an altar prepared for Him. All then knelt and worshipped, as the shepherds had so many centuries before. This was the tradition of *Las Posadas,* the inns, followed for generations in Spain and its New World colonies.

Meanwhile, at the church, another group sang praises to the Holy Family. At about 10:00 P.M., a young man dressed in full Comanche attire entered and threatened to shoot the image with his bow and arrow! Several worshippers pled with him not to do this terrible deed, and a woman, an actress in this annual fete, explained to him that here was the

King of Kings, here slept the Lord of Lords. Then
the Mexican garbed as a wild Comanche changed his
manner, fell to his knees, and tenderly kissed the
image, then peaceably left the lighted church.

Shortly after that incident, the quiet was abruptly
broken when an Indian woman snatched up the image, and a crowd was soon chasing her. The Child
was finally recovered, whereupon a great dance was
held in celebration. Thus with medieval pageantry,
the elements of suspense, excitement, and considerable beauty, intermixed with all the unexpected out-
bursts of savage natures, the Nativity was celebrated
in the New Mexico of long ago. Missionaries had
introduced the miracle plays and elaborate church
festivities which Indians had modified to fit their
understanding of Christianity.

In a similar manner Christmas was kept in Spanish Texas. Legends connected with the holidays developed among the unlettered people. One attempt-
ing to explain the origin of the margil vine is worth
repeating. Near the Mission of San Antonio de Valero
(later called "The Alamo"), founded in 1718, lived
an Indian boy named Shavano. He was born poor,
but he was also born a dreamer. Perhaps his dreams
could be traced to the time when as a baby on the
Rio Grande he had played the part of the Christ
Child in a Christmas presentation. Now he was about
to witness his sixth Christmas at Valero. Unfortunately, Shavano had no gift for the Holy Infant. He
told Padre Antonio Margil, founder of the mission,
his troubles. He said that he had only a few arrows

and blue-jay feathers and pebbles to give, but Padre Margil told him that love was enough. This did not convince little Shavano. During his moody dreaming one day he saw a little green vine at the foot of a poplar tree that he used as his hideaway. Liking the plant, he dug it up, transplanted it to one of his mother's earthen jars, and then placed it in the mission chapel. There he saw the blankets, furs, feathers, bison horns, and beads given by other Indians as presents. His gift looked forlorn in comparison.

Before dawn Christmas morning, the pageant, *Los Pastores,* began. The chosen "shepherds" walked from mission to mission while "Satan" tried to divert their steps. Over the chapel hung a lamp symbolizing the star of Bethlehem. When the shepherds entered the mission, they cried out, "Milagro, milagro!" Surprised, little Shavano rushed in to see what the miracle was, and with tears of joy beheld that his vine had miraculously grown and twined itself about the crib, its bright green leaves and scarlet berries ornamenting the creche. This plant, the margil vine, still grows in San Antonio Valley and remains the people's favorite Christmas decoration.

First mission in present Arizona, the architecturally outstanding San Xavier del Bac, south of Tucson, has for nearly two and a half centuries observed the Day of Days in the same manner. Here at Midnight Mass, announced by church bells, Indians gather. These Papagos have prepared a crib for the Christ Child, and the figure is carried back to the high altar and placed above the tabernacle. A Papago

The Blessing of the Figurines

choir of a dozen or more voices intones the Kyrie
in Latin. The worshippers may not understand the
words, but their reactions proclaim that they feel
the spirit of the Holy Night. As the Indians leave,
each in the long line pauses to take his turn swinging the crib. Among the Yaqui of Arizona, the same
ceremony prevails on *Noche Buena* (the Good Night,
or Christmas Eve). Shortly after midnight when the
rites are completed, everyone in the church receives
tamales, the baking of which had been contracted
for some time before when one of the village families was chosen for the honored task.

CHAPTER IV

A California Festival of Good Will

FROM ITS beginning, Christmas in Spanish California was well worth remembering. Yet the earliest holidays celebrated within the area which would later become the Golden State were tragic. For example, December 25, 1542 found Juan Rodriguez Cabrillo, discoverer of coastal California, lying upon his deathbed, slowly succumbing to an infection which had resulted from an accidentally broken limb, an injury probably sustained when Cabrillo was exploring San Miguel, one of the Santa Barbara Channel Islands. He died on January 3, and the expedition, under a Levantine navigator, Bartolome Ferrelo, continued the voyage of discovery begun with so much more hope.

During the following two generations only a scattering of expeditions from Mexico touched the coast of California. No more important sailing took place until that of Sebastian Vizcaino in 1602. Vizcaino's exploration of the Pacific shores was to be the most thorough and significant of any made up to that time. Under his direction, California's second Christmas came about, but here again, it was not a time for joyful celebration. Vizcaino and his men were enduring numerous hardships, matching in some ways those of his predecessor, Cabrillo. They had reached the Bay of Monterey, which the eager Vizcaino would earnestly publicize because of its great breadth. There, in a safe cove, they remained from December 17 until January 3 while brief land scouting was undertaken. Yet only frustration awaited the explorers, for it would take over a century and a half for Vizcaino's dream of founding a settlement at Monterey, which he named for Mexico's viceroy, to be realized. In the meantime of cold, hard facts, scurvy was making inroads on his men. Forty of them were already severely ill, sixteen were to die. With nearly exhausted supplies from the long voyage from Mexico, they met "unusual weather for California" on Christmas Day, for the Santa Lucia Range experienced a rare storm of great severity, and the Spanish sailors could see snow on the mountains near their new-found port. By New Year's the water holes were frozen to the depth of a man's palm, and their water bottles were iced. Still, religious rites would be dutifully observed. Confession and Holy Communion were held as usual.

Although Vizcaino had produced good maps and a relatively reliable report on much of the coast of Upper California, his expedition, like the bleak Christmas that he had spent at the site of Monterey, was a failure. His recommendations came to nothing, partly due to his enemies in Mexico. It was not until 1769 that fear of encroaching English and Russian forces on Spain's northern borderlands decided the reforming and enlightened Spanish government to settle and fortify Upper California. As a result,

the "Holy Expeditions" were sent out in the autumn
of 1769. Leaders of the party were Don Gaspar de
Portola, in charge of the armed forces, and Father
Junipero Serra, who would be the founder of the
Franciscan missions. Two contingents had gone by
land, another two by sea; they met at San Diego,
and there the first of what would be a string of
twenty-one missions was founded. That winter Portola's expedition moved north in an attempt to discover Monterey, the long-sought bay, the value of
which Vizcaino had so overemphasized. On the way
Portola's men discovered San Francisco Bay, but did
not recognize the site of Monterey. Disappointed,
in early December they turned south again, toward
San Diego. Father Juan Crespi left an account of
that first Christmas of the Franciscan fathers in California. His diary tells us that since Christmas Eve
was a Sunday, they observed it with two masses.
The pioneer band rested in the Valley of El Osito
(Little Bear) de San Buenaventura, not far from
present Ventura, where Crespi noted:

> More than two hundred heathen of both sexes came to visit
> us in this place, bringing us Christmas gifts, for many of them
> came with baskets of pinole and some fish, with which everybody
> supplied himself, so that we had something with which to cele-
> brate Christmas Day. Blessed be the providence of God, who
> succors us more than we deserve! Their gifts were returned with
> beads, which greatly pleased them.

Fond of decorations, these Indians of coastal southern
California had to make their own beads, laboriously
ground from shell and then pierced and strung. Thus

the Spanish-manufactured glass beads were prefer-
able to the do-it-yourself variety and must have
been a welcome Christmas gift. That day the spirit
of the Nativity was uppermost for this good padre,
who meditated on an alien coast:

> The cold is so biting that it gives us good reason to medi-
> tate upon what the Infant Jesus, who was this day born in
> Bethlehem, suffered for us. We made three leagues and a half,
> and went to stop a little farther to the south of the estuary
> of Santa Serafinia close to a small village of Indian fishermen,
> from whom a great deal of fish was obtained, in exchange for
> beads, with which all provided themselves. So we celebrated
> Christmas with this dainty, which tasted better to everybody
> than capons and chickens had tasted in other lands, because of
> the good sauce of San Bernardo [who was noted for abstemious-
> ness], hunger which all had in abundance. And, there was not
> lacking a Christmas gift of good baskets of pinole and atole.

These latter two foods were made of acorns and
tasted to Father Crespi just like the breast of chicken!
On Christmas Day four years later, Fathers Serra
and Palma saw the new church of the Carmel priests
dedicated at Monterey. This rude structure was built
of logs and had a tule-thatched gable roof. Only
slowly did the sturdy adobe missions with red-tile
roofs with which we are so familiar arise as evidence
of the permanency of Christianity and civilization.

The necessity of finding a land route from Mexico
to California through the Arizona desert and the
plan to found San Francisco led the Spaniards to
authorize Captain Juan Bautista de Anza to lead an
expedition overland to California. His first trip in
order to explore the overland route had been success-

ful in 1774. The next year he set out on his second journey, this time taking along 240 settlers. Father Pedro Font accompanied these pioneers. In his diary is recorded that year's Christmas, celebrated in the Cahuilla Valley. There the party camped on Christmas Eve. Contrary to Father Font's wishes the soldiers, tired from their long, dangerous trek, were rationed their "refreshments." Font, however, did not believe that the relaxation they all merited should include drunkenness. He told the commander, Anza, that this was indeed a poor way to celebrate the birth of Jesus. Inebriation was a sin, and the giving of alcohol was likewise sinful. Despite these serious admonitions, the commander gave his men a pint apiece, but told them not to get drunk or they would be punished! Thus Anza had salved his conscience but not suited the Franciscan father. As a consequence, the people sang lustily and danced wildly from the effects of their indulgence. At least for a few hours they forgot the rugged mountains, the heavy rains, and their tired, sick, and highly temperamental animals, but the realities remained.

That Christmas in the desert was not entirely a mockery, however, for at half an hour before midnight on the Holy Eve a soldier's wife gave birth to a baby boy, Salvador Ygnacio Linares, the first white child born in California. Font had consoled the mother when she feared that she might die. Heavy downpours and the birth kept the party at their camp during Christmas Day, when three masses and the baptism took place. Font's sermon, properly enough, was a condemnation of drunkenness.

By the mid-1770's the missions were beginning to prosper agriculturally. Cattle raising had started to progress. Now the holidays could be celebrated in abundance. At Christmas a steer or bull was usually slaughtered. By that period, too, the childlike neophytes at Santa Clara, San Diego, and other missions looked forward to the Christmas season. As the Indians of New Mexico and Arizona had already been doing for a century or more, they enacted the scene of the Nativity, and he who played Joseph and she who played Mary were especially honored throughout the coming year. The *Pastorela,* an age-old musical piece representing the shepherds of the Bible story, was composed anew by Padre Florencio of Soledad Mission, and this was a great favorite, performed on Christmas Eve.

When, in 1822, Mexican officials arrived in Upper California, they brought merely a change in political personnel, for the Spanish customs of two generations were unaltered. The golden day of the missions, however, was ending, and the age of the great ranchos was about to dawn. The rancheros, mostly of pure Spanish blood, were excellent horsemen, but they celebrated Christmas much as had the Indian neophytes, though with more understanding of the Christmas story.

Noche Buena, Christmas Eve, meant jollity, plus religious ceremony. During the evening bells rang continuously, as they had at the missions. As night approached, the great rancheros began to arrive at the church, each escorting his gaily decorated *carreta*. The *carreta* was a rude cart drawn by two oxen which were attached to the yoke of the vehicle by their horns. The plodding animals and the clumsy cart moved at about the speed of five miles an hour, yet this was the only means of conveyance known to most Mexican Californians. Usually, the farm cart had no cover, but on this special occasion it was garbed with a canopy of silken bedspreads. The fabric was worked with beautiful flowers, and the fringe served as a screen and reached to the axles. Other *carretas* had as their covering gay *rebosos*, shawls made of Chinese crepe. Flowers and figures were embroidered on these, also. Even the horses, proudest of many a rancher's possessions, and indispensable to pastoral California's civilization, were gallantly trapped out. Their riders wore a short graceful jacket embroidered in silver or gold. Trousers were expanded from the thigh to the ankle, the side seams being open or strung together with silver buttons or clasps in the form of tiny shells. Before the 1830's many rancheros still wore knee-breeches and *botas*, the latter being leather leggings, the ancestors of our Western cowboys' chaps. Unlike chaps, however, *botas* were fastened at the top by a wide, tassled garter.

At Christmas, too, the best horses were brought out. Saddles of black or red with stamped floral designs were displayed. Headstall and reins were mounted with silver, making the riding equipment worth hundreds or even thousands of dollars.

Everyone knew everyone else at one of these Christmas fetes, and many families were closely related by blood and marriage, for Mexican California was medieval and feudal in many ways. Like Europeans of the Middle Ages, these *Californios* always loved a pageant.

Most interesting of all their colorful festivities was *Los Pastores,* the pageant of the shepherds, a kind of sacred drama, which we encountered in New Mexico. The main characters were the Archangel Michael, the Devil, a lazy, clownish fellow named Bartolo, and the shepherds. Most admired by the boys and the crowd was the Devil! Next most popular was St. Michael. The Devil, of course, always sported horns, a tail, and the cloven hoof. The *Pastores,* or shepherds, went from house to house enacting the same scenes. The first in their tableaux represented them watching their flocks by night; the second was concerned with the appearance of an angel announcing the birth and calling upon the shepherds to go and adore the Christ Child. Meanwhile, the Devil used sarcasm and tricks to slow or to keep the shepherds from going on their way to Bethlehem. Lazy Bartolo, on his sheepskin, cracked lame jokes, which pleased the unsophisticated crowd. The third scene was in the stable, with the Infant, Mary, and Joseph visible. When the shepherds entered the street the angel and the Devil crossed swords, but the Devil lost. Then Satan chased some Indian boy in the crowd. At the plaza outside the first church of Los Angeles the main scene of the play often took place.

The *Pastores* dined at every house where they stopped. They were generally received with sweetcakes, *buñuelos,* and other delicacies. Here in California the *buñuelos* were fried crisp in grease.

On the adobe walls of the homes that they were visiting these strolling players stuck candlewicks in large vessels of melted tallow, giving themselves light for their next performance. Privileged people on this special night, they had the perfect right to invade courtyards, which on other days, as in all lands of Hispanic culture, were guaranteed to the privacy of the family residing within. Furthermore, the shepherds entered the homes of the *gente de razon,* strictly translated as "reasoning people," but in our jet-age vernacular, "V.I.P.'s." Here they were always treated well, enjoying the fullness of the hospitality of a Spanish home.

At San Jose the shepherds must have had a strenuous evening in 1847, for after a party of about thirty people had waited a couple of hours for their arrival, passing the time by dancing to the strains of a guitar, someone announced that the awaited players were "tired out by the previous performances that day & that their visit at that place would be on the morrow." True to their word, they did appear the next day, dressed in fantastic disguises and carrying staves trimmed with lace and colorful ribbons. Two men were masked as devils with horns; another approached his hosts as a hermit in a gray friar's gown with a wool sheepskin mask; while yet another played the clown, a black wool skin mask

covering his features and a rod with a cowbell
attached to it in his hand; his pocket was full of
"trumpery," as one gringo visitor described it. A
note of the sublime was introduced by a little girl
with huge blue wings, representing an angel. Finally
the performers began their traditional recitations, in-
terspersing their words with humorous gestures, jokes,
and what we today would call Hollywood slapstick.
Altogether, our American reporter, untutored in such
strange rites, was disgusted with the low-comedy
effects.

Unlike the pageant of *Los Pastores,* the *Pastorela*
was a high and more refined show for the Christmas
season. All the crude passages injected into the former were left out, while beautiful, realistic scenes
were added. A particularly appealing one dealt with
the Annunciation to the shepherds, followed by tableaux of combats between angels and devils, and
moving glimpses of hell; even the lack of good
scenery and props failed to blunt the genuine emotions of awe and shock which the players roused.
Alfred Robinson, who had come to California in the
Mexican period and had become a *Californio* culturally and economically, noted that many of the
rancheros had leading roles in the *Pastorela.* For
months ahead rehearsals were held about three times
a week at the residence of Don Antonio F. Coronel,
a leading southern California figure. Fine costumes
and scenery were prepared, and one fete took place
in the old Los Angeles courthouse.

On Christmas morning, the ranch-life theme, in-

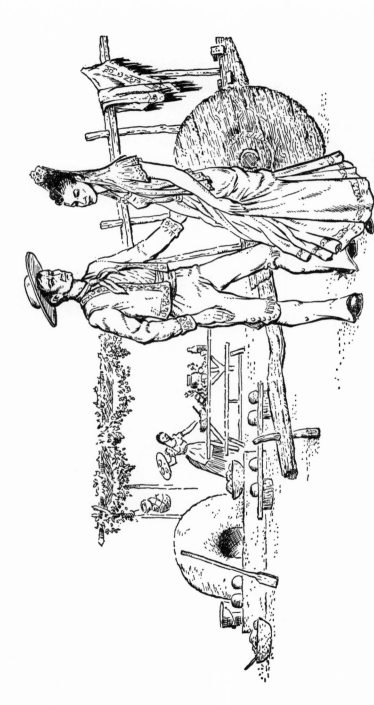

In California, December 25 Meant "Fiesta!"

evitable in a cattle kingdom where "leather dollars" were the daily currency, predominated. Feats of horsemanship were demonstrated, and music, dancing, and games combined to draw the whole people together in a festival of good will.

CHAPTER V

With the Explorers

THE FRENCH and Spaniards of the American West had, by 1800, become settlers in trading post and village, at mission and army camp; for many of them life had grown sedentary and, to some extent, even conservative. Unlike them, the first Anglo-Americans venturing beyond the Mississippi were strangers indeed in unknown country. With little time for self-examination and no moment for self-pity wherever they might be, they used the pause of Christmastide to bring back in memory past holidays enjoyed in civilization. Most of these adventurers were homesick during this brief holiday interlude. Happy memories of comfort, friends, and evident success sometimes made the present seem all the more miserable and the coming days appear the bleaker. On the other hand, explorers usually got inspiration from Christmases past and the spontaneous friendship of their fellows in the Christmas of here-and-now to see their destiny in a better, broader light.

In the 1790's, the new United States stopped at the Mississippi on the west and the thirty-first parallel on the south. Ours was a one-ocean and no-Gulf nation, but already Yankee traders to China and the far Pacific had begun to make the American flag known in the Orient and the South Seas. China's silks and teas, Oregon's sea otter and beaver, and the strange treasures of Hawaii enticed them westward. One of these intrepid New Englanders was Captain Robert Gray, and his ship, the first American vessel to sail around the world, was called the *Columbia*. Hunting for the breeding grounds of the sea otter, Gray discovered the mighty river which was named for his ship. Although Gray's log of the *Columbia* has been lost, his master mariner, John Boit, kept a diary which lets us see how these men spent the winter of 1791 at Clayoquot Sound, located on the west coast of Vancouver Island. Of that Christmas celebrated in the Pacific Northwest, Boit wrote:

> This day was kept in mirth and festivity by all the *Columbia*'s Crew, and the principall Chiefs of the Sound by invitation din'd on board ship. The Natives took a walk around the work shops on shore, they was supprized at seeing three tier of wild fowl roasting at one of the houses—indeed we was a little supprised at the novelty of the sight ourselves, for at least there was 20 Geese roasting at one immense fire, and the Ships Crew appear'd very happy, most of them being on shore. The Indians cou'd not understand why the Ship and houses was decorated with spruce bows. At 12 Clock fir'd a federall Salute, and ended the day toasting our *sweethearts* and *wifes*.

The Pacific Northwest which Captain Gray and other New Englanders found so rich in peltries had also attracted the attention of other citizens of the new republic who sought knowledge of the Far West for its own sake. One of these was Thomas Jefferson, member of the American Philosophical Society as well as author of the Declaration of Independence. As early as the 1780's he was encouraging adventurers to explore the Oregon country. When Jefferson became President in 1801, as always, he looked westward. Even before the purchase of Louisiana he had decided to sponsor the exploration of the Missouri Valley. Setting in motion the organization of an American expedition to the Pacific, he specified that the explorers should take careful scientific note of flora and fauna en route, make way for trade treaties with the Indians, and discover trade routes through the new-found lands. For this task was chosen Meriwether Lewis, private secretary to Jefferson, a man experienced in military affairs on the Western frontier. Lewis was only twenty-eight; he chose as his assistant and partner, William Clark, the younger brother of George Rogers Clark. Despite his thirty-two years, Clark was already a man of practical accomplishments and frontier service.

During the summer of 1803 the expedition sailed down the Ohio River for St. Louis, where the winter was profitably spent gathering information from fur traders experienced in navigating the Missouri. On May 14, 1804, the party set out in three small craft, pushing up the Missouri, already being trapped by energetic American and Canadian fur men. By October they were in the land of the friendly Arikara tribe of present-day South Dakota. Later that month Lewis and Clark selected winter quarters near present Bismarck, North Dakota, in the land of the Mandans. By that date they were 1,600 miles up the Big Muddy.

In log houses of their stockade camp where they would remain for five months, the two young leaders and their twenty-odd companions observed their first wilderness Christmas.

25th December Christmass Tuesday—I was awakened before Day by a discharge of 3 platoons from the Party and the french [boatmen], the men merrily Disposed, I give them all a little Taffia [rum] and permited 3 Cannon fired, at raising Our flag, Some Men Went out to hunt & the others to Danceing and Continued untill 9 oClock P.M. when the frolick ended &c.

Thus wrote Captain Clark. Sergeant John Ordway was impressed first of all that the day was cloudy and next that

we fired the Swivels at day break & each man fired one round. our officers Gave the party a drink of Taffee. we had the Best to eat that could be had, and continued firing danceing & frolicking dureing the whole day. the Savages did not Trouble us as we had requested them not to come as it was a Great Medician day with us. We enjoyed a merry cristmas dureing the day & evening untill nine o Clock—all in peace and quietness.

So passed an unforgettable holiday. The party was too busy to speculate as to where each member might be a year hence, as many other pioneers moving westward later would do. Christmas of 1805, however, found Lewis and Clark's expedition far from the scenes of the previous year. Now they had completed half their trek, and with the loss of only one life. The men, accompanied by the Shoshone Indian girl, Sacagawea, as interpreter and guide, were encamped at the mouth of the Columbia, that mighty River of the West which Gray had rediscovered less than

Exchanging Gifts at Fort Clatsop

a decade and a half before. Wrote Clark at rudely built Fort Clatsop:

at day light this morning we we[re] awoke by the discharge of the fire arm[s] of all our Party & a Selute, Shouts and a Song which the whole party joined in under our windows, after which they retired to their rooms   were chearfull all the morning. after brackfast we divided our Tobacco which amounted to 12 carrots one half of which we gave to the men of the party who used tobacco [no ardent spirits were supplied], and to those who doe not use it we make a present of a handkerchief, The Indians leave us in the evening   all the party Snugly fixed in their huts. I recved a pres[e]nt of Capt. L. of a fleece hosrie [hosiery] Shirt Draws and Socks, a pr. Mockersons of Whitehouse a Small Indian basket of Gutherich, two Dozen white weazils tails of the Indian woman, & some black root of the Indians before their departure. Drewyer informs me that he saw a Snake pass across the parth to day. The day proved Showery wet and disagreeable.

we would have Spent this day the nativity of Christ in feasting, had we any thing either to raise our Sperits or even gratify our appetites, our Diner concisted of pore Elk, so much Spoiled that we eate it thro' mear necessity, Some Spoiled pounded fish and a fiew roots.

Just two months before Lewis and Clark returned to St. Louis, in September of 1806, Lieutenant Zebulon Montgomery Pike, who had previously attempted to find for the United States government the source of the Mississippi, now set out from St. Louis himself. This time his purpose was to explore the headwaters of the Arkansas and Red rivers and to make a peace treaty with the belligerent Comanches. Moving up the Arkansas, Pike and his score or so of men sighted the Rockies. They were in what is now Colorado. Failing to climb the peak named for him,

Pike declared that it could not be mounted, and thereupon sought the Red River.

On Christmas Eve of 1806 Pike's party was hungry and greatly in need of game. Fortunately, four buffalo cows were killed, giving them a fair meal. After the bison hunt, all the men were assembled again that night, and, according to Pike, they

appeared generally to be content, although all the refreshment we had to celebrate that day with, was buffalo meat, without salt, or any other thing whatever. My little excursion up the river was in order to establish the geography of the sources of the [supposed] Red River.

Two historians of our century, A. B. Hulbert and Stephen Harding, claim that this was probably the first Christmas celebrated in Colorado, if not in the entire upper Arkansas Valley. Pike's camp, with its unexpected game which staved off starvation, was on the north bank of the Arkansas, below the mouth of Squaw Creek.

On Christmas Day the party rested and dried buffalo meat. The memories of past holidays haunted them all:

Having been accustomed to some degree of relaxation, and extra enjoyments; but here 800 miles from the frontiers of our country, in the most inclement season of the year; not one person clothed for the winter, many without blankets, (having been obliged to cut them up for socks, &c.) and now laying down at night on the snow or wet ground; one side burning whilst the other was pierced with the cold wind. . . . [Yet] We spent the day as agreeably as could be expected from men in our situation.

The near future brought them nothing to raise their spirits. Amid great hardship, the explorers crossed the Sangre de Cristo Range, and in February built a log fort in southern Colorado. Not long afterward a hundred Spanish soldiers from New Mexico arrested them and forced Pike's party to accompany them to Santa Fe, where his records and other papers were seized. Eventually, Pike was set free and brought back East in his memory many impressions of the virtually unknown Southwest. One of these memories was of that barren Christmas on the Arkansas.

The romance of Western wanderers has always fired the imaginations of adventurous-hearted Americans. One of the most dramatic of all these men on the nineteenth-century frontier was the "Great Path-finder," John C. Fremont. Actually, the important discoveries of Fremont were few; others had trod before him most of the lands he visited, but his knack of publicizing with a powerful impact the things that he did made Fremont a national hero. His five expeditions to the Rockies and beyond in the forties and fifties left for those who would pry into Christmases-long-gone some fascinating accounts of the holiday in the unsettled West. On his second expedition in 1843, Fremont was in northeastern California. His party had come to the south end of another of that area's lakes and this one Fremont named Lake Abert for the chief of the Topographical Corps. It was twenty miles long and found to be quite salty. As the Americans had a hard time getting pure water, they were forced to dig holes near the lake, but even this was difficult work. They retired supperless the first night, and after the next day's two-hour march came finally to a pure, cold spring near the lake where they found some coarse grass. Luckily for them, there were flocks of ducks on this lake, just as there are today. After another day, Fremont moved south, across the plain, which was covered with sagebrush. On Christmas Eve he reached a smaller lake and went into camp, where on Christmas morning Fremont was awakened by the pistol and rifle shots of his men. To make the celebration unanimous, Fremont fired off their howitzer. For a change, the soldiers had something to commemorate — good food. It included meat, a little brandy, and coffee, with that rare luxury which few trail blazers tasted, sugar. For some years this place was called Christmas Lake. The Christmas salute was the last time Fremont's famous cannon was fired until it was used years later in Virginia City, Nevada.

Christmas of 1845 found Edward M. Kern, for whom today's rich agricultural Kern County, California, would later be named, camped with Fremont's third expedition. The adventurers were exploring the Humboldt River-Carson Lake-Owens River region. Wrote Kern of his reaction to that day:

Our Christmas was spent in a most unchristmas-like manner. Our camp was made on the slope of the mountain, at some Indian wells of good water. The yuca tree is here in great abundance, furnishing us a plentiful supply of fuel. The camp-fires blazed and cracked joyously, the only merry things about us, and all that had any resemblance to that merry time at home.

The animals, on account of grass, were guarded about a quarter of a mile from camp, higher up the mountains.

December 25—Christmas day opened clear and warm. We made our camp today at some springs among the rocks; but little grass for our animals. Dined to-day, by way of a change, on one of our tired, worn mules, instead of a horse.

He concluded that they also ate that "swinish food" so popular in the California Indian diet, acorns.

On his fourth expedition, Fremont spent another chilly Christmas. Writing later to his wife, the indomitable Jessie Benton Fremont, he described his doings of the day:

Like many a Christmas for years back mine was spent on the summit of a wintry mountain, my heart filled with gloomy and anxious thoughts, with none of the merry faces and pleasant luxuries that belong to that happy time. You may be sure we contrasted much of this with the last at Washington and speculated much on your doings and made many warm wishes for your happiness. Could you have looked into Agrippa's glass for a few moments only! You remember the volumes of Blackstone I took from your father's library when we were overlooking it at our friend Brant's? They made my Christmas amusements. I read them to pass the heavy time and forgot what was around me. Certainly you may suppose my first law lessons will be well remembered. Day after day passed by and no news from our express party. Snow continued to fall almost incessantly on the mountains.

There are many, many accounts of Christmas humdrum in the years when the Far West was being mapped and trailed and finally plowed, but probably no other record of a celebrant keeping the day with a thick tome of Blackstone! In the San Juan Range, eight days' travel from Taos, Fremont's men dined that holiday on the carcasses of dead mules. One man froze on the trail about this time.

After Fremont's day, general explorations of the West for trail and pass sites ended; most of the routes had been discovered, the rivers followed, and the mountains sighted and conquered. Yet, in 1853, the federal government sent several parties to explore routes for a potential transcontinental railroad. One of these expeditions was led by Lieutenant Amiel W. Whipple. By Christmas Eve of that year Whipple had reached Cosnino Caves in north central Arizona. This was his Camp 89, a sheltered spot on the edge of a forest with plenty of water and grass for the animals. There the group of surveyors decided to rest for three days. At sunrise on December 24 the temperature was 3° below zero. According to Whipple:

Christmas eve has been celebrated with considerable éclat. The fireworks were decidedly magnificent. Tall, isolated pines surrounding the camp were set on fire. The flames leaped to the treetops, and then, dying away, sent up innumerable brilliant sparks. An Indian dance, by some *ci-devant* Navajo prisoners, was succeeded by songs from the teamsters, and a pastoral enacted by the Mexicans, after their usual custom at this festival. Leroux's servant, a tamed Crow Indian, and a herder, then performed a duet improvisated, in which they took the liberty of saying what they pleased of the company present—an amusement common in New Mexico and California, where this troubadour singing is much in vogue at fandangoes. These last entertainments are interesting to a stranger from their singularity. The plaintive tones of the singers, and the strange simplicity of the people, lead one's fancy back to the middle ages. In this state of society, so free from ambition for wealth or power, where the realities of life are in a great measure subject to the ideal, there is a tinge of romance that would well repay the researches of a literary explorer. Their impromptu ballads alone would make an interesting collection.

On Christmas Day, Whipple wrote that the temperature was nearly at zero.

Balduin Möllhausen, a German artist with Whipple's party, gives us an even more moving description of that Christmas Eve:

> As night came on, our company was seated in picturesque groups round the fires, which glowed larger and brighter in the darkness. The cooks were running about busily with their hissing frying-pans and bubbling coffee-pots, some were singing, some cheerfully gossiping, some only wrapped in their blankets and calmly smoking their pipes.

All, however, were relaxing in the warming Christmas spirit, which was about the only tepid thing, save the blazing fire, in that snowy woodland. The next morning opened a glorious day:

> Various dainties that had been hitherto carried in closed cases were brought forth to be eaten up at once, partly with the view of lightening the load of the waggons, but at the same time with an eye to the glorification of our Christmas dinner in the wilderness. When we left Albuquerque, some of the party had bethought themselves of the festive season, and procured a chest of eggs, which, carefully packed, had travelled in safety thus far. Others had brought a stock of rum and wine, and all these luxuries were now produced to do honour to the Christmas banquet.

Möllhausen felt that:

> The marvellous combination of wood and mountain and valley must have tended to remind every one of their Great Creator,

and awaken feelings of devout gratitude. This feeling is closely
allied to those of love to one's neighbour, and compassion for
the brute creation; and there was no one, I imagine, in our whole
expedition who did not at this time sincerely grieve for the
hardship suffered by our poor beasts, who for their Christmas
cheer had to scrape away snow a foot deep to get at the scanty
grass and moss beneath.

All officers had been invited to Lieutenant Johns's
tent and advised to bring along their tin drinking
mugs. Johns had prepared a steaming punch. None
seemed to have previous engagements, and all listened
in good will to the lieutenant's flowery speech, enun-
ciated in this magnificent scene framed by snowy
branches under a deep blue star-specked firmament
into which the fire blazed upward. This is what he
said:

Let us now forget for a few hours our hardships and privations,
the object of our journey, and the labours still before us; and
here, under a roof of boughs, and on the spotless white carpet
that God Almighty has spread for us, far as we are from our
homes, let us think of our friends, who, very likely, are thinking
of us as they sit round their firesides; and drowning our cares
in a social glass of toddy, drink to their health, and to our own
happy return.

Toasts and various jokes, all of them rough but
kindly, followed round the merry circle and echoed
through the once-lonely ravines. Not far away, the
Mexicans who had been allowed a supply of excess
gunpowder, were taking out their celebration in
booming noise. If any Indians had been lurking nearby, what must they have thought of the medley of
Indian chants, Mexican *solís,* Southern Negro songs,

and army ballads of this strange gathering! Most of Christmas Day itself was spent "in perfect quiet, in thinking over past times and our distant homes, where church bells were now summoning all to the religious celebration of the season."

CHAPTER VI

The Fur Men Make Merry

IT HAS BEEN said that the early history of North
America was written on a beaver skin. In a broad
sense this is true. The cleverest and busiest of ro-
dents, though he never knew it, lured to Canada its
first French settlers and stimulated their exploration
by many a route, even to the Great Lakes and farther west. Meanwhile the Dutch of upper New York
and their English neighbors in New England developed new regions through trapping and trading
for the little animal's coveted pelt. This soft and
glossy dark-brown fur, destined for some Old World
celebrity's hat or cloak, was to play an even greater
role in the trans-Mississippi West. Based on the search
for the mountain beaver or his lowland cousin of
the desert wastes, there appeared in the first forty
years of the nineteenth century the remarkable epic
of the Mountain Men.

The Mountain Men! Even the name sounds unique
and powerful, and of such character were the hunters
who won the name by trapping nearly every stream
from the Missouri to the Rockies and beyond. As
no other white men before them had, they knew
the Western mountains, their vital passes, and the
rivers issuing forth from the snowy ranges. The fur
men had trekked the forests and learned the secrets

of their game and plant life; they had scouted the plains in river raft and buffalo-skin boat or had blazed a dusty trail on mule back. These men were the first to unroll the map of our Far West and investigate its last great mysteries. One of their number, Jedediah Smith, who might have been a prophet in another wilderness, had the honor of becoming the first citizen of the United States to reach California overland, while his fellows discovered Yellowstone and Great Salt Lake.

Living and trading among scores of Indian tribes, adopting the natives' techniques of fighting, hunting, and surviving, donning the moccasins and buckskin of the first Americans and most of their earthy outlook on life's meanings, these trappers were often taken for Indians. To them this case of mistaken identity was the greatest of compliments. After all, both Mountain Man and Indian shared a savage bravery. Pure freedom was theirs, and little else really counted. Life might be threatened daily by tomahawk and grizzly claw and its zest a little chilled by avalanche and hunger, yet every peril was but part of the price paid for life as the hunter wanted to live it. The spiritual ancestor of all American Westerners and the first of a long line of trailblazing gamblers, the fur man saw life for what it was, the real prize he sought. To him, civilization was not life. Perhaps once or twice a decade he peered at the settled man's homespun swatch of civilization on the Missouri or New Mexican frontier. This was enough of a look to do him a long time, he told the inquirer with gestures and few words. He did not miss the plow or steeple.

Yet the Mountain Man, unlike the Indian, was allied with white culture through his trade with the big fur companies of St. Louis. Although deeply hidden, he did carry the elements of the culture that he had abandoned. Into much of the West the fur gatherer brought the remembrance of Christmas and a minimum of its practices. If formal Christianity was not introduced by this rugged and fabulous American, at least some of the oddest Christmases ever kept on United States soil were observed in his unmapped winter camps, carefully selected spots away from Indian eyes or prevailing winds.

Christmas at a fur-trading post could be a dangerous proposition. Here the trappers had come for many reasons. The post was a haven against the storm as well as an armed fort and a meeting ground. It was also a place in which to make merry, and for the rough-and-tumble fur man, fun was as dangerous as his livelihood, and sometimes more so. An example was the celebration of 1837 at Fort Laramie, in present-day Wyoming. That post was then still a private establishment and had not yet become a military fort. A cannon mounted on the bastion had been heavily loaded that day so that it could give a grand send-off for Christmas. In order to make the report even louder than it usually was, an old pair of buckskin pants and several moccasins were rammed into the cannon's mouth. When at last the gun was filled nearly to its muzzle

The gunner refused to touch off the cannon, as he said he was sure it would burst. Dave Crow, one of the trappers, and a particular friend of Rose's, took the iron rod from the fire and touched it off, and, as the gunner predicted, it flew into a hundred pieces. One of the splinters broke Crow's leg.

Soon afterward Crow died, for his limb had not been bandaged properly by a fellow trapper whose good intentions did not make up for lack of medical knowledge.

Some of the most lavish celebrations of the early nineteenth-century West could be found at fur-trading posts. One of these places, Fort Manuel, named for Manuel Lisa who had been a prominent Spanish fur trader during Spain's ownership of Louisiana, had been founded by Lisa at the mouth of the Big Horn in 1807. There, at sunset on Christmas Eve of 1812, three guns were fired and whisky made the post loud and lively. On special occasions such as this the fur posts' clerks enjoyed dried-apple pie and the luxury of cream to symbolize the importance of the annual celebration.

When Stephen H. Long's exploring expedition was in the Rockies in 1819 its holiday season was punctuated by the visit of several French Canadians employed by the American Fur Company who came to dance and sing a bit before their surprised hosts. These seemingly wild men were adorned with paint in the "Indian manner, clothed with bison robes, and had bells attached to different parts of their dress. So completely were they disguised, that three of their employers, who happened to be present, had

much difficulty in recognizing them." Their dance
was called *La Gineolet*. Enthusiastically, Long's men,
months removed from any sort of frolic, recipro-
cated generously for the evening's unexpected entertainment by passing out to the visitors whiskey, meat,
and some flour.

At Fort Clark in 1833, none other than a German
nobleman, Prince Maximilian of Wied, come to the
Far West for scientific study, heard *engages* of the
post fire a volley to welcome Christmas. They repeated the midnight firing early the next morning.
To mark the occasion, these French Canadians were
given an allowance of better provisions than the
parched maize, boiled in water and eaten without
fat, upon which they had been subsisting for some
months.

Holiday celebrations in the mountains were usually "taken out in drinkables instead of eatables,"
as one who knew the situation plainly described it.
These grand fetes have been sketched by several
literate fur gatherers and their visitors. Charles Larpenteur, trapper on the Upper Missouri for forty
years, did not drink and therefore missed at least one
Christmas "dinner," that of 1838, which at Fort
Union turned out to be quite a memorable liquid
repast. He comments on the results as follows:

At the height of the spree the tailor and one of the carpenters
had a fight in the shop, while others took theirs outside, and toward evening I was informed that Marseillais, our hunter, had
been killed and thrown into the fireplace. We immediately ran
in, and sure enough, there he was, badly burned and senseless,

but not dead yet. We were not at first sure whether this was the mere effect of liquor, or had happened from fighting; but we learned that a fight had taken place, and on examination we found that he had been stabbed in several places with a small dirk.

The fort's tailor had such a knife and therefore was accused. Silently, he threw it down on the table, and everyone present saw that it was bloody. Immediately, he and the carpenter were placed in irons. Since Christmas frolics, as all Mountain Men knew, "could not be brought to a head much under three days," the trial took place four days later. With as much dignity and legalistic form as the wilderness would permit, witnesses were examined and the verdict of guilty of murder announced. The judge condemned the offenders to be hanged, but since it was not thought safe to execute his sentence, he promptly changed it to thirty-nine lashes apiece! This in itself was severe punishment, since the executioner used a large ox whip with the expenditure of considerable muscle.

Thus Christmas, if not always the spirit of Christianity, was encountered. The amount of homesickness that thoughts of Christmas aroused among the Mountain Men and other early adventurers can never be measured, but it is a frequent and almost standard entry in their recorded musings. Ross Cox, who was among the Flatheads in the northern Rockies at Yuletide, 1821, wrote:

I thought of my preceding Christmas off Cape Horn, and was puzzled to decide which was the most enviable—a tempestuous storm in the high southern latitude, after losing a couple of men—or a half-inundated island, without fire, at the foot of the rocky mountains covered with sheets of snow. In my slumbers I imagined I was sitting at my father's table surrounded by the smiling domestic group, all anxious to partake of a smoking sirloin, and a richly dotted plumb-pudding, while the juvenile members recounted to each other with triumphant joy the amount of their Christmas boxes; but alas! "Sorrow returned with the dawning of morn, And the voice in my dreaming ear melted away!"

Peter Skene Ogden, famous fur trapper for the Hudson's Bay Company, spent his Christmas of 1824 in the Flathead Indian region of Idaho and observed, "Christmas may it be a merry one to all our friends, to me I must confess it is rather dull time no doubt a good *Stock* of merry ones are in Safe keeping for *me*." That day he had seen the tracks of a war party near camp, which may have affected his words more than a little, and beaver trapping had not been successful of late. Yet, symbolic of the day, a child had been born to the wife of one of his free trappers. The following Christmas, spent in the wilds of Oregon, was made special by Ogden's decision to remain in camp where all hands participated in prayers read aloud. Ogden, like Jedediah Smith and a few other outstanding fur men, was deeply religious, and seldom did natural perils prevent his regular meditations and study of the Scriptures. On this second Yuletide, prospects were little better than a year earlier, as the trappers had only twenty pounds of food.

Yet futile dreams of plum pudding and steak could become merely poor imitations of delicious Western realities at many a Mountain Man's lavish Christmas party, for these men could, with the proper ingredients present in their hunting grounds, prove themselves excellent chefs as many an outdoor man before and since their day has done. The plains and mountain Indians themselves were no mean cooks.

In the White River region at Christmas, 1842, Rufus B. Sage partook of one of these savage yet magnificent feasts:

This great annual festival is observed with all the exhilarating hilarity and good cheer that circumstances will allow. Several little extras for the occasion have been procured from the Indians, which prove quite wholesome and pleasant-tasted. One of these, called *washena,* consists of dried meat pulverized and mixed with marrow; another is a preparation of cherries, preserved when first picked by pounding and sun-drying them (they are served by mixing them with *bouillie,* or the liquor of fresh-boiled meat, thus giving to it an agreeable winish taste); a third is marrow-fat, an article in many respects superior to butter; and, lastly, we obtained a kind of flour made from the *pomme blanc* (white apple), answering very well as a substitute for that of grain.

The above assortment, with a small supply of sugar and coffee, as well as several other dainties variously prepared, affords an excellent dinner,—and, though different in kind, by no means inferior in quality to the generality of dinners for which the day is noted in more civilized communities.

For the Christmas of 1847 at Fort Union, Montana, James Kipp, a grisled veteran of the fur business, planned to give all the employees of the fur company and the Indians round about the fort a real treat—a treat, that is, according to the fastidious culinary standards of Eastern and European civilization. Carefully he fattened a large, small-boned heifer, rare for that area, and just before Christmas slaughtered it. The animal had been in fine condition, and Kipp thought that the meat would be a wonderful surprise for the men. They all sat down expectantly while old Jim built up a mood of suspense concerning the mysterious secret treat he had promised them. Yet, after eating only a little of the beef, the diners fell silent, and then, abandoning any pretense of etiquette, one by one turned down the meat entirely and set about eating their familiar bison meat, also on the festive board. They unanimously condemned the roast, which might be good enough, they allowed, but its fat tasted to them like unfit food, downright sickening. At last Kipp offered a plateful of the spurned beef to a squaw, who, like all Indian women, ate separate from the men. Surely she would accept the rare viand. This daughter of the early West, not given to much talk, was finally prodded to comment, and even she declared that, although this strange meat was edible, it was both coarse and insipid! It has been said that once a man has eaten buffalo meat he is never satisfied with any other. This Christmas dinner which went awry seems to support that claim. So much then for Eastern delicacies on Western palates!

When Benjamin Bonneville, Western adventurer and self-promoting ex-soldier, was among the Nez Perces on Christmas Eve, 1832, the Mountain Men and Indians about him began a *feu de joie*. This included a circle of bonfires built around the lodge of the head chief who had invited all the hunters and trappers to a Christmas festival on the morrow. Here was a cheerful mountain valley, well protected from the severity of a Rocky Mountain winter. In the gathering of tepees various kinds of skins were spread on the ground, and upon these piles of venison, elk, mountain mutton, and other meats were heaped, all served with bitter and aromatic roots used by the Indians as condiments. Captain Bonneville, remembering his upbringing, offered a short prayer. Then all were seated about the mounting fires, and the banquet began. Entertainment took the form of games of skill and strength, in which animal spirits and the pride of physical achievement were displayed by whiteskins and redskins alike.

W. A. Ferris of the American Fur Company, John Jacob Astor's old outfit, kept a diary of his perilous wanderings in the Rockies early in the 1830's. Ferris tells us that in 1832 he spent Christmas near the Blackfoot River, receiving there the trappers' best treatment, limited though their hospitality had to be. New Year's Day was even a bigger holiday among these Mountain Men than Christmas, since many of them were of French ancestry. Feasting, dancing, and the old Canadian custom of rough but friendly exercise in the form of riding, shooting, and wrestling, made the holiday season a semicivilized North American version of the Olympics. The next Christmas Ferris passed agreeably on Thompson's River with his host, eating buffalo tongue, a great plains delicacy, dried buffalo meat, fresh venison, and wheat-flour

Red Man and Mountain Man Keep Christmas

cakes, the last-mentioned topped with buffalo marrow which took the place of butter. And there were those rare Eastern luxuries, rum, sugar, and coffee, the indispensable trinity for the many rounds of toasts which hailed a fur man's Yuletide. Ferris concludes that though crude tin cups symbolized the day, "We were at peace with all mankind and with ourselves." Few could ask more of Christmas, and yet cynicism unfortunately crept into and closed his report: these fine sentiments lasted only until "the next favorable opportunity offered for taking advantage of the ignorance and necessity of the Indians."

A German artist, not alone among his countrymen in this endeavor, ventured westward at the tag end of the forties to paint the Indians and trappers in the sunset of their wild golden age. Rudolph Friederich Kurz found many excellent subjects among the fur traders of the Missouri Valley, but experienced a Christmas in 1851 which was far from jolly. Since all hands were busy the entire day, they could only vary their daily routine with "an extra course at dinner of cake and stewed dried apples served with cream."

As was usual among the French Canadians, New Year's brought a round of kissing. Complained the fusty German, newly initiated into what he considered a highly undignified pastime, "I was constantly disturbed by the half-breed girl with her kisses and New Year's greetings. . . . When one asks a girl what she would like at the New Year she replies always, 'a note,' i.e., a bank note. Less than a dollar a man could not offer her; she herself thought that too little. Kisses are dear!" Thus the naivete of which Ferris had spoken was not a universal Indian failing.

There was neither commercialism nor cynicism in the wilderness Christmas of Frederick Gerstaecker, another German, who observed the holiday in 1841 in a cabin on the White River. Gerstaecker had been feeling melancholy during the previous days about his happy Christmases in the Old World and the loneliness of the oncoming Yuletide in northwestern Arkansas. He was a writer born, both warm and detailed in his recording of human reactions to interesting situations, and so let him describe the scene:

In good time we arrived at old Conwell's, Slowtrap's father-in-law. He lived in a block-house, surrounded by mountains covered with trees, close to the bank of the White river, which was narrow enough to be bridged by a tree. The family were assembled round the fire; Conwell himself was absent. A matron of pleasing appearance rose from her seat on the entrance of her son-in-law, and cordially shook his hand, while two fine boys of eleven and eight jumped up to welcome him; another person in the room, a young graceful girl, who at first kept modestly in the background, then came forward to greet her brother-in-law, who addressed her as Sophy; neither was the stranger overlooked, but received a hearty welcome from all. I, who, a few minutes before, had felt so deserted and miserable, now experienced a silent joy, as I looked on the amiable honorable countenance of the mother, the mild expression of the daughter, and the open, happy faces of the two boys. It was as if I had found new relations, and was once again at home.

This was the sort of scene, multiplied thousands of times, which filled the memory of many fur trappers as they gorged themselves in some far-distant Indian village or marked the day in a winter camp snowed in in some Rocky Mountain valley. Few were as fortunate as Slowtrap to have a home on the far edge of the frontier. Others seldom turned east toward the Missouri or Arkansas settlements to pick up for a few days the routine of domestic life.

The Oregon country, comprising today's Washington, Idaho, Oregon, and those parts of Wyoming and Montana west of the Rockies, is now called the Pacific Northwest. A century and more ago it was noted as the paradise of trappers. Years before the missionary efforts of Marcus Whitman, Jason Lee, and others, American and British fur gatherers competed for economic control of the area. Eventually, the Hudson's Bay Company won temporary supremacy, but Americans had arrived early, too, and they were determined not to surrender permanently this vast domain of rich forests and well-watered valleys.

To follow up the discovery of Captain Gray in the *Columbia* and the land explorations of Lewis and Clark, two groups of fur men were sent out in 1811 by John Jacob Astor, who hoped to control commercially the north Pacific coast and the Columbia Valley. There furs would be gathered and shipped by sea to connect with the lucrative China trade, then enriching New England's energetic merchants who had opened the whole world to American vessels and who were becoming the new nation's first millionaires. One group of fur men, coming by land, was called the Overland Astorians. They reached the mouth of the great "River of the West," as the Columbia was poetically and hopefully dubbed, and at its mouth founded the rude post called Astoria. Of that first Christmas in the recently completed fort, Gabriel Franchere said in his diary:

> The 25th, Christmas-day, passed very agreeably: we treated the men, on that day, with the best the establishment afforded. Although that was no great affair, they seemed well satisfied; for they had been restricted, during the last few months, to a very meagre diet, living, as one may say, on sun-dried fish.

The cheer was all of the interior-decoration sort that season, for outside the gloom of drizzling rain had continued uninterrupted since October, and it knew no break for holidays. The monotonous downpour continued until New Year's Eve, when once more a starry sky was seen.

It takes more than good weather to make Christmas Christmas. One man who knew how dreary Yuletide could be was a Dr. Bigelow, a Western wanderer who found himself all alone in the Oto country of Nebraska about 1850. Those who have been in a similar situation might take comfort, not only because misery loves company but because few men have experienced such a holiday-gone-wrong as he describes:

> . . . and lying on my back looking up, when the night was fine, at the glittering starry sky, through the hole at the top of my tent, I inhaled the fragrant smoke produced by mingling some tea with the dry willow leaves in my pipe, the only Christmas indulgence I could afford, and fancied the stars looked kindly down upon me, as they used to do at home, though they seemed,

like myself, to be trembling with cold. On Christmas morning, when I went out into the air, I beheld a flock of prairie fowls, sitting among the trees on the bank of the river, and I am ashamed to say how my heart beat, and with what delight, after living so long upon tough wolf's flesh and a scanty diet, I looked forward to the sensual joys of a roast worthy of Christmas.

A grand looking cock was sitting just within reach of my bullet, but my irresistible, covetous desire to get two birds at once, induced me slightly to change my position. I trod on some dry twig that was hidden by the snow, it snapped under my foot, frightened the fowls, and the whole flock instantly flew off.

Hope and despair, disappointment and relief alternated for the next few days of Bigelow's prairie experience. Finally, early in January, a very welcome half-breed Indian brought him help and a much-delayed holiday feast.

The British, feeling almost patriotically bound to import as much of Merry England as frontier conditions would warrant, probably enjoyed their Western Christmas more than did the American Mountain Men. By all accounts the first Yuletide ever kept in Montana occurred at Saleesh House in 1809, and like the one two years later at Astoria, it was "squally with showers." The rain caused leaks everywhere at the post, even in the warehouse where the precious furs were stored. According to Ross Cox, a careful observer, by 1813 Saleesh House was no longer plagued with a faulty roof. Rather, he found the place comparatively pleasant, and settling himself by a blazing fire in a warm room, he soon "forgot the sufferings we endured in our dreary progress through the woods." Warmth from within was supplied by the meat of mountain sheep which Cox's hunters had just killed, plus arrowroot, used in place of potatoes, fifteen gallons of prime rum, a bag of rice, and plenty of tea and coffee.

Yet Cox's contemporary, David Thompson, a first-rate explorer in his own right, said that Christmas was usually kept by British fur men he knew by pursuing their usual hard tasks. In fact, he remarked, the men were all glad to see the day pass, for "we have nothing to welcome it with."

This seasonal defeatism was certainly not evident at Nisqually House in 1833. Wrote the factor of that post, erected at the base of Puget Sound:

Wednesday 25th—This being Christmas day I gave the men a liberal Regale of eatables and drinkables to make up in some measure for the bad living they have had all year here, and they enjoyed the feast as might be expected men would do who lived solely on soup since they came here. Weather still very cold—

Thursday 26th—The men were allowed to rest from their labors, today as they are rather fagged after yesterday's indulgence—A hurricane or whirlwind passed and broke down the largest trees in its way like straws.

Regales became a tradition at Nisqually, as they did in other strongholds of the fur trade. As late as Christmas of 1849 the post's journal, never elaborate in its descriptions of social matters, did mention such a fete. At a regale, presents were always given employees and neighboring Indians. That year the record noted that "some of the Beef killed on Friday proving rather tainted was selected for present use, and some given out to be smokedried." Apparently the donors believed that it was indeed better to give than to receive—spoiled meat!

Yet, at John McLoughlin's Fort Vancouver, most historic and important Hudson's Bay Company post in the Northwest, Christmas was always a grand occasion and generosity was in all respects genuine. McLoughlin, a magnificently dignified old Scot, as canny and courageous as he was dramatic and wise, was called the "White Headed Eagle" by the Northwestern Indians who respected him as the leading figure of the vast region over which he ruled. At Yuletide he allowed the Company's servants a small amount of spirits. According to an eyewitness, Palmer, quoted by Hubert Howe Bancroft, historian par excellence of the Pacific Slope, the result for Christmas, 1845 was:

. . . such ranting and frolicking has perhaps seldom been seen among the sons of men. Some were engaged in gambling, some singing, some running horses, many promenading on the river-shore, and others on the large green prairie above the fort. HBM's ship of war *Modeste* was lying at anchor about fifty yards from the shore. The sailors also seemed to be enjoying the holidays—many of them were on shore promenading and casting sheep's-eyes at the fair native damsels as they strolled from wigwam to hut, and from hut to wigwam, intent upon seeking for themselves the greatest amount of enjoyment. At night a party was given on board the ship, and judging from the noise kept up until ten at night, they were a jolly set of fellows.

No work was required of any Company employee on Christmas, New Year's or Good Friday except that of feeding and caring for the animals. On

Christmas and New Year's Day all the men were invited to the chief factor's room where McLoughlin gave them the traditional regale of cake and rum. Each man usually got a half-pint or pint of liquor to take with him. Due to this practice little work was expected on the following day. Except on these holidays, however, no liquors were ever allowed to anyone, and none was sold to the Indians.

Writers of our day have described Fort Vancouver both as spacious and as lavish in accommodations as a modern national park hotel which it resembled in its rustic setting. The Reverend Samuel Parker who was visiting the famous post during the holidays of 1835-36 knew the truth of this claim. Of the gay trappers he encountered there on Christmas morning, he said:

. . . they dress themselves in their best attire, accelerated movements are seen in every direction, and preparation is made for dinners, which are sure to be furnished in their first-style, and greatest profusion; and the day passes in mirth and hilarity. But it does not end with the day; for the passions and appetites pampered through the day, prepare the way for the night to be spent in dancing, and loud and boisterous laughter, shouts, and reveling, consume the hours designed for rest. They continue these high-strung convivialities until they pass the portals of the new year, when labor and toil resume their place.

One of the most interesting Christmases celebrated by Mountain Men and preserved for posterity, was witnessed and recorded by Osborne Russell, a man of both thought and action. His presence in the Weber River country of pre-Mormon Utah in 1840 proves his rugged character, while the following account of

Christmas among the trappers and Indians is evidence
of his intelligent observation which has maintained
his reputation as one of the best sources of information we have today on the Mountain Man and his
ways.

It was agreed on by the party to prepare a Christmas dinner
but I shall first endeavor to describe the party and then the
dinner. I have already said the man who was the proprietor of
the lodge in which I staid was a Frenchman with a flat head
wife and one child. The inmates of the next lodge was a half-
breed Iowa, a Nez Percey wife and two children his wife's
brother and another halfbreed; next lodge was a halfbreed Cree,
his wife (a Nez Perce) two children and a Snake Indian. The
inmates of the third lodge was a halfbreed Snake, his wife (a
Nez Percey and two children). The remainder was 15 lodges
of Snake Indians Three of the party spoke English but very
broken therefore that language was made but little use of as
I was familiar with the Canadian French and Indian tongue.

About 1 o'clk we sat down to dinner in the lodge where I
staid, which was the most spacious being about 36 ft. in cir-
cumference at the base, with a fire built in the center around
this sat on clean Epishemores all who claimed kin to the white
man (or to use their own expression all that were gens D'esprit),
with their legs crossed in true Turkish style—and now for the
dinner.

The first dish that came on was a large tin pan 18 inches in
diameter rounding full of Stewed Elk meat The next dish was
similar to the first heaped up with boiled Deer meat (or as the
whites would call it Venison a term not used in the Mountains).
The 3rd and 4th dishes were equal in size to the first, containing a boiled flour pudding prepared with dried fruit accompanied by 4 quarts of sauce made of the juice of sour berries
and sugar Then came the cakes followed by six gallons of strong
Coffee ready sweetened with tin cups and pans to drink out of
large chips or pieces of bark supplying the place of plates. On
being ready, the butcher knives were drawn and the eating
commenced at the word given by the landlady As all dinners
are accompanied with conversation this was not deficient in that

respect The principal topic which was discussed was the political
affairs of the Rocky Mountains the state of governments among
the different tribes, the personal characters of the most distinguished warrior Chiefs, etc One remarked that the Snake Chief,
Pahdahewakumda was becoming very unpopular and it was the
opinion of the Snakes in general that *Moh-woomha* his brother
would be at the head of affairs before 12 ms as his village already
amounted to more than 300 lodges. . . . Dinner being over the
tobacco pipes were filled and lighted while the squaws and children cleared away the remains of the feast to one side of the
lodge where they held a Sociable tite a tite over the fragments.
After the pipes were extinguished all agreed to have a frolic
shooting at a mark which occupied the remainder of the day.

The above was characteristic of Christmases celebrated by those fur trappers who had intermarried
with Indians, and a majority had done so, several of
them finding native "princesses" as their mates, and
a few rising to real authority within the red man's
society.

Near the end of the heyday of the fur men a typical scene was enacted at Fort Edmonton. The year
was 1847, the place well north of the international
line. Trappers, however, were always international-
ists in equipment and procedures and through their
nearly savage culture and basic psychology. The
occasion as depicted by Paul Kane, an artist who
painted both the fort's dwellers and their visitors,
might have been duplicated at many of the other
posts in the Rockies. He begins:

Towards noon every chimney gave evidence of being in full
blast, whilst savoury steams of cooking pervaded the atmosphere
in all directions. About two o'clock we sat down to dinner.
Our party consisted of Mr. Harriett, the chief, and three clerks,

Mr. Thebo, the Roman Catholic missionary from Manitou Lake, about thirty miles off, Mr. Rundell, the Wesleyan missionary, who resided within the pickets, and myself, the wanderer, who, though returning from the shores of the Pacific, was still the latest importation from civilised life.

The dining-hall in which we assembled was the largest room in the fort, probably about fifty by twenty-five feet, well warmed by large fires, which are scarcely ever allowed to go out. The walls and ceilings are boarded, as plastering is not used, there being no limestone within reach; but these boards are painted in a style of the most startling barbaric gaudiness . . . altogether a saloon which no white man would enter for the first time without a start, and which the Indians always looked on with awe and wonder.

The room was intended as a reception room for the wild chiefs who visited the fort; and the artist who designed the decorations was no doubt directed to "astonish the natives." If such were his instructions, he deserves the highest praise for having faithfully complied with them. . . . No tablecloth shed its snowy whiteness over the board; no silver candelabra or gaudy china interfered with its simple magnificence. The bright tin plates and dishes reflected jolly faces, and burnished gold can give no truer zest to a feast.

Perhaps it might be interesting to some dyspeptic idler, who painfully strolls through a city park, to coax an appetite to a sufficient intensity to enable him to pick an ortolan, if I were to describe to him the fare set before us, to appease appetites nourished by constant out-door exercise in an atmosphere ranging at 40° to 50° below zero. At the head, before Mr. Harriett, was a large dish of boiled buffalo hump; at the foot smoked a boiled buffalo calf. Start not, gentle reader, the calf is very small, and is taken from the cow by the Caesarean operation long before it attains its full growth. This, boiled whole, is one of the most esteemed dishes amongst the epicures of the interior. My pleasing duty was to help a dish of mouffle, or dried moose nose; the gentleman on my left distributed, with graceful impartiality, the white fish, delicately browned in buffalo marrow. The worthy priest helped the buffalo tongue, whilst Mr. Rundell cut up the beavers' tails. Nor was the other gentleman left unemployed, as all his spare time was occupied in dissecting a roast

wild goose. The centre of the table was graced with piles of
potatoes, turnips, and bread conveniently placed, so that each
could help himself without interrupting the labours of his companions. Such was our jolly Christmas dinner at Edmonton;
and long will it remain in my memory, although no pies, or
puddings, or blanc manges, shed their fragrance over the scene.

As evening arrived, the great hall was prepared for
a dance, and such a dance as no city-bred Easterner
could have imagined! It is a wonder how even such
energetic outdoor men as these could have moved
after such a feast. Yet, when Harriet invited everyone in the fort to this affair, all arrived gaily dressed
and ready for some strenuous entertainment. From
his description of it, the ball must have been as welcome a feast to Kane's artist's eye as the wondrous
meal had been to his stomach.

Indians, whose chief ornament consisted in the paint of their
faces, voyageurs with bright sashes and neatly ornamented moccasins, half-breeds glittering in every ornament they could lay
their hands on; whether civilised or savage, all were laughing and
jabbering in as many different languages as there were styles
of dress. English, however, was little used, as none could speak
it but those who sat at the dinner-table. The dancing was most
picturesque, and almost all joined in it. Occasionally I, among
the rest, led out a young Cree squaw, who sported enough beads
round her neck to have made a pedlar's fortune, and having led
her into the centre of the room, I danced round her with all
agility I was capable of exhibiting, to some highland-reel tune
which the fiddler played with great vigour, whilst my partner
with grave face kept jumping up and down, both feet off the
ground at once, as only an Indian can dance. I believe, however,
that we elicited a great deal of applause from Indian squaws
and children, who sat squatting round the room on the floor.
Another lady with whom I sported the light fantastic toe, whose
poetic name was Cun-ne-wa-bum, or "One that looks at the

Stars," was a half-breed Cree girl; and I was so much struck by her beauty, that I prevailed upon her to promise to sit for her likeness, which she afterwards did with great patience.

After their boisterous evening of innocent fun, all retired quietly at midnight.

CHAPTER VII

Down a Prairie Chimney

EVEN while the Mountain Men were trail blazing in the Rockies and beyond, the first tier of territories and potential states west of the Mississippi was being settled by farming folk migrating from farther east. These pioneers of Minnesota, Iowa, Missouri, and Arkansas were never culturally cut off from Western European civilization as were the explorers and trappers. The settlers, like their French and Spanish counterparts farther south and west, clung to the deep traditions of their past, if not to the prejudice, luxury, and formality of the East. Most of them had been relatively poor farmers on thin soils of their native states, and now they had a chance to achieve some individual improvement and at the same time serve social progress. They were an optimistic and domestic lot, and usually quite devout. Isolation did not modify their simple faith or prevent their proper observance of that day which best symbolized it. In condensed form, Christmas was the Westerner's Christianity graphically at its best.

On the Missouri frontier in the 1840's Independence had become the gateway to the West, the door through which experienced Santa Fe traders, Oregon-bound farmers and missionaries, and ambitious gold seekers would pass. An artist, Alfred S. Waugh, who went this way, spent the Christmas of 1845 at the outfitting post. This season in the wilderness, full of strange sights and ways, roused in the homesick Waugh the images of past childhood and lost acquaintances. Yet with true pioneer spirit he had sense enough to conclude, "What's the use of sighing?" A friend introduced him to Western hospitality, already developing into a tradition, and "made the day look like Christmas at home."

Missouri slaves, like those of the Louisiana Creoles, had special reason for welcoming Christmas and its Yule log. According to custom, as long as the log burned they did not have to do any work. Therefore the slaves always selected the largest and greenest one they could find, not from the woodpile, where the log had had time to dry and would burn quickly, but from the wood lot, where green wood was usually found. They noted its slow reduction with vested interest, and when the Yule log was only a brand, the final remnant was given to an old mammy who would preserve it to be used the next year to light the long-anticipated log. Furthermore, by unbroken tradition, any work that had to be done while this very welcome fire was blazing had to be paid for!

Early on Christmas morning the children and all the slaves awoke, shouting "Christmas gift!" at everyone they saw. Later, the filled stockings of the youngsters were expectantly examined. The early French and Spanish children had no tree in their Missouri homes near the Mississippi, but rather placed their shoes beside the hearth for the Christ Child to fill. The French had their famous crèche and the Spanish their *posada,* or inn. The *posada* was concerned with the old tradition of seeking lodging for the Holy Family. In the crèche scene were the Holy Family, the Magi, their camels, the donkey upon which Mary rode, and oxen in their stalls. Mexicans in frontier Missouri observed the still-popular Mexican custom of breaking a gaily-decorated *olla* or jar, filled with candies and gifts. This was the *piñata,* and all children eagerly awaited its arrival. Not, however, until the Germans began settling in and near St. Louis late in the forties did the Christmas tree at last arrive between the Missouri and the Mississippi.

Iowa was on the forefront of the frontier in the 1850's, yet primitive conditions never completely blighted a Christmas lighted by the human heart. During Christmas Eve, logs were rolled in and burned in the pioneer cabins along the Iowa and the Nishnabotna. The burning of the Yule log gave one of the few forms of variety to these settlers, who did not even have evergreens and certainly could give no elaborate presents. Not until the seventies did the edge of settlement pass beyond northwestern Iowa. As late as 1856 a colonizer in Boone County remembered bagging three prairie chickens in one hour's hunting on Christmas morn.

Near the Mississippi in Clinton County, a seven-year-old girl named Mary would remember even better the Christmas of 1842. In her parents' log cabin, built in a clearing of the bottom lands near the river, stockings were hung by the fireside. Next morning, each of them held a "nice fat brown doughnut and some pieces of gaily colored calico." Her older sister made a rag doll, also of ever-faithful calico, and this surely was as appreciated as any china doll from far-off Paris. Meanwhile, the head of the pioneer household shot a wild turkey in the woods but a few yards off. Maple sap had been gathered on an island in the Mississippi, and the industrious mother prepared sugar cakes for her brood.

The pioneer housewife, so extolled by later generations, deserved her laudations. She had to display an ingenuity not needed by Easterners and a canniness for solving life's myriad of little problems at which Americans still marvel. At Christmas, the one time which called for gaiety, luxury, and light, she outdid herself. Mrs. Santa Claus of the Old West wore sunbonnet and calico, and she baked in a Dutch oven. As prime mover of Yuletide, she was busy for days in advance baking her mince pies made of dried berries that she had so carefully gathered and preserved. Home-rendered lard for the crust was painstakingly prepared. There were always lots of turkey, roast venison, or pork, with potatoes, nuts, and maple syrup to go with the baked goods. After dinner, all the family sat before the large fireplace and enjoyed stories of earlier Christmases "back home."

Even in the early days of the first tier, there were stores of a sort, though they were far away, and children eagerly awaited the holiday season when their

father would come home from the annual buying
spree loaded with bundles and with pockets sus-
piciously bulging. When at last the big day came
and the secret treasures were unveiled, the younger
generation would find such luxuries as a slate pencil,
a shotgun, some colored handkerchiefs, or mittens and
other clothes made by Mother. On this farming
frontier, Christmas Eve introduced a round of fairs
and suppers calculated to achieve charitable as well
as social goals, and almost inevitably ending with
a country dance and a merry sleigh ride home. One
such sleighing party in Hamilton County, Iowa, at
Yuletide, 1857, got much more than its festive-
bound members had bargained for when a pack of
about a hundred wolves and coyotes (so witnesses
declared) chased a four-horse sleigh, which, fortunately, got through safely. Many a romance was
kindled at these Christmas Eve parties when love
was imparted along with the consumption of venison, elk, buffalo meat, corn bread, and pumpkin pie.

One interesting Iowa custom was born in Boone
County when a number of neighbor men gathered,
elected a captain as seriously as if they were choosing a wagon master for a long and perilous covered-
wagon journey, and then visited the homes of their
friends. Upon reaching a given house, they would
fire their guns and then call out, loud enough to
shake down the icicles, the name of the surprised
resident. As this became a yearly procedure, probably the surprise eventually wore off, but not the
cameraderie. All the chilly wayfarers were invited

in by the man of the family amid mutual joking, laughing, the shaking of hands; and the drinking of steaming coffee followed. Next the contingent of merrymakers would reload their arms and go on to the next house. Sometimes they would grow more reverent and sing a hymn as they departed. All in good fun, they had a few hours of strenuous walking in the winter air and innumerable cups of coffee, and then returned at midnight to their own warm homes.

Santa Claus began appearing at Iowa church suppers in the late sixties. It was the Sunday school, quite appropriately, which gave importance to the Christmas tree. Iowa had its pioneer community tree in Franklin County by 1868. In the second-floor courtroom of the courthouse at Hampton three religious denominations held their services. A group representing this trinity of good will planned a tree for all the village. But where would they get an evergreen in that part of Iowa? It was prairie land, which would be good for corn, but certainly was not lumber country. The nearest railroad was then fifteen miles away. Then someone, as "someone" inevitably does, remembered that cedars grew along the Iowa River about twenty miles distant. In spite of freezing weather, the Reverend L. N. Call volunteered to go select a tree. He and a deacon set out and after a cold trek finally returned with a great shaggy lord of the forest.

The courtroom was jammed that Christmas Eve. Children had been brought in by wagon, cart, and horseback from all over the countryside. The tree was bright with candles and popcorn garlands, while red apples in strings added color. On the lower branches and at the base were the presents. After the children had experienced the full beauty of the tree, the proceedings began. First there was singing, followed by Scriptural reading, and then a prayer. After that packages were opened. As the small supply of songbooks available contained only familiar Christmas songs, few carols were sung. The ministers had chosen religious tunes appropriate to the occasion. In a broad sense, of course, any Christian music would be fitting for the holiday. Thoughtfully, a special committee had provided a sack of candy for each child, while parents and Sunday school teachers brought other gifts. The needy and old were not forgotten on this fast-growing frontier; they had their presents, too. As a tasteful farewell to a first Christmas-tree party, a child recited Clement Clarke Moore's already Well-known " 'T was the Night Before Christmas."

As late as 1872, none of the children in North Madison, Iowa, had seen a Christmas tree. The Sunday school therefore wanted to provide one for them. Here again the prospects of getting a tree seemed very poor, so efforts were made to insure against any Christmastide disappointment, in case none could be had, by planning a church party and a play. That ever-present frontier institution, the Methodist circuit preacher, offered a prayer which was followed by speeches, dialogues, song, and tableaux. Yet here again there were men persistent enough to see that

Christmas would not be treeless. A townsman charged only a dollar for the one he procured, but he had really earned that sum. In crossing a river to get the tree he broke the ice and fell in. Decorated with popcorn and candles, the ten-foot tree seemed well worth the frigid dousing—even to the victim!

Minnesota was in general even farther off the path of settlement than Iowa, but this fur-trading region as early as 1827 welcomed Christmas with a serenade of musicians. They wasted no time in being early celebrants; their concert began at three o'clock in the morning! This incident occurred at Fort Snelling, where the Minnesota River meets the Mississippi. Before the 1820's were over, Indians in that region had become accustomed to call at the post and shake hands with the white men there. Year after year these natives would appear at the front door, first of the fort, and later of pioneer cabins which comprised a growing settlement. As they did at other fur posts, Indian women kissed the commander. The bigger occasion for such official osculation was New Year's, called "kissing day." Indians, half-breeds, and traders quickly adopted French-Canadian Christmas customs, which, where there were no missionaries and no attempts at family life, often took the obvious route of drinking, fighting, feasting, and dancing. The *voyageurs*' usual diet of corn and suet was always amplified with a holiday ration of sugar, flour for cakes and puddings, and rum. Christmas was sweet if not serious. When he was exploring the Mississippi in 1805, seeking its source in Minnesota,

Zebulon M. Pike gave his men extra meat, flour, and tobacco for Christmas. This sweet flavor of Christmas was finally joined to its genuinely sacred nature in the 1880's when Bishop Whipple continued the custom of giving victuals. He sent candy to all the Indian churches and mission stations of northern Minnesota, for this was the only time during the whole year that most of the Ojibways got a taste of candy.

Even by mid-century, though the population of forested Minnesota was but 6,077 and this number for the most part was engaged in such rugged pursuits as mining, fur gathering, and lumbering, a refined spirit had made headway. Settlers went to church on Christmas, attended balls and parties, and had their first Christmas trees. Christmas fairs were held at Stillwater and other mushrooming towns. To these Eastern delicacies of ice cream, sauces, and jellies was added the spicy zest of wild Minnesota cranberries.

When store-bought toys were impossible to get, or a severe winter storm had cut off farm from town, the children of early days were told that "Santa Claus had not learned the way to Minnesota yet." But the spirit of the Magi had, long before. By 1860, frontier youngsters were receiving drums and dolls, books, neckties, candy, nuts, and popcorn. The decorations for the few Christmas trees were great in both variety and origin; they might include yellow soap cut in the form of stars, gilt paper from some box brought west in a covered wagon, ribbons from the mother's Sunday-best gown, now worn out, colored beads used in the Indian trade, berries from the backland, and the handiwork of local tinsmiths. As early as 1849, when St. Paul was a hamlet on the shore of the Mississippi, its bakers and confectioners were expansively preparing for the holidays. Pipes, toys, tobacco, cigars, and drygoods vied with their Christmas cakes for popularity. The steamboat had brought Eastern manufactured goods to Red Wing, and these were taken over the ice to St. Paul. Even that early, sleighing parties and amateur dramatics were being held. The custom of morning calls had sprung up a full decade earlier, but it was more typical of New Year's Day than the week before.

One can never forget the Swedes in any discussion of Minnesota. Before the Civil War had begun, Scandinavians were already arriving, and they imported the fascinating custom of setting out sheaves of unthreshed wheat on Christmas Eve. In the true Christmas spirit shivering birds were thus given a Yuletide meal.

The American frontier, which had reached western Missouri and Iowa in the 1840's, leaped to the Pacific when gold was discovered on the West Coast and then moved backward to people the mining camps of the Sierra Nevada and the Rockies. Not until the next decade, that of the fifties and early sixties, did the edge of civilization touch the border of the Great Plains, that semiarid wilderness of grass which had been mistakenly called the Great American Desert,

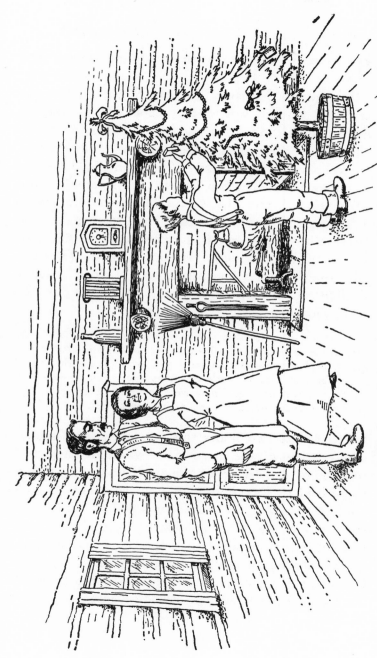

Hard-come-by Evergreens Symbolized the Day

but which would soon prove to be America's Wheat Belt.

In spite of the name, "Bloody Kansas," given the territory when it was rent by abolitionists and pro-slavers hoping to win Kansas for their extreme views, this new frontier, even in the fearsome 1850's, paused to do honor to the Prince of Peace on His day. For example, on November 25, 1855, James H. Lane from the Office of the Executive Committee, issued a Thanksgiving proclamation, but strange to our twentieth-century minds, he named Christmas Day as Kansas' Thanksgiving Day for that year. The next Christmas found a Southerner, A. J. Hoole, later a Confederate lieutenant colonel, writing his mother from Douglas:

> What sort of a Christmas have you all spent? For my own part, it has been very dull. I went over the river squirrel hunting, walked over the ice. After I got over I heard that there was to be a meeting of settlers on that side a mile above. So I went up to the meeting. There were about 12 or 15 there; one got up and endeavoured to explain the object of it.

For the next two hours this amateur orator spoke. The purpose of the meeting he was addressing was to appoint a delegate to the proslavery convention to be held in Lecompton on January 2, 1859. According to Hoole, the speaker was drunk. The audience was in the same condition. Several members had brought four bottles of liquor, and one of them got so intoxicated that he fell down while "another got about a hundred yards off, and there he lay." Thus passed one holiday in Bloody Kansas.

It seemed to be a highly inappropriate time and place for keeping Yuletide. A pioneer missionary in this land of civil strife, the Reverend Cyrus R. Rice of Hartford, Kansas, was despairing of good will. There were no trees and no plum puddings, though Christmas morning in 1855 proved a sunny one. After a good breakfast, Rice saddled up and started for Osawatomie, but he had not gone far when his horse went down in the deep snow. As the animal was unable to move a leg, Rice had to dismount and with his hands pull the snow away so that the steed could rise again. For the next two days and nights, the missionary received shelter from a Missourian who managed the Pottawatomie Agency. Perhaps it was the combination of hard luck, cold, and the lack of amenities which formulated his pessimism, for Rice concluded, "Let me say here, I did not try to preach Christmas and New Year sermons in those days, for I could not feel any Christmas or New Year's spirit in the cold air. I never heard 'Merry Christmas' or 'Happy New Year' once. The people I met, as well as myself, were not in a merry mood. We were enduring a bitter cold winter."

Rice should have been at Shawnee Mission that day. It was "cold, bitter, freezing" there, too, as George D. Brewerton, a special New York Correspondent in Kansas, tells us, and "Christmas joys were left on t'other side of those far-off Allegheny mountains"—at least for the most part. The morning and afternoon were given over to humdrum routine, work which could only be defended as a "self-defence to occupy the mind and drive away those confounded visitors, the Blue Devils." But the evening would compensate for a poor beginning. At the home of the mission's superintendent, Brewerton was greeted by a large open wood fire and plenty of children. These all delighted him. "Colonel" Brewerton, as he was usually known, was no stranger to rugged Western life. He had served in the army during the Mexican War in California, had come to know and to admire Kit Carson, and had served in various border posts once peace returned. In 1852 Brewerton had left military service to become a writer, and now was in this trouble spot representing the New York *Herald*. He would stay here a spell and study law in Kansas. A tall, well-built man with the full beard and mane-like hair which many Easterners expected of a frontier character, Brewerton had not, however, been hardened by long years of a rough existence. Throughout his days he would love to tell children his true adventures, and so it is in keeping with his character that for him this otherwise bleak holiday should be saved from melancholy and eventual oblivion when he met a pretty little girl. He says:

It may interest the New York juveniles to know that in the Far Western country, a child's first Christmas salutation to everyone it meets is Christmas gift—Christmas gift! They catch you always, if they can. We tried to get ahead of a blue-eyed curly-headed little lady this morning—a daughter of Mr. Woodson, the Secretary of State—but Miss Betty was too smart for us, and cried "Christmas gift," before we could open our mouth.

Unfortunately, the cheerful sound of Christmas greetings which the Reverend Mr. Rice missed were fifty miles too far north for his ears.

Although most of them were very cold indeed, not all early Kansas Christmases were so plain as the one described by Rice and Brewerton, for the internal turmoil of territorial days was resolved in a greater Civil War, at the beginning of which Kansas at last became a state in the Union which was preserved. During the seventies settlers moved farther out on the plains, using barbed-wire fences where there was no wood, building houses of blocks of prairie sod where there were no other materials, and erecting windmills to pump the water which was seldom found upon the surface. A farmer in the former Osage Indian lands, C. E. Cory, remembered how one holiday was made worthy of its name, though the heroes of this particular occasion were some supposedly wild frontier characters, a party of young and naturally boisterous Englishmen and Scots who had recently arrived in frontier Kansas. Here is what resulted:

One Christmas, I think of 1875, they thought to inject a little of good English Hallow-mass into the life of the prairies. So, early that morning, they loaded up an old-fashioned sled with everything good to eat. A snow of four or five inches had freshly fallen and sledding was good. The load was all the team wanted to pull. With bells of all sizes and on all points of the harness, and men on top, they scurried over the prairies and dropped their Christmas greeting at the doors of the cabins; a ham and a package of coffee at one place, a sack of corn-meal and a pound of tea at another, a turkey and some sugar at a third; and so until the load was ended. They had a peculiar notion that that was a good way to spend Christmas. You would better understand that those Christmas morning rollickers looked like angels. They were not that by a long way, but they acted like them.

By that period the average emigrant family in its house made of blocks of prairie sod could observe, as did Percy G. Ebbutt:

> We had a very quiet time, but managed to get up a very good spread, with a regular Christmas pudding. For the latter a special journey had to be made to town for the various ingredients, all of which we obtained without much trouble, with the exception of suet. As our staple food was pork, and there were no butchers in town, we were rather in a fix, and thought our pudding would suffer, until at last we got hold of some buffalo suet from a hunter returning from the west. Despite a few minor accidents our pudding was a great success, and we had quite a banquet with roast sucking-pig, wild ducks, and prairie fowls.

Never having heard of such twentieth-century terms as "togetherness" or "hi-fi," Hezekiah Brake and his fellow Kansans on the frontier certainly knew how to make short shift of loneliness and supply a Christmas tune. When the young folks arrived for a holiday party, he "heaped the old chimney with logs so often that half a cord of sturdy oak was consumed ere the gay revelers left us." On the plains, mistletoe was lacking, but nonetheless, "osculatory feats" were not. They danced, too, and "in the absence of a parlor organ, a good-natured fellow *whistled* the tunes, and Lottie and I enjoyed the performance more than any other couple present," wrote the middle-aged chronicler.

While the Kansas farmers were snug against winter blasts in their soddies, refugees from European tyranny and poverty began to come among them. In the seventies, Germans of Russia, fugitives from czarist rule, a tyranny nearly as ruthless, though not so efficient, as that of the Soviet, had brought with them their Christmas customs. The Reverend Francis S. Laing, O. M. Cap., describes these for us:

On the eve of Christmas a lady dressed in white with girdle of blue, and with face veiled, appears in each family as herald of the "Christ Kindlein" (Christ-Child). The tinkling of a little bell without, a knock, and she enters with the greeting, "Gelobt sei Jesus Christus." She inquires for the youngest child, has it say a prayer as evidence of diligence in this regard, and then gives it Christmas presents. The older children are frequently chastised with a rod because of delinquencies which are recounted. Gifts follow: a quantity of nuts are thrown in the air and as the children scramble for their possessions the apparition is gone. Each child . . . in Christmas and Easter calls on its sponsors (at baptism) to wish them a happy feast, and is rewarded by sweets, which it bears away in a white cloth.

The Swedes in early Kansas offered their Christmas festivities as the best examples of imported Scandinavian customs. Christmas Eve's celebrations were strictly family affairs, centering around a fine supper followed by the exchange of presents beside the tree. Then about half past five on Christmas morning the young and old together met at church for services. The old Swedish hymn "Var Halsad Skona Morgonstund" pealed forth from the churches, which were lighted by tall Christmas candles. Festivities, varied in both color and joyousness, continued for a full week.

Nebraska escaped the bloodshed of Kansas, since it was too far north and too cold for cotton and the importation of slavery, but otherwise pioneer conditions were similar—the long, treeless plains, the bitterly cold winters alternating with hot, dry summers, and ever isolation. There were many complaints about the mails of the early days, for homesteaders forgot the enormous problems of transportation involved in delivering a letter and only remembered the classic examples of poor service. One of these extreme cases, though probably far from rare in the fifties, occurred when a man ninety-six miles from Brownsville, Nebraska, wrote a letter to the editor of the *Nebraska Advertiser* in that town, inviting him to a Christmas ball to be held December 21, 1856. If he expected either an answer or a personal appearance, he was to be disappointed, for the correspondence was not received until March 14, 1857, eighty-four days later. When, however, such parties did take place, despite the mails, they were well attended. Guests found none of the traditional evergreens in the land of grasses, but rather oak branches from the scant growth along rivers. Yet, ingeniously, the settlers wrapped cotton about the twigs to make a "white tree."

The Reverend S. Hermann, a missionary among the Plains Indians, reported from Omaha in January, 1865, of his recent holiday:

We had a Christmas festival at Bellevue and one at Fort Calhoun. The one at the latter point was the first in the history of that town. About sixty dollars were spent to decorate the tree, and procure presents for the Sunday-school; besides thirty-five volumes of Church Books, a gift from the Church Book Society, which I procured from the school. Few old parishes display more interest in their Christmas festivals than this missionary point where service was held, for the first time, six months ago. The parish at Bellevue also took great pains and raised about the same sum of money for their festival.

Typical of the Nebraska settlers were the Thorns, a family who had moved to the territory, enjoyed good harvests for their hard work, and as their cattle and hogs fattened, they built a fine house which they tried to weatherproof with strips of listing. Then came the terrible blizzard of 1883, which proved fatal to many a settler. Their windows were so frosted that they could not see for five days. On the fifth day the sun outside and the fire inside finally thawed a spot about the size of a teacup in the window pane. Robert Thorn, heavily bundled, and with a bed cord about his waist, the other end tied to the house, managed to care for the hungry cattle in his dug-out stable. This record storm had arrived just two days before Christmas. For the holiday the family had killed and dressed forty young turkeys to be taken to market five miles away. They had laid the plucked carcasses out to freeze in preparation for their start to town the next morning but, due to the storm, Christmas and New Year's had come and gone while the roads remained impassable. When at last the teams got through, the holiday craze for turkeys had passed, and it was difficult for the unfortunate Thorns even to give the birds away.

Another typical sod-house family was that of Martin Block, who with his wife and boy of twelve and little girl of four, worked hard and slowly prospered. The year 1865, which saw the nation at peace again, had been a twelvemonth free of mishap for the Blocks, blessed with their good crops and plenty of potatoes, corn, and wild fruits in their storehouse. Martin Block had always believed in the power of Christmas, and he intended to keep the holiday that year. He would make the day happy for his family. Yet, how would he get the "fixings" for Christmas? The trip eastward to Omaha would take three days. That, according to his wife, was entirely out of the question, but she knew Martin well enough not to argue with him. He was determined to go. Since their mules were needed for loading firewood, Block decided to go without animals, to set out on foot for a hundred-mile walk! He reached Omaha all right, bought a packet of gifts and a few delicacies for the table, including a twenty-five pound bag of wheat flour to replace the usual supply of corn meal. With a total of fifty pounds on his back, Block started home. The load forced him to rest often. At the end of the second day he found that his mileage was not good; he'd only covered thirty miles. At dusk on Christmas Eve he came upon a lone covered wagon with two starved horses near it, and since wagons alone on the plains were a rarity, he knew something was wrong. Then he saw a woman gathering firewood. She told him that her sick husband was inside the wagon, helpless. The couple had a farm about twenty-five miles west of Block's place, and in building their house, her husband had been pinned beneath a falling beam. His crushed leg did not heal quickly. Bad had become worse. Inexperienced as a farmer, he had not been doing well anyway. His wife finally decided that she would have to take action, packed the family into the wagon, and set out for Omaha where she hoped to get a winter job until her husband recovered. In the true Samaritan spirit, Block took charge of everything, and at midday on Christmas he reached home with the strangers. No man to be merely swayed by temporary holiday sentimentality, he kept them all until spring, when the invalid could plow again. With seed lent by Block, the man planted a crop which succeeded. Thus was harvested for one family along the Platte River the kindliness of a determined Christmas giver.

If daily life in Nebraska was bleak and a livelihood precarious, even at holiday time, then survival on the Dakota plains was an exaggeration of these conditions farther south. Yet stories of Christmas seem to be spawned and to thrive best in such unpromising surroundings. As every student of Western life knows, the pioneer doctor was a vital part of the farming frontier. One Christmas Eve in North Dakota, a doctor was called to a remote settler's cabin. This particular man of medicine was also learned in prairie lore and he knew what to expect of stiff winds. He was well aware that a severe storm was approaching on the treeless wastes, and he knew all the important landmarks as well as the necessary short-cuts. But the stars were hidden that night, making it much unlike the first Christmas in Bethlehem. The snow fell ever more thickly and the biting wind increased its harshness. Instinctively, the doctor's bronchos were led the right way when the man's lore failed him. In time they reached the lee side of a settler's haystack. From this vantage point the traveler glimpsed a sod shanty and wasted no time in dashing for it. This was the home of the sick woman who was awaiting him! In appearance, the visitor looked like Santa Claus, for his dress was snowy fur from head to foot. Believing that they had at last met their seasonal hero, the children excitedly looked for his traditional pack and peered out the frosted window in hopes of finding reindeer instead of horses! Only disgust and disappointment met the boy of six and his little sister of four. Reluctantly they left for bed, though hope was not entirely dead within their young hearts, for they had remembered to hang up their stockings. Betty wanted a baby sister and Bobbie said that he hoped for something to play with. Both got what they wished, for that midnight twins were born to their mother. Not expecting a double blessing, she had only prepared clothes for one, but the doctor, who through grit, and perhaps destiny, had reached his goal when he had given up hope of doing so, was not dismayed by this minor misturn. He took off his coonskin coat and gave it to shelter the newborn girl and boy. Christmas morning, as all good stories, and especially true ones, ought to have it, dawned beautifully, and before many hours had passed the latter-day Magi arrived bearing gifts. These were no Oriental potentates, but only kindly neighbor ladies coming to provide baby clothes for the Christmas arrivals.

Yuletide could easily go from the sublime to the ridiculous, as often happened on the frontier. The Christmas of 1862 at Yankton found hotels busy and merchants trading wildly, and "on Christmas the town was tight, though I saw but one fight," reported Moses K. Armstrong, who would survive many a political argument. He further noted that this one brawl was between a supporter of Todd, a big man in local politics, and the other vehemently defended Jayne, his opponent. "On the second round the Todd man threw up the sponge, and the Jayne man broke his thumb," concluded Armstrong. He might have added that politics and Christmas seldom mix!

Poverty never precluded the possibility of a beautiful Christmas, as we have already learned. The Suttons were a pioneer family who had always had a tree in their Ohio home. Now they had settled in the Dakota country, and Christmas was coming again. Mrs. Sutton made up her mind they would break no tradition this first year in the West. She had her way, although in an unusual manner. Pictures of the presents that they all wanted were cut from a Montgomery Ward catalogue and hung by strips to the tree. Her son Ernest got a double-barreled shotgun, or at least the vivid *picture* of one, while his father "received," visually, a saddle and a pair of gloves. The only real gift came from Sister, and it was for all the family—a doily to keep hot dishes from scorching the table. It had been knitted from a long rope of assorted colored yarn. The simple treat for Christmas Day was seed popcorn, and this, at least, was not made of printed paper!

CHAPTER VIII

Celebrating Texas Style

TEXANS are known not only for tall stories but
also for openhanded hospitality. They displayed
this attribute early. For example, on the Gulf Coast
in 1828, to a stranger in their midst, D. W. C.
Baker, a kindly lady gave some hominy beaten in
a wooden mortar and some fresh milk. This was
a simple enough gesture, but so different from the
treatment that outsiders had sometimes received in
other countries at other times when fear might cause
hatred and ignorance might breed cruelty. It would
have been hard to conceive of frontier Texans allow-
ing a Babe to be born in a cold manger, no matter
how crowded their border-town inns.

During the nine perilous years of the Texas Republic, 1836-45, Christmas was nonetheless a jolly
season. True, no decorated tree had yet appeared
and the giving of presents was not customary except among the Germans of New Braunfels and
other European-founded colonies. On Christmas Eve,
however, and especially on the following day, neighbors assembled in small groups and usually drank
punch with whisky, the "national drink," to celebrate the great occasion. Afterwards dances were
almost *de rigueur,* and the discharging of holiday

firearms became virtually an inevitable display of the country's youthful enthusiasm.

Gustav Dresel, a German who visited the Republic, wrote of Houston, Texas, on Christmas Eve, 1838, a night spent with some nearly destitute but wholeheartedly Christian people:

They said they wanted to let me have some cheer and invited me to supper in the little cabin that now contained at least a cooking stove, a table and some chairs, and suchlike. I later found out that A. had pawned his breastpin to procure flour, meat, etc. The young wife treated us to German pastry and sang native songs. A short time afterwards we succeeded in obtaining a position for A. as secretary to the Minister of War, which enabled the little family at least to defray their living costs. . . .

His next Christmas Eve, that of 1839, was observed simply with a friend as they spoke of their native land while Dresel read him German poems. In his thoughts, Gustav Dresel was home again in the Rhineland. Feeling that the Americans he had now known for over a year did not give their best to celebrate Christmas, he planned a new form of enjoyment for "these backwoods people." Frankly, Dresel remarked, "I did not want to wallow on the buffalo skin, sunk in melancholic reveries, while all Germany, jubilating, dancing, drinking, and kissing, rejoiced at having safely got over another year and at finding everything as it had been before." With this noble cause in his single-track mind, Dresel set out for town, and directly bought up "as much whisky as our saddlebags would hold"—four jugfuls. Almost as quickly he found that "Texians" were not wanting when it came to organizing a frolic. Soon he had more than enough abettors in his mirthful scheme. Dresel and his crew went forth, visiting farm after farm, waking the neighbors there, and getting the unappreciative watchdogs to barking. Some frontiersmen, fearing an Indian or Mexican attack, seized their firearms, but alarm soon gave way to loud guffaws, and the drowsy farmers were sharing in the imported custom. At one place Dresel was invited in by a leading citizen after he and his companions had fired salutes to the official and his very pretty daughter. As the German put it, "The housewife fetched a stag's horn, the young daughter baked a maize cake, and we contributed the remaining two jugfuls of whisky." As a reward for his efforts, Dresel received eggs, sugar, and hot water, and from these ingredients an eggnog was soon being passed around. And so the gift giving became mutual. "We returned by daybreak only," he concluded, "to our scattered homesteads. All were satisfied with the execution of my queer notion and declared that I was a 'hell of a Dutchman.' "

As the Republic passed into its later period, the Christmas eggnog, traditional in the Anglo-Saxon East, became universal. Here, on the Texas frontier, it included the white and yolk of eggs, sugar, and both whisky and brandy, with "new milk to thin it, somewhat pleasant, but of a bilious nature." The slaves brought from the Old South still maintained their week-long Yuletide holiday and still dressed in their best array in the land of the Alamo, as they had in the realm of the palmetto. William Bollaert attended a candy pull on the day after Christmas in 1843, where

Some 50 or 60 lads and lasses congregated to assist at this sport. A quantity of molasses is boiled down until it becomes thick; it is then poured out into dishes and plates, each one taking a portion in their hands and commence "pulling," or elongating it until it gets cold, when it takes on a yellow appearance and hardens, but the great fun and sport is to approach slyly those persons whose candy appears to be well pulled and snatch it from them, this produces great hilarity, and for the first time since I have been in Texas, this party made me think of the Christmas gambols at home—indeed, with the excitement of "candy pulling" the stiffness of the American character one sees in Texas was thrown on one side.

A much different sort of Texas Christmas was celebrated by Adolphus Sterne in 1842, when he visited an abandoned town en route home. He wrote:

Christmas day, a rainy, nasty, mean, day it is and the poor fellows who *take a drop* on Christmas are to be pitied, not a single thing in the shape of Liquor in Town, no matter we had a most Splendid dinner (except wine).

At least their holiday went off peacefully and in the proper spirit, probably due to the lack of drinking. As a sample of what could happen if the stuff was flowing too swiftly and widely, during the Mexican War a Texas group in northern Mexico reached the dilapidated town of Seralvo, population roughly two thousand. Physical surroundings were boresome that twenty-fifth of December, 1846, so:

Texans Believed in a Noisy Welcome

This being a holyday, some of the Boys seemed determined to celebrate it. There was plenty of muscal to be had in the place. Two wagoners who had been there an hour before us, were taking regular knock-downs in the street when I came up. Headys Co. was in advance to day. As I came up to camp in the evening, the second fight was just commencing, there were some blows given and received that were worthy of deaf Burk and boxing Bill. The Col. (Field) interfered, but to little purpose. All was quiet in my Co.

Yet even that early in the development of frontier life a wholly alcoholic Christmas was not characteristic. Bollaert's experiences at Huntsville in 1843 are evidence of this. In 1846, Ferdinand Roemer, another German, was staying in New Braunfels. There he saw a German Christmas tree, a young cedar, decorated in the best finery of the outpost. It seems that a tree in the settlement was already a young tradition, for in 1849 the local orphanage had acquired one of its own.

The Reverend L. C. Ervendberg was a Protestant minister at Port Lavaca in 1844. He had been brought west by Prince Carl Zu Solms-Braunfels, owner of a huge Texas tract and fabulous founder of a colony in that region. The clergyman arrived to serve the settlers just before Christmas. With him came the festive Old World holiday, and, inevitably, the German tree, which he used on the Holy Eve. But it was not the sort of Christmas tree that Europeans were used to; no *tannenbaum,* or pine tree, greeted merrymakers there on the Texas coast. Though a tenderfoot, Ervendberg had improvised as admirably as any grisled pioneer might. He had decorated a large oak with many little lights and hung upon its gnarled boughs numerous presents for the colony's children. As the lord of a Continental estate would have done, the prince provided both the tree and the gifts for his settlers. When Christmas Day itself arrived, Ervendberg celebrated the Lord's Supper.

Half a decade later, in 1849 at Castroville, the Abbe Domenech, who spent six years in central Texas, chronicled his participation in the services held at Christmas:

I was awakened at eleven o'clock by the harmonious voices of a choir of young men who sang a German Christmas hymn in compliment to me, for the 25th of December was my birthday. I rose to thank them, but they had already disappeared. The temperature had become milder, it was a starlight night, and our little cottage was filled with colonists who came to congratulate us, bringing at the same time cakes and pork.

The abbe's contribution would come the next day when he lighted a red Bengal fire, which was viewed with awe by the populace attending Christmas services in the colony's little church. The whole building was illuminated by this light, and, as the gentle cleric, himself moved by the scene, describes it, a minor aurora borealis greeted the congregation, "the gold, the crystals, the chandeliers, the hangings, the flowers, were all dazzling."

Another Christmas, this time at Brownsville on the lower Rio Grande, Abbe Domenech held service for "a crowd of every age, sex, and creed," as non-Catholics also participated in the best of interdenominational accord. Fireworks were set off by army officers of the nearby garrison, and the day terminated with a feast "which had never before been celebrated with so much solemnity on the frontiers of Texas."

Yet near the same Castroville where the abbe had been so pleasantly feted, a tragedy proved that the frontier was still the sharp and ruthless edge of danger and Christmas Eve need not necessarily mean peace on earth when men of good will were not about. Four Alsatian settlers—a butcher, an eleven-year-old boy who lived with him, and two young colonists fresh to Texas—had set out that silent night to fetch their cattle and to cut wood near the San Hyronimo. Their day had been long and hard, and weary bones coaxed them to rest. Under a tree the tired four fell asleep. From out of the plains came some marauding Indians who swiftly pinioned the two youngest to the earth with arrows while the others fought bravely, though without arms. There was evidence at the scene that they had broken two Indian lances before they were shot to death.

Other newcomers remembered more peaceful Christmases. For example a British recipient of happy Yuletide hospitality was Cecil Roberts. He noticed that on Christmas Eve at Española New Mexicans had practiced an age-old custom of placing little fires in front of each doorway. Upon arriving at the town of Lamy, in the late eighties, he was not charged for his hotel room "because it was Christmas, and they were having a good time. They had a Christmas tree here, and the mistress of the house gave me a gingerbread cow, for she said that as it was Christmas every one in her house must have a present of some kind." And so a child's cookie, given to a full-grown man, possibly did more for Anglo-American relations that magic day than a score of consulate parties.

It was this same spirit of kindliness expressed in gift-giving that the Texas governor, James S. Hogg, remembered as a child in the late fifties. When a generation later a reporter asked the dignified states-man what Yuletide had meant to him, he remi-nisced, "My first impression of Christmas was made by Santa Claus. I thought that in a great battle with the devil God had won and sent Santa around to celebrate the victory by making presents to the children on His side." From such a mood of triumph and joy over evils both physical and psychological the frontier best honored the birthday of the Saviour.

Yet while he was journeying through Texas in the early fifties, Frederick Law Olmsted stopped at San Augustine in east Texas to spend the holiday, only to be disillusioned. The town itself was a poor stage upon which to behold a Yuletide of the tinsel-and-ribbon variety, for there were no more than fifty houses and a dozen dilapidated shops, almost all front-ing on the plaza. A resident told Olmsted, and evi-dently the wayfarer took it seriously, that only one man in town was not a habitual drunkard, and "this gentleman relaxed his Puritanic severity during our stay in view of the fact that Christmas came but once that year." No better impressed by another

Yuletide custom, Olmsted looked out on Christmas Eve from the window of his inn and there glimpsed a band of Christmas serenaders. Their talents, it seems, were entirely lost upon an unappreciative audience, for, Olmsted said:

A band of pleasant spirits started from the square, blowing tin horns, and beating tin pans, and visited in succession every house in the village, kicking in doors, and pulling down fences, until every male member of the family had appeared, with appropriate instruments, and joined the merry party. They then marched to the square, and ended the ceremony with a centupled tin row. In this touching commemoration, as strangers, we were not urged to participate.

Frontier boisterousness would puzzle many another newcomer, unable to see how those who could give the last of their food to a total stranger on the Holy Night could also join wholeheartedly in vandalism. It is difficult, too, to understand the actions of Peter on Good Friday with the holiness of Peter the carrier of Christianity to the Italians, but both were one man. With the better examples of family life and a diminishing of dangers, the rougher kind of celebration would pass away, while the touching scenes of goodness, worthy of the season, would persist in Texas history.

CHAPTER IX

Of Argonauts and Holly Wreaths

DURING seventy-seven years that Spaniards and
Mexicans settled and owned California, the vast
interior valleys of their province, secret storehouses
of untapped wealth, remained unclaimed either by
missionaries or rancheros. The padres sought only
souls and the rancheros were interested in being near
the shore line so that they could market their cow-
hides and tallow. And so the untamed Indians of
the interior remained in full possession of their unmapped homeland.

Then came a sturdy Swiss of realistic dreams, John
August Sutter. In 1839 Sutter obtained from the
Mexican government a grant to much of the wilderness that was the Sacramento Valley. At the conflu-
ence of the Sacramento and American rivers he founded New Helvetia, his fort, which was also the adobe
capital of an agricultural empire-to-be. With Indian
labor and the help of American pioneers who came
overland to California after 1841, Sutter soon erected
shops, developed fertile fields, and then sought to
extend his enterprises into the foothills where lumber might be cut.

Forty miles east of Sutter's Fort, on the south fork
of the American River, Sutter decided late in 1847
to send workmen to a place called by the Indians

Coloma, which means "beautiful vale." Here in the foothills of the Sierra Nevada he planned to make use of the river and nearby pine forests and set his men to building a sawmill for his vast realm. But Coloma had a far greater destiny in the story of the American West. At this spot on January 24, 1848, just thirty days after Sutter had hosted one of old California's most lavish Christmas dinners at New Helvetia, James Wilson Marshall, moody boss of the crew digging the tailrace for the mill, discovered gold. From that moment, early on a chilly morning, modern California began. A mass migration, the world's greatest gold rush, soon started to transform California from a Latin-American backwash, a strategic but far-flung outpost of the United States, into the new Western empire, populated by more than a hundred thousand settlers.

The news of this discovery may have been, as some enthusiasts have claimed, the greatest journalistic "copy" of nineteenth-century America, but it was certainly a slow-spreading story. Not until May of 1848 did San Francisco and other northern California towns realize that the metal existed in really important quantities, and the year was ending before rumors which had reached the Middle West by summer finally received official recognition from President James K. Polk in his annual State of the Union message. Those zealots who came earliest for gold, history's neglected "forty-eighters," were few in number, but they received greater rewards in pay dirt for less really hard work than did many of the glamorous Forty-niners whom history has more kindly—and more voluminously—remembered.

In southern California, little touched even in the fifties by the events occurring in the Mother Lode country, Christmas was celebrated in the old Spanish ways. Farther north, at San Jose, Chester S. Lyman mentioned a Christmas Eve religious service conducted by a "Methodist exhorter recently from Oregon," but few people were present at the meeting. Lyman gave his workmen a holiday along with an extra dinner including pies.

The miners, however, celebrated their holiday and recent strikes up in the diggings. Francis D. Clark. a young fellow who had arrived in California in 1847 and had set out on November 1 from Monterey with three Mexican *carretas* and six yoke of oxen, participated in a "Christmas jollification" with a party of youths in their log cabin called "Independence Hall." On the banks of the Mokelumne, filled with adventurous spirit, cameraderie, and a disregard of both danger and trivia, these young men characterized on that holiday the thousands of Americans who were manning the gold rush and winning a frontier. Of his companions, Clark wrote:

What cared we if whisky was $20 a bottle, flour $2 a pound, one pound can of oysters one ounce [of gold], fresh beef one dollar a pound, salt fish two dollars, &c., &c? Were not the banks paying out gold *on demand* upon *personal applications?* Oh what happy days those were when after a hard day's work we returned to our domicile to partake of the feast the "Cook of the Mess" had awaiting us. 'Tis true we had no luxuries, but we possessed robust health and an excellent appetite, and our sleep was as sound on the pine boughs which formed our mattress as ever enjoyed since on a mattress of softer material.

The most appropriate present one could have sent home from California that golden Christmas was what James Clyman enclosed to his friend, Hiram J. Ross, in a letter dated that day: "Enclosed you will find a small specimen of gold. It is found in all shapes and sizes up to twenty pounds in weight."

Possibly the most thoroughly recorded Yuletide merrymaking in early Western history took place in the golden days of '49. Aware that they were making history, scores and even hundreds of Argonauts preserved their doings in diaries, letters, and accounts to the press. Several diggers stumbled on good luck that day. From Georgetown, Charles T. Blake wrote his partners that "we took out fifty-nine dollars in about six hours, bailing about ¾ of the time!!!! The washing of the dirt is generally the least part of the work in Canon digging." Yet another stranger to pick and pan, John Clifton, spent Christmas "in a mudhole digging for the precious metal and it was precious little we obtain." Furthermore, he complained of a great carousal at Kelsey's Dry Diggings, where even the men at work were forced to join in the drunken brawl; Clifton and his father claimed to be almost the only exceptions.

The Christmas spirit was not always evident on the Holy Eve. William Wellington White had quit work for the day and was returning from Dry Creek when he shot a hare. While he was busy skinning

Animated Was the Golden Yule of '49

it, an Indian came along and tried to buy the animal, offering White two ounces of gold, which he
refused, "preferring to make a Christmas dinner of
it for our mess, for we had nothing but bread, bacon
and beans. That hare was good enough for us but
too good for an Indian." Even the holiday could
not overcome all prejudice.

On the Trinity River, William Kelly, a man of
education and the rare ability to observe keenly and
to write fluently, characterized a typical Forty-niner's
holiday. That fabulous personage, so often stereo-
typed in dress, conversation, and deeds by fiction
writers, according to Kelly observed Christmas "if
not with a devotional reverence, at least by an ab-
stinence from all labour on that day, which, from
earliest childhood at home, we are taught to look
forward to with a rapturous eagerness." Kelly and
his fellows secured a loin of grizzly bear meat, some
six bottles of wine, and two pounds of raisins, which,

together with the contents of our own larder and cellar, furnished us such a dinner as dwellers in the mountains are rarely
enabled to enjoy, each member of the mess undertaking that
portion of the preparation he was best prepared to deal with;
one agreeing to bake, another to roast the venison, another to
boil the bacon, one gentleman taking in charge the manufacture of short and sweet bread, a second choosing for his department the pies, made from preserved apples; but Captain S——r's
was the *chef-d'oeuvre* of the feast, being a plum-pudding, made
ship-shape, not to be excelled in composition, which he launched
into a liquid so truly exquisite and congenial, as to leave one
in doubt whether to prefer the pudding or the sauce. The part
assigned to me was to rig a table, and get the Sheffield ware in
order, which I managed admirably by means of the front and
end boards of the waggon, making shins of willow sticks, that

squeeled and bent, not being far enough advanced in years to "groan" under the superincumbent profusion, a purified-waggon-sheet serving the purposes of the cloth; and, if the cutlery was not all to match, it was matchless in its peculiar variety, a sufficiency being secured by supplying the carvers with bowie-knives, and short swords in lieu of their legitimate instruments.

Christmas dawned as glorious as a day in May, greeting the miners dressed in holiday garb.

Every tent was prepared with some hospitable welcome, manufactured specially, and every estrangement was forgotten and forgiven. . . . Our dinner-table was quite a spectacle in its way in the diggings, with its studied instrumental arrangements, its bear meat, venison, and bacon, its apple-pies pleasingly distributed, its Gothic columns of plain and fancy breads, interspersed at becoming intervals, and its Cardigans flanking the whole gastronomical array; the plum-pudding alone being reserved for second course, from the motives of expedition and economy, as waiters were only to be had by express order from the cities. We had two guests, natives of the *ould* country, settlers in Oregon, who were about returning home, as gold mines, it was said, had been discovered on Rogue's River, which runs through their own territory, one of whom brought me, as a present, a noble dog that I often desired to possess, as their vigilance about a tent at night supersedes the trying necessity of keeping guard.

As it has been said that the only friendship that can be bought is a dog's, this gift of man's best friend was a highly appropriate Christmas gesture in the lonely mountain camp.

Thoughts of home for William Downie, founder of Downieville, and his friends at the forks near the town he would soon establish, brought forth patriotic sentiment reminiscent of Fourth of July celebrations:

I had a small representation of the stars and stripes in my possession, and we determined that on this day it should adorn our
house. So I climbed upon the roof with the flag in one hand,
a pistol in the other. I made a short speech, waved the flag and
fired a few shots and finished up by giving three cheers for the
American Constitution. Then I fixed the flag on the gable
point, and we all shouted for joy when we saw it unfurled to
the breeze for the first time in the fastnesses of the Sierras. . . .
After we had done justice to Christmas, we went prospecting
in different directions and met with very good success.

In towns, both those serving and others far removed from the diggings, Christmas received an even
better "send-off." San Francisco, a wonder of the new
West, had been born almost literally overnight due
to the gold rush which it supplied and stimulated.
From a little settlement of a few hundred in 1848,
the town had grown suddenly into a crowded em-
porium, a city which had not yet found its soul, but
with plenty of backbone and brains to serve it while
it sought one. John W. Audubon, son of the Western painter and naturalist, found no merry Christmas
in 1849 in "this pandemonium of a city." He ex-
claimed:

Not a *lady* to be seen, and the women, poor things, sad and
silent, except when drunk or excited. The place full of gamblers,
hundreds of them, and men of the lowest types, more blasphemous, and with less regard for God and his commands than all
I have ever seen on the Mississippi, [in] New Orleans or Texas.
. . . Sunday makes no difference, certainly not Christmas, except
for a little more drunkenness, and a little extra effort on the
part of the hotel keepers to take in more money.*

---

* Reprinted by permission of the publishers, The Arthur H. Clark Company, from John W. Audubon, *Audubon's Western Journal, 1849-1850*, ed.
Frank Heywood Hodder, Cleveland, 1906, page 193.

Yet a man of more faith, and therefore light in the darkness, could see many uplifting prospects for this city of all future and little past. William S. Jewett, an artist, but not necessarily a futile dreamer, had noticed with his keen eye that on this Christmas Day there were already many churches in San Francisco; two of them at least were filled for the holiday, the Episcopal and the Methodist. He himself attended the Episcopal service, finding there a large congregation of most respectable people, who sang the hymns well and in harmony. For the fire-and-brimstone brotherhood, who saw only retribution as the salvation for the sinning community, Christmas Eve of 1849 offered a powerful warning, for on that day one of the town's frequent devastating conflagrations occurred, destroying the Parker House and its plush monte tables.

Meanwhile, the first state legislature of California was assembling at San Jose in an adobe structure erected that very year on Market Square. California, like Texas, never reduced to territorial status, had written its own constitution and put it into effect even before Congress had admitted the Golden State as the thirty-first member of the American Union.

Christmas, 1849 was not so sedentary a holiday for many Californians-to-be still en route to the mining camps. By land and sea the trails led to the diggings and the sparkling promises by which men had been attracted from all over the troubled world. Christmas at sea was quite a different experience from camp life. During the rush by water, some Christ-

mas celebrations were undistinguished, while for a
few the day passed as others aboard ship, only the
calendar mutely telling passengers that this was the
birthday of the Christ Child. Off Mexico in 1853,
Ida Pfeiffer, eager to reach California, noted only
"many hurras and the drinking of much Champagne
and other wines" to set off the day. Garrett W. Low
observed another Christmas without a carol, 2,500
miles from familiar things in old New York. His
ship seemed devoid of any season's greetings. Said
Low, "It is as though some dark and horrible fate
awaits us all in the near future. As though we were
quietly sailing to our deaths. I would to God Rev'd
Thorne would sing a carol. It might break the spell
and cheer us all up. Even the sailors are glum." No
great catastrophe awaited them, but the pessimistic
Mr. Low might be forgiven for expecting it with
such a Christmas to pass far from home.

If no calamity was in store to liven up life on
the bounding main, at least there would be action!
The officious and unimaginative captain finally gave
in to the urgings of passengers and crew and agreed
to organize a holiday celebration of sorts. A game
of "King" was hit upon as liable to amuse his bored
and downcast passengers. Too late for Christmas, the
diversion took place on December 27, 1850. A Mr.
Whippet was elected King after receiving twenty-
nine votes, while Thorne, a minister, was the runner-
up with twenty-two. As an honor guard four sailors then solemnly conducted Whippet to the throne,
made of boards and covered with canvas. His Majesty

wore a green paper crown while the coronation was undertaken by the captain. As the new sovereign seated himself upon his makeshift throne, the seat gave way and he sank waist-deep in water, for a tub had been placed beneath the seat. The minister was as properly shocked as his fellows expected him to be, but most of the sailors were highly amused. Later inquiries showed that even in this regal election there had been some shenanigans. Seventy-eight votes had been cast; this would have been all very well, except that there were only fifty-three persons aboard ship!

At least Low's Christmas included some break in dull routine, but Enos Christman, a would-be gold digger, wrote that the passengers on his ship had for about three days been forced to fast "under the promise of an excellent dinner for which the cooks and stewards have all been busy making preparations." Yet the chicken and turkey were so scanty that the passengers' shares "amounted to but precious little, and with the addition of two small potatoes each, all arose from the table with appetites still craving." Some mischievous and hungry boys, who could hardly be blamed for their act, stole part of the captain's dinner, and he raged at them, threatening at the height of his fury to blow up the ship! Yet, for all the excitement and the poverty of victuals, the spirits of the youthful adventurers aboard the California-bound ship were not permanently downed. Horseplay was in the ascendant; and the holiday took on something of the atmos-

phere of a picnic in some friendly country town
the voyagers had known. As the day ended, Christman tells us, "the violin appeared, and with dancing,
singing, and a little drinking, quite a time was had.
Now eleven o'clock, all is quiet and while I have
been writing, my old comrade, Atkins, made drinks
of lemonade. I now take up my bowl to drink 'a
happy Christmas to friends we've left at home!' "
Thus he said farewell to the most unusual holiday
of his eventful young life.

Aboard the brig *Orleans* the passengers, en route
to San Francisco, were dancing, but they could boast
"lots of chicken fixens today for dinner." Such was
possible for them because they had set sail from New
York late in the season and were only eleven days
out. Off Lower California that same day, William
G. Johnston, who had gained his sea legs long before, still had little about which he could complain:

Christmas was observed by our being served with a really
good dinner; that is, good for the "Glenmore." The beef and
pork were about as they should have been; we had beans both
boiled and baked, pumpkins and potatoes, and mince pies. The
good cheer made us forget some past discomforts. Several whales
were in sight, and among them one very large one which, the
sailors said, was a species called sulphur bottom. Besides a good
dinner and the sight of whales, there was the prospect of a
storm. The sky became black with angry clouds; some brilliant
flashes of lightning formed as fine an electrical display as any
I had ever seen, and there was some deep-toned thunder which
added to the grandeur of the scene. Sails were reefed, and other
preparations made for the coming storm, but it came not, and
there was but a light discharge of rain.

Another Christmas observance in which Nature
was a talented but far less welcome holiday guest
was taking place far to the northwest, on the California coast near present-day Arcata. It is a strange
anecdote to relate, but then, Josiah Gregg was a
unique trail blazer in the West. Author, doctor,
linguist, scholar, botanist, Gregg had been a sickly
frontier boy who left the Missouri woodlands to become a merchant-freighter on the rough Santa Fe
Trail in the 1830's. The trip from Independence,
Missouri, to the Mexican pueblo of Santa Fe took
over three months of travel by wagon train, but hardship and sunshine seemed to be just what the frail
young man needed, and on the Great Plains, threatened by hostile Indians, he soon had found the wilderness to be his only true home, and the lore of wild
things and wilder people his chief interest in life.
Always a wanderer and always an acute observer,
the brilliant, unclassifiable Gregg knew the Far West
from Missouri to New Mexico, from Chihuahua to
California. He had served as interpreter and correspondent in the Mexican War, and upon hearing of
gold discoveries, went north to California. Not content with mere grubbing for gold, Gregg saw more
glittering treasures in the horizon than he would
ever find in a miner's pan. And so it was natural
for this solitary figure to turn his back upon the
frontier and seek unknown lands. He had been told
by Indians and myth-filled prospectors that there
was somewhere to the west, beyond the Coast Ranges,
a great harbor, not yet found, but surely rich in

the yellow metal. With little need for urging, Gregg was on his way, accompanied by seven other men, no strangers to the unknown, but not as well stocked with the love of knowledge for its own sake as was he.

They left the diggings in the fall, not a good time for adventure in the north. Soon Gregg, who by his very nature was only fit to travel and live alone, began to infuriate his companions by stopping every so often to make careful scientific investigations and to write exhaustive notes. He did not hurry, though winter had already reached them. Endless arguments followed, and out of this friction the Mad River received its name. Yet, as explorer, Gregg persisted. On Christmas Eve they had their dinner unexpectedly furnished by a band of elk.

After the holiday had passed, the party followed an Indian trail south along the eastern shore of the bay, "Trinity Bay," as Gregg had called it. He had discovered Humboldt Bay, last major harbor on the California coast to be sighted. That was his Christmas gift to scientific knowledge. Everything after that was an anticlimax, for his path would lead to death in the unknown region before February had gone. It is appropriate enough that such a life as Gregg's should end far off the path of settlement, and that he should be buried in an unmarked and shallow grave in the wilderness.

Other pioneers, endowed with the more conventional hopes and fears of mankind, had considerably more to celebrate in California that season. Most of them were safe in camp, dreaming of their own private pile of gold to be discovered in the next turn of the stream. An exception, however, was William Lewis Manly. His party had set out from the Middle West, passed through Salt Lake and Pinto Creek, Utah, and then took a short cut to southern California, discovering Death Valley on the way. This scene of their sufferings was so named because of the casualties sustained there, for it was indeed the valley of the shadow of death. At Christmas, however, the valley was yet to be crossed. The emigrants were at its edge, at Amargosa Valley. Years later, Manly told of their plight:

On Christmas day, they came to a rough, rocky mountain that could not be passed over with any wheeled vehicle. Now, I know how this holiday was spent. We must prepare to pack ourselves and oxen with the small quantity of provisions left (had been living some time on rations). Some of the poor oxen had to be slaughtered for Christmas—scarcely a morsel else to be prepared for the sorry festival. No one felt merry, but awful sad, when he could put in his hat his allotted part of the grub still left. Some were almost tongue-tied and walked on in silence. As the water here was quite brackish, they had to move as soon as possible and try to find better water for themselves and the oxen. No merriment was indulged in in this Christmas camp of 1849. As they tramped over the rough, rocky country, their badly protected feet left blood in their tracks.

Yet, on that day, the first sermon heard in that part of Nevada was preached by the Reverend James W. Brier. Manly tells us that at dusk on Christmas Day he suddenly came upon Brier, his heroic wife, Juliette, and their two sons. Brier was "very cooly delivering a lecture to his boys on education. It seemed very strange to me to hear a solemn discourse on the benefits of early education, when, it seemed to me, starvation was staring us all in the face, and the barren desolation all around gave small promise of the need of any education higher than the natural impulses of nature." Yet, after a century, this does not amaze us as it did the direct, down-to-earth Manly, that a mother and father with the faith of the Briers would celebrate the holiday with a consideration of cultural matters. In the Atomic Age and its shadows, we still erect skyscrapers and cathedrals and look to the future. And, after all, the Brier boys lived to profit from their parents' admonitions.

Meanwhile, to the north J. Goldsborough Bruff was wintering in the Sierra. There he recorded a temperature of forty-nine degrees, a highly appropriate figure for that year and the men who made it famous. He noted also that his companion, one Poyle, "chopped up the fragments of the old ox, most of it integuments from the neck & shoulder; put it in a bake-kettle with water to stew slowly; adding the squirrel, cut up." Somehow these two men found three leg bones of a deer which they cracked for the marrow, a gill of mustard seed, pepper, salt, and some ginger for flavoring. All these oddments went into the stew which bubbled and steamed for an hour and a half, and the resultant dinner was topped off with strong black coffee, the universal beverage of Forty-niners. That was just the lunch. Christmas supper was yet to come. It consisted of the baked hind quarter of an ox, which had died of hunger and cold, but this sad fate did not lower its values for Bruff. The meat did prove tender but tasteless. Then, with their aftermeal pipes asmoke, Bruff and his friend talked of "the affairs of the world, our future prospects, discussed ancient history, policy of England; and lastly, enquired of each other and explained, how our friends at home were now enjoying themselves."

All this conversation about old acquaintances, mince pies, and turkey stirred Poyle's cravings for something more cultural to add distinction to the day. He suggested carolling, storytelling, and an eggnog of sorts, concocted of coffee, imagination, and mixed with memories. Taking up Poyle's plan, each man sang two or three old songs and related several anecdotes, the sort that always go well with campfires. Once more they smoked, and then turned in. As Christmas faded, their nightly visitors crept forth. These included lynxes, catamounts, and "panthers." Nevertheless, the evening was a beautiful one, and the thermometer's fall to 41° did not cool the mood. After all, a little child was with them. This was four-year-old William Lambkin. Billy had been abandoned by his father, whom Bruff considered an "inhuman wretch." Only a week later, however, Billy died from eating caustic soda biscuits, and was tenderly buried by Goldsborough Bruff.

Others remembered their first Christmas en route to or newly arrived in California in terms of rare gustatory treats. Most of these dishes and drinks would not have been thought much in the East, but on the frontier they would be talked about for a lifetime. Lorenzo D. Aldrich had fish and pie on Christmas Day for the first time since he had left "the States," while C. C. Cox, a newcomer to Santa Barbara, wrote of a bottle of cordial which he had carried along as a symbol of civilization and good living. The symbol now disappeared, being readily sacrificed in a toast to the health of "absent friends."

Although the early fifties witnessed an increasing number of gold seekers' arrivals in California, for these newcomers workdays remained long, holidays few, and luxuries still rare. Christmas was the prime luxury and for many, the only holiday, decked out in hope and holly. It was even more welcome than Steamer Day at San Francisco or mail day in camp. David Rohrer Leeper, who has preserved much of the fleeting era in which he lived, tells us to what lengths miners might go to provide entertainment.

As a straw of the prevailing flush times it may be mentioned that Seth Kinsman, the noted hunter and antler chair-maker, and myself were tendered fifty dollars each to preside as the *orchestra* for a Christmas ball at Uniontown in 1852. Kinsman's repertoire consisted mainly of an alternation of "The Arkansas Traveler" and "Hell on the Wabash," and mine was little more varied on pretensions. He responded. My conscience had not yet reached that degree of elasticity.

Sometimes just chatting was the best form of entertainment one could find, and even that might be the most appropriate. For example, although Nelson Kingsley enjoyed the beautiful weather of Christmas, 1850, and unlike many another miner, could rejoice in such rare "eatables" as fried ham, cheese, and oysters, fresh despite a trip all the way from Boston in sealed cans, he doted on good company. That day he got it. At a friend's cabin Kingsley met a Mr. Smith from Connecticut who had arrived in September. This Yankee told his eager hearers, "old timers" of a year or so in California, all the "news" (probably eight months old!) of New England and provided an intellectual meal such as the miners had not experienced in many months. Consequently, to Kingsley he "seemed an old friend, tho' I never before spoke with him. Many a pleasant 'yarn was spun' during the evening which made the time pass away pleasantly."

Other Argonauts, enjoying the best time of the year, found less peaceful ways to make Christmas pass. Chauncey L. Canfield has given us a purportedly true account of one, Alfred T. Jackson, whose diary he published. Whether real or fictionary, the events at Selby Flat were typical of the lively Yuletide mining camp where a prank was refined into high frontier art. According to Jackson's story, the landlord of the Flat's only hotel had boasted for weeks that he would provide his guests with a real turkey dinner, but most Selbyites were skeptical, and, being real Forty-niners, they were willing to back up their opinions with cash bets. Those who were in on the secret and knew that the landlord had arranged a month before for the delivery of a dozen birds from Marysville, took all bets offered. A week before Christmas, the potential dinners arrived, fat and gobbling. The men who had bet on the turkeys wanted to be paid, but since the wager was on a Christmas feast, the stakeholders decided to wait until the meal itself before giving out the money. It seemed a sure thing anyway, so no one objected. Meanwhile, the condemned turkeys were fattened up while the hotel proprietor advertised the "big feed" at two dollars and a half a head. He even promised mince pie for dessert! But then came the shock; two days before Christmas word spread that the turkeys had disappeared. Everyone was upset, and most especially the hotelkeeper. He had no clues as to who the thieves might have been but, like everyone else at Selby Flat, he suspected the "Saleratus Ranch boys," who were usually at the bottom of any deviltry. And so he demanded that their cabin be searched by the deputy sheriff, but that officer had no warrant. As a result, a very plain dinner was served amid such gloom as only the sorrow caused by losing a rich claim could have surpassed. Only one lone mince pie brightened a bit the dreary day at the mining-camp hotel. Not even a Christmas dance livened things enough to make holiday cheer. Finally, unwilling to remain mystified any longer, fifty of the dinner guests went down to the Saleratus Ranch to see how the hands there had dined. To their surprise, they found no turkey thereabouts, only old pork, some beans, and the remains of tasteless boiled beef. After their amazement had sunk in, the turkey-hungry crew began to suspect that some Indian had stolen their promised gobblers. Then the writer, Alfred Jackson, was asked to go to a cabin owned by Jack Ristine and one Carter. There the turkeys were found at last. All those who had bet on their being no turkey dinner at the hotel were in on the plot! They had stolen the birds, taken them down the creek, killed and picked them, thrown the feathers in the fast-running waters, and then six of the culprits helped Ristine and Carter to prepare a really tasty meal. For a chosen few a good supper had resulted. After the last morsel was downed, the diners buried the turkey bones in the bank of the creek—three feet deep.

Christmastide hunger was not the only cause for "raising the dander" of the honest miners. In the Coloma region, where gold had been first discovered, Walter G. Pigman spent Christmas night of 1850, and as a very disturbed miner complained of "the Spaniards" who had a hoedown at Dry Diggings. "Such noise!" he said. "Singing and whooping, blowing of horns and beating of pans, singing the Spanish songs, passing around from camp to camp and compelling the inmates to get up and treat. What a dismal night—more like the suburbs of hell than anything the mind can imagine."

Anglo-Saxon miners seldom appreciated such revelations of Latin holiday folk customs, but on their own part they could be just as noisy. In at least one case it cost them more in gold dust to do so. The occasion was the first ball ever held in Weaverville, something of a "city" as camps went in the northern mines. The last thing a gold digger could be accused of being was a pinchpenny, and the word "piker" was used by these open-handed miners for the few among them who did things in a small way. And so it was decided as the holiday season of 1852 drew near that the "big blowout" should take place in the Independent Hotel where tickets would be sold at ten dollars each. As there were only two ladies present, some miners had to lead while others followed. For once, and probably for the first time since they had left the Big Muddy, these rough fellows doffed their flannel shirts, and, according to the memories of one of their buddies, John Carr:

. . . more boiled shirts were worn that night than ever before on one occasion in Weaverville. . . . One fellow would buy a "rig"; he would dance a while in it and then lend it to some other fellow for a while, who would use it for an hour or so, and then pass it around, and in that way the "store clothes" were kept well occupied. Boots were used in the same way. The ball passed off in fine style, and everybody was well pleased.

Being both perceptive and voluble, Dame Shirley, who came to the mines with her ailing husband, has left letters of life in the diggings which have been profitably mined by generations of historians. Never losing a chance to record something interesting, whether she approved of it or not, she wrote at length of a "Christmas Saturnalia" at the Humboldt in 1851.

The bar was re-trimmed with red calico, the bowling alley had a new lining of the coarsest and whitest cotton cloth, and the broken lamp-shades were replaced by whole ones. All day long, patient mules could be seen descending the hill, bending beneath casks of brandy and baskets of champagne, and, for the first time in the history of that celebrated building, the floor (wonderful to relate, it *has* a floor,) was *washed*, at a lavish expenditure of some fifty pails of water, the using up of one entire broom, and the melting away of sundry bars of the best yellow soap; after which, I am told that the enterprising and benevolent individuals who had undertaken the Herculean task, succeeded in washing the boards through the hopeless load of dirt which had accumulated upon them during the summer and autumn. . . .

The revel of Christmas had begun about dark, ushered in with "great hurrahs." At 9:00 P.M. the celebrants had an oyster and champagne supper, gay with toasts, songs, speeches, and dancing which lasted all night. They were dancing still when Dame Shirley fell off to sleep, and dancing when she awoke. Three days of carousal continued, and on the fourth, the perverters of Christmas lay in drunken stupors, and "barked like dogs" or "hissed like serpents." Sheer exhaustion finally ended the obstreperous affair.

The gentler sex played a role, and not so far-removed and unsympathetic a one as Dame Shirley's, in a Christmas celebration at Shingle Springs just the year before. As the great holiday approached, the miners learned that a real live woman would be at the springs cooking a holiday dinner. Since none of them had seen a member of the opposite sex during their careers as gold diggers, all were overjoyed at the prospect. In great excitement they dressed in their best array, such as it was. And what a sight that must have been! Here was one young Tennessean boasting a pair of fancy drawers, an elaborate shirt, such as a river gambler might have envied, and the uniform headgear of the mines, a large slouch hat. Perhaps he felt he would be the Beau Brummel of the sluice boxes. Others brought forth odds and ends of masculine finery, which pleased the individuals who wore them, if no one else. After grand preparations with soap, comb, and brush multiplied manyfold, about a hundred men arrived for the feast. They were not to be disappointed as our turkey-dinner hopefuls had been at Selby Flat. In fact, in this Christmas episode reality was to prove far better than expectation. There was not just one lady present, but three, all of whom were busily preparing a meal on an improvised table of rough boards. It is doubtful if any of the rugged men noticed that there was no tablecloth and that most of the crockery was cracked. Tin cups had held their bitter coffee for a long time and tasteless food had been their lot. Now here was a meal both good and abundant, but the dessert was best of all—the privilege of gazing as long as one liked upon the cooks "as they flitted about their work."

Christmas in the California towns of the 1850's was as differently celebrated as the faces, brains, and hearts of mankind are varied. If one were a pessimist in this sea of youthful American optimism, he might want to quote the Sacramento *Union's* opinion of merrymaking at the state capital in 1855. We can almost hear the editor "harrumph" as he put aside his quill!

. . . a formidable troop of bacchanalians paraded the streets on Christmas Eve, making night hideous with discordant noises. They erected barricades across the streets at several places, and blockaded the entrances of stores and dwellings. Next day, quite a number of inebriates were to be seen on the street.

And, if one were a "croaker" whose favorite pastime was complaining, he might believe with a Shasta correspondent to the San Francisco *Bulletin* in 1857 that:

The mountain towns of our State do not seem to observe those old time-honored holidays as the towns and villages of the older States. One seldom hears the sound of a gun or firecracker on Christmas and New Year in our streets. When the report of a pistol is heard, everybody looks in the direction whence came the sound, as if to catch a glimpse of some victim of the murderer.

The complainant signed himself, "Aloha," which was quite an appropriate pen name after all, for the wild and woolly sort of celebration was fast disappearing in the populous parts of California, now turning to farming and the hum and humdrum of normal town life as mines petered out. At a very early date San Francisco, California's, and indeed the whole West's, metropolis, learned to celebrate in the grand fashion. In 1851 George Tisdale Bromley, hungry for every bit of to-do he could find in a region ready-made for the spectacular, noted that:

The Christmas of 1851 was duly observed in San Francisco with the merry greetings of the season. At Barry & Patten's, Billy Blossom's, and the Blue Wing, everybody received the assurance of the distinguished consideration of everybody else during the day, and at night a Christmas banquet was given at Jones' Hotel, which stood at the corner of California and Sansome streets. . . .

The paying a dollar and a half for a meal made up of beans, bear steak, codfish hash and potatoes from Australia, it was worth all it cost. The roast turkeys were a sensation to most of us, who had not seen a turkey since leaving our eastern homes.

This particular dinner lasted from nine at night until two o'clock the next morning. Bromley was impressed by the high-flown oratory, remarking that, "The speeches, as I remember them, were fully up to the average of the after dinner speeches of the period. The remarks of Collector King seemed to me more like a Fourth of July oration than any after Christmas dinner speech, and it paved the way for his going down to San Jose when the legislature was in session and running for the United States Senate, although he did not get there."

By 1866 San Francisco was growing up, culturally as well as economically, though it still was as Western as a prairie schooner. James F. Rusling, an army man on tour, was there at the time and noted things social as carefully as he did the material developments of the West. Of the holidays, he said:

Christmas and New Year in San Francisco were observed very generally, and with even more spirit than in the East. The shops and stores had been groaning with gifts and good things for some time, and on Christmas Eve the whole city seems to pour itself into Montgomery street. Early in the evening, there was a scattering tooting of trumpets, chiefly by boys; but along toward midnight, a great procession of men and boys drifted together, and traversing Montgomery, Kearney, and adjacent streets, made the night hideous with every kind of horn, from a dime trumpet to a trombone. New Year was ushered in much the same way, though not quite so elaborately.

Noisemaking to welcome the Yuletide and comparatively reserved celebrations for New Year's sounds strange to us today. Californians themselves, almost all comparative newcomers, found many of the customs strange, too. An editor defended Western Christmas keeping, which had been attacked by some Yankees, insisting that it was as big a day in the land of gold as Yuletide ever had been in the ice-bound East, for here Santa appeared in full dress for children. Sarcastically, he concluded:

> When San Francisco gets a little older and has made herself perfect, it could not be a bad idea to send Christmas missionaries to Boston, to enlighten her people, who have a great many good traits, and know how to keep Thanksgiving as well perhaps as Californians. Let us not, on this merry day, forget the poor Massachusetts people, and the heathen generally.

A fair observer could hardly poke fun at the mince pies, eggnog, and roast turkey; neither could he ignore the growing number of Christmas trees and the increase in churches and their charity parties for orphan children. In 1856, the Music Hall held a festival and dressed up a Santa Claus to match its beautifully decorated tree. Even in the mountains, at Sonora, for example, children were being entertained by Presbyterian, Methodist, and other church groups. By the sixties California society was no longer so predominantly masculine, and a large number of children were now to be considered as family life gradually replaced the lonely miner's existence.

Traveling in California during the early days of the Civil War, William H. Brewer stopped in San

Francisco at Christmas of 1862. He attended Midnight Mass, marvelled at the beauty of the holiday observances, and discussed California's contributions to the ancient festival:

> The customs of Europe and of the East are transplanted here —churches are decked with evergreens, Christmas trees are the fashion—yet to me, as a *botanist*, it looks exotic. With us at home, and in Europe, the term "evergreen" seems almost synonymous with "cone-bearing" trees, and so the term is used here. Churches are decked with *redwood*, which has foliage very like our hemlock—it is called evergreen, but it is hard for the people to remember that nearly *all* California trees are evergreen. While at Christmas time at home the oaks and other trees stretch leafless branches to the wintry winds, *here* the oaks of the hills are green as they were in August—the laurel, the madroño, the manzanita, the toyon, are rich in their dense green foliage, roses bloom abundantly in the gardens, the yards are gaudy with geraniums, callas, asters, violets, and other flowers; and there is no snow visible, even on the distant mountains. Christmas here, to me represents a *date*, a *festival*, but not a season.

Since Brewer still thought of Christmas in terms of Santa Claus, snow, cheery firesides, and holly, he became homesick. A southern California enthusiast of a few years later would have chided this visitor, for to Charles F. Lummis California was the real "Christmas country"; the same sort of climate prevailed there and almost identical scenery as where Christmas was begun nearly two thousand years before. Mistletoe grew on the California sycamore, and here the Christ Child would have found a more comfortable manger than anyone could image Boston being able to provide Him any December 25.

The children of post-gold-rush California were a

fortunate breed. Even at far-off Weaverville and Big Flat Christmas trees had appeared for the youngest generation while adults enjoyed their shooting matches, age-old eggnog custom, and snowballing. In that country snow was often two feet deep before New Year's, so winter sports could always be depended upon. A ball for the benefit of the school netted $475 one holiday. Still, old-timers nostalgically complained that "the holidays are not the gay and festive times they used to be in Weaverville. The great crowd of miners are gone to Cariboo, Idaho, and Montana, and the gold miners are letting up. The saloons look deserted and we have settled into a quiet country village." A quiet country village is just what many of the stable citizenry wanted at Weaverville and elsewhere.

Belying the alcoholic name of their town in the Kern River country, the children of Whiskey Flat in the late sixties were enjoying the best of pioneer Christmases in their snug log cabins. In this mining camp of southern California there were still few store-bought things, and these had to be shipped in by freight wagons from Los Angeles. So parents put their offspring to bed early in order to work for several nights before the holiday on toys and tree decorations. A family Christmas did not vary much on any American frontier, and here in a boom-town of the California mountains one might find the familiar stockings on the mantelpiece, the tree with its candles in wooden holders, and strings and strings of popcorn. Handmade dolls, some with heads ingeniously carved from potatoes, others of linsey-woolsey, jackknives aplenty, and little six-shooters whittled by a doting father, were in evidence beneath the tree. Practical presents always dominated the gay scene—mittens, for this was the dead of winter in the hills—shoes, and good, warm stockings. Homemade Christmas usually proved the most unforgettable. One little girl called her aging potato-face doll with its hardening and darkening features her "old grandma doll," and loved it all the more for its homely essence.

Perhaps some in the mining regions still believed with the Cornish among them that if a miner's mules were brought to the surface on Christmas Day their breathing the outer air that holy morn would insure good health for the beasts throughout the coming year in their work below. It is more likely, though, that schooling seemed more important in later days than the airing of work animals. One memorable though humble teacher, Patrick Curran Tonner, made Christmas a lot better for San Jose Rancho in 1873. He had recently started his little school in a wooden building there. Although the enrollment began with twenty pupils, soon it had risen to seventy. Christmas was coming, and Tonner felt that it had to be properly celebrated in this outlandish part of southern California, so he decided to assess the school trustees. One of them had to pay $200, another $100, and others lesser sums until the kindhearted Irish schoolmaster had collected $500. With this he bought presents for every man, woman, and child in the neighborhood and rode about the community on horseback to deliver the gifts to those who would not come in person to celebrate with him the festival which he had organized. Throughout the coming year the figure of Santa Claus hung over the door of his little schoolhouse, but it seems to us that Santa in the flesh trod the broad boards of the classroom just inside.

Southern California was slow in becoming Americanized, since the rush for glittering ore did not touch it as effectively as it had the northern section of the state. By the end of the gold rush, however, some families, most of them from the South, had arrived to become cattle ranchers or merchants. Perhaps the first Christmas tree in this still predominantly Latin-American community was seen in 1857. On Main Street between First and Court in Los Angeles was a long row of adobe houses occupied by the well to do. In this block resided an Englishman, Dr. Carter, and his wife. They were intelligent and civic-minded folk and, as the year grew old, proved their public concern by preparing a communal Christmas tree. Now, the tree custom was new even to the East in those days, and completely unknown to those of Spanish ancestry, so the Carters had to explain what they were doing. Many families were invited to their hearth to enjoy the tree, and almost as many pairs of hands eagerly decorated it. Of course, children, then as now, were the honored guests, and for them the kindly British couple served special treats. Carter himself was Santa Claus.

Music and songs, dancing and games opened the happy party while a jolly pattern of chatter supplied the background environment that always makes Christmas sociability a success.

Yuletide of a few years later, early in the sixties, threatened to be as complete a failure as the Carters' festival had been a triumph. The rainy season had arrived in Los Angeles especially early. William H. Brewer, who was in town on Christmas Eve, 1861, said that the rains interfered with the social functions, yet people were still lively enough that night to enjoy a fandango and to play monte for large stakes of silver coin. Six to seven inches of rain were recorded in forty-eight hours, and with the downpour several squat and square adobe houses crumbled, melting away into formless mud. Of course Los Angeles in its eighty-year history was used to rainy holidays, but that Christmas had brought really "unusual weather," and the precipitation, which lasted a week, cut off all transportation. No wagon, no rider, and not even a pedestrian could reach the little town. Most people took the situation in stride, but the family of Andrew Boyle had been invited to dine at the home of a local vineyardist, Don Mateo Keller. As yet no bridge had spanned the Los Angeles River, which was nearly dry in summer, but had become a monster this winter. The Boyles could get no holiday supplies, since they were on the opposite shore of what a few weeks before had been a dusty and shallow arroyo. Then the stranded family decided to send a Mexican servant, Jesus, to swim the flood and bring them food for the duration of the storm. A strong young fellow, he succeeded in getting across and took a note of regret for Keller, who certainly understood why his dinner guests were absent. On his part, Keller sent food back with Jesus. While west of the river, the faithful messenger received a well-deserved Christmas dinner from Don Mateo. Then he put the supplies on a board, wrapped it securely, and swam back, pushing the little raft before him. Everything was delivered safely and was well received on the birthday of the Saviour, for Whom the messenger had appropriately been named.

Thus in many ways California, opulent but comparatively isolated, observed its first American Christmases. Through this whole story of the land of gold run those threads perfectly in harmony with the first Christmas—the hopefulness and youthfulness of the Christmas keepers, the hospitality seldom stinted, and the courage and good sense to enjoy basic things, whether they be a whittled toy or homemade entertainment.

CHAPTER X

When It's Yuletide in the Rockies

A GOLD RUSH has been compared to a fever, and
indeed the love of gold is similar to a disease.
For many adventurers of a century ago it was an
incurable malady. Once infected by the pleasantest
of epidemics, thousands of men would have no other
life but that of prospecting. It was the great adventure of the mid-century. Lust for quick wealth
and the gambling "instinct" fascinated many, bored
with the customs and routine of the East. The California gold fields had been the training grounds for
those who would strike it rich in diggings throughout the Great West. It seemed logical to these men
that mountainous regions outside California might
be rich, or even richer, in gold. Their assumption
proved valid, and in the late fifties and early sixties
gold and silver were discovered in rich veins from
Nevada to Colorado and from Montana and Idaho
to the Colorado Valley of Arizona. The rushes that
followed brought to these formerly empty wilder-
nesses enough population, power, and general economic importance that territories were carved out,
and, in a short time, statehood was granted to Nevada
and Colorado.

The Rocky Mountain West was blessed with scenic
magnificence to match the mineral treasures. In

California, most of the gold had been dug in the foothills, covered with Digger pine, scrub oak, and chaparral. But the Rockies were more inspiring. Here were mighty peaks, great gushing springs and sparkling cataracts. Deep in awesome canyons, cut through millenium by millenium, rushed some of the wildest and most beautiful of American rivers. No straggly foliage, but rather majestic evergreens framed the stage where wealth would be discovered. Yet the miners had to pay for the majesty of their stage. Winters were more severe than the Forty-niners had encountered in the California foothills, and the transportation problem was greater in the rugged fastnesses of the central and northern Rockies. Supplies followed longer, more tenuous life lines to the civilized frontier. Thus Nature supplied a perfect backdrop for a Christmas wonderland and countered it by challenging man to survive at all, much less to import his holiday customs and Yuletide luxuries.

The first important discovery in Colorado was made at Cherry Creek, a branch of the South Platte, where Denver was soon to rise, a cluster of wooden shacks and stores. That was in 1858, only a decade after the incident at Sutter's mill, and in a sense Colorado's first Christmas symbolized the rapid development and quick success of the little camp. The firstcomers felt they had something to celebrate, and with admirable confidence they held a meeting on December 21 to arrange for a Yuletide feast. Christmas dawned bright and beautiful, as if by prearrangement. The miners lolled about their cabins smoking their pipes and spinning yarns of their alleged prowess in hunting as well as in achieving unheard-of strikes. Meanwhile, the "culinary professors," as some wit called them, worked over the food supply, turning a choice saddle of venison or peeping fondly at the cooking pastries. One chef, probably as new to his pastime as he was to mining, molded fresh rolls of butter into fancy shapes, while another cracked nuts. From a log cabin a head would appear and cry for "more wine for the pudding sauce." Finally, the big meal was ready, and the bill of fare, surpassing in every way what far-off Delmonico's was offering New Yorkers that day, included:

PLATTE RIVER GOLD DIGGINGS BILL OF FARE.
Christmas _____1858
Soups:
Oyster soup. Ox tail.
Fish:
Salmon trout, with oyster sauce.
Boiled.
Corned beef, buffalo tongue, mutton, pork, ham, beef tongue, elk tongue.
Roast.
Venison, a la mode; buffalo smothered; antelope; beef; mutton; pork; grizzly bear, a la mode; elk; mountain sheep; mountain pig.
Game.
Mountain pheasants; mountain rabbits; turkeys; ducks; sage hen; prairie chickens; black mountain squirrel; prairie dog; snipe; mountain rats; white swans; quails; sand hill cranes.
Extras.
Potatoes baked; potatoes boiled; rice; beans, baked and boiled; beets; squashes, fried; pumpkins, stewed.

Desert:
Mince pie, currant pie, apple pie; rice pie; peach pie;
mountain cranberry pie; tapioca pudding; bread pudding;
rice pudding.

Fruits.
Brazil nuts; almonds, hazel nuts; filberts; pecans; wild
currants; raisins; prickly pear; dried mountain plum.

Wine List.
Hockheimer; madeira; champagne; golden sherry; cherry
bounce; hock; Monongahela whiskey; claret; brandy;
Scotch whiskey; Ja. rum; Bourbon whiskey; Taos lightning.*

Even aside from the last-mentioned supply, the
company was in good spirits. It gave votes of thanks
to the wagon-train guide who got them all through
from Nebraska, and then witty toasts and long and
lustily-shouted songs were in order. First of all, the
miners sang "The Star-Spangled Banner," already an
unofficial national anthem, and then they toasted
women and song: "May they both attain that which
ruins the one and improves the other; viz: old age
—B. Franklin." There were toasts to homes, old and
new, and finally such ditties to stimulate good fellow-
ship as "The Girl I Left Behind Me" and "Rosalie,
the Prairie Flower." Then it was time for more toasts,
though by now the suspicion was rife that it was
the wine more than the sentiment which led to so
many encores. At any rate, the compliments were
duly paid to the press, to mines, to the new homeland,
and even in honor of doctors and ducks: "May the

* Reprinted by permission of the publishers, The Arthur H. Clark Company, from *Colorado Gold Rush: Contemporary Letters and Reports, 1858-
1859*, ed. LeRoy R. Hafen ("Southwest Historical Series, Vol. X), Glendale,
California, 1941, pages 193-94.

quack of the former be as harmless and of as little use as that of the latter." When the merry company had run out of people, places, and institutions to drink to, they finally saluted the past, present, and future.

Adjourning at last to the town of Auraria, just across the creek, a rival camp which within a year would be incorporated into Denver, they found that place crowded with other celebraters. Some of the men there had built a big fire and were energetically dancing about it, a pastime which they kept at until midnight. Groups of Indian braves and their squaws filled the background of this interesting scene. Wrote an observer, moved by the frenzied gestures and twisting shadows, "It was a picture that Rembrandt would have contemplated with delight."

A dozen years later, Denver was no longer a muddy mining camp but the capital of a prospering golden territory and headquarters for miners and their equipment throughout the Rockies. Rose Georgina Kingsley, an Englishwoman, wrote her enthusiastic account of wintertime in Colorado. Her father, the already internationally famous British novelist, Charles Kingsley, edited the work, which he found delightful. The reporter was at Denver in the Christmas season and there noticed the evident bustle, the merry holiday air of the energetic Westerner. None of the activity had been slowed by six inches of recent snowfall. Always interested in people and their doings, she noticed that:

The toy-shops are gay with preparations for Christmas-trees; and candy stores filled with the most attractive sweetmeats; the furriers display beaver coats, and mink, ermine, and sable, to tempt the cold passer-by; and in the butchers' shops hang, besides the ordinary beef and mutton, buffalo, black-tailed deer, antelope, Rocky Mountain sheep, quails, partridges, and prairie-chickens.

The streets were filled with sleighs, each pulled by a horse with a collar of bells, and the small boys of Denver had made for themselves little sleds which they tied in back of any passing cart or carriage and then were whisked along the streets until a sharp turn or an especially rough spot upset them. Snow had spoiled the ice, so there was no outdoor skating that holiday, but already roller-skating rinks had been built in this mile-high city of brick and stone.

Like many another Briton of her generation, the visitor was fond of Colorado and the Rockies. The general cheerfulness of the people especially appealed to her. True, this was no newer England, this Alp-like land with its hardy, hurrying folk, but the rougher side of its nature was already being polished, without the loss of frontier romanticism. In the clear air of the deeply-wooded valleys, settlers were building soundly for the future. It was this combination of wholesome family life, at its best at Yule-tide, and the newness and wonders of nature, which appealed to an English gentlewoman. And so she was delighted when a friend welcomed her on a sunny Christmas afternoon to his home, there to dine on turkey and mince pie. But the biggest thrill for the globe-trotter came later when all the guests were summoned to the Christmas tree in a spacious Victorian parlor. It was decorated with raw cranberries and snowy popcorn, as there was no holly to be found. Everyone had put something on the tree for the little Negro girl who was nurse for the landlady's baby. While the colored child pulled eagerly to open her packages, she put the baby on the floor; she was little more than a baby herself. Forgetting her more adult duties, she became all child and opened a large parcel containing a new pair of shoes. Upon the young face was a smile from ear to ear, and none who watched her would forget with what ecstasy she capered about like a carefree puppy. It was a wonderful day all around, glamorized by games and music, which began at sundown. The greatest thrill for the British visitor was when her host led the company in "God Save the Queen," for this was the first time she had heard her national anthem since leaving home. Best of all, since most Americans did not know the words, she was urged to sing them all through.

We are coming to see that no matter which phase of its development the West was passing through in its reactions to Christmas—the homesick stage, the period of rowdyism and drunkenness, or a time of pure courage in the face of peril and privation, it was always generous and hospitable and the Day of Days, above all others, brought out these basic traits.

Another visitor from the British Isles, Emily Faithfull, spent a pioneer Christmas near Colorado Springs at the mountain estate of a wealthy friend. Once more the Christmas tree impressed a stranger:

decked out with the usual bonbons, presents, and gay-colored candles, and placed in the library for the special benefit of the eldest little girl of the house, who had not only many gifts herself, but had prepared presents for all the servants and children of the retainers on the estate, who trooped in freely at the appointed hour, taking their places on the sofas and arm-chairs with the true American spirit of brotherhood and equality.

Indeed, Christmas was as democratic as the West itself. There was little of the Old World's or the East's class-bound customs associated with the holiday here, except, perhaps, at the old fur-trading posts or in European-born Sutter's medieval-like fort, New Helvetia.

Typical of the republican spirit and frontier religion was the holiday of the Crawford family in Routt County, Colorado. In 1876 they invited all their neighbor-settlers in to enjoy the Christmas tree.

Besides the four older people, there were three children, two young men two miles above us, and an old German three miles below us on the river. Our tree was necessarily small, for we had but few things to decorate it with. Mrs. Bennett made each child a cornucopia from a large sheet of writing paper and trimmed it with pink ribbon. I made home-made candy to fill them with, and we managed to have something on the tree for every one present. I don't think we ever had a happier Christmas. Our thoughts went back to other Christmas times, in our old far-away homes. Here we were, shut in by the deep snow, no way to get out except on foot—with snow-shoes—over 150 miles to the nearest settlement. For months at a time I have not heard a woman's voice.

Down in southern Colorado, life at Trinidad in the seventies was even harder. For example, at Christmastide, 1872, there were fears of a Ute attack, yet preparations were made by Sister Blandina Segale and her companions to decorate a tree for the classroom of their Catholic school. Two Italian musicians with them hustled to see that the tree was well loaded. Next Christmas, the senior class made secret preparations, like the true Vigilantes, whose name they adopted, but unlike that vengeful group, these students were busily preparing for a Yuletide surprise for certain families and their children who knew Santa but by rumor. Clothes and shoes were gathered up, and boxes of candy decorated the tree for the needy. At the Academy young girls gave their last-year's dresses, almost new, to deserving folk. Most surprising of all, yet so true to the meaning of Christmas, they all visited the jail on Christmas Day, the one where Billy the Kid was located in December of 1880.

Christmas keepers in the Old West were as resourceful as they were charitable. One Coloradan of the seventies, J. S. Campion, caught his own Christmas dinner, a deer which he had shot the day previously. He had also laid in turkey, but the *piece de resistance* was venison. As the deer proved to be fat, by rugged pioneer standards it was perfect. The kidneys were completely covered with tallow. Campion had hung the quarters out to freeze all night and then thawed them in snow water before turning cook. Tenderness was thus insured. The plum pudding which

Campion prepared was over a foot in diameter, and he could hardly pull it out of the pot, even with the aid of his husky guests. Following the pudding came a welcome punch bowl, the contents of which had been concocted in a tin bucket, which on any ordinary day was used for watering the horses. After all, this was the only container that the miners owned capable of holding as much punch as they would inevitably drink. Although Campion could find no holly in the vales of the Rockies, Colorado offered him the shining berries of the Indian arrow-wood and of the barberry bush, and, of course, ever-greens covered the snowy mountainsides.

Gold was the teething ring of Montana, a frontier territory born in the diggings of the early sixties. Here, Northerners and proslave Southerners, buried their animosities, at least temporarily, in the same holes from which they dug their pay dirt. The Civil War was probably forgotten on Christmas Day of 1861 at Cottonwood, where Granville Stuart, co-discoverer with his brother James, of gold in the upper Missouri, celebrated with understandable earnestness. Years later he remembered that day: "We went up to Cottonwood to Pete's grand ball," he reminisced. "Had a fine supper and then danced all night till sunrise. There were a few students of toxicology occasionally, but they were well behaved and gave the rest of us no trouble. Snowed a little last night."*

---

* Reprinted by permission of the publishers, The Arthur H. Clark Company, from *Forty Years on the Frontier, As Seen in the Journals and Reminiscences of Granville Stuart,* ed. Paul C. Phillips, Cleveland, 1925, I, 192.

More famous as a gold outpost in the northern Rockies than Cottonwood could ever become was Virginia City, Montana. The camp had been named for the fabulous Nevada silver camp of Washoe. A friendly Easterner, fascinated by the Christmas celebration there in 1867, felt he was in a wonderland. From that day on, A. K. McClure had the new West in his heart, and he was convinced that Westerners were the best of American party givers. McClure observed, "Holidays in the Rocky Mountains are the most festive of all our festive occasions." The weather itself helped to win him over, for the air was soft and clear in that high and cold camp as Christmas morning dawned. Only a short while later at the miners' chief saloon, "The Pony," diggers were seen frolicking about the crowded tables and they would not leave until a new day had started. One might visit lively games of billiards, while outside street auctions became unusually active. As if it were market day in the East, stores "were swarming with customers of all classes from the unshorn and unshaven mountaineer to the fashionable belle."

After seeing all this, McClure went up to the Planters', a large inn where any sort of special meeting or general celebration might be staged. On this day a ball was to be held, and tickets were selling fast at twenty dollars apiece. The visitor certainly was not going to pass up this rare chance of taking part in a Rocky Mountain social. Evidently he thoroughly enjoyed the experience, and wrote:

For the first time in the Far West I found nearly as many ladies as gentlemen at the ball; but they varied rather more in their ages than is usual in Eastern gatherings of the kind. Young misses of ten and twelve years not infrequently aided to fill up the dance, and as a rule, did their part very well; while my partner in the only active participation I had in the ball (the promenade to supper) was a grandmother who owned to nearly sixty winters. She was, like all Western ladies, fond of social parties, and looked with just pride upon her children and grand-children as they "tripped the light fantastic toe" to the best of music. Supper came with midnight; and it would have done credit to any Eastern town thrice our population.

This meal consisted of such luxuries as oyster soup from oysters shipped three thousand miles. Westerners liked to announce the money and trouble expended in bringing such a luxury west, though they had many dishes in their own country just as delectable, including the "elegant" salads, rare jellies, game of various kinds, and candies imaginatively molded in different forms, and served with fruits, wines, and nuts at this party.

Midnight brought no anticlimax of silence and humdrum to McClure, for between Christmas and New Year's music set the mood at Virginia City, and the traditional rounds of visiting and square dancing, typical of the West at its early best, could be enthusiastically noted.

Mrs. Nat Collins, who in time would become a "cattle queen" of Montana, spent her first winter in Virginia City in dire want. Her little log cabin had only one window, but that was the least of her problems. Flour was selling in that boomtime mining camp for $110 per sack of a hundred pounds and eggs brought two dollars a dozen. Besides, she had a sick brother to tend. Undaunted, Mrs. Collins went from door to door finding jobs to do. She cooked for the hungry miners and made a simple living. The holiday season seemed a mockery until:

. . . on Christmas morning I opened the rude door of my little cabin—which I had myself made since first I occupied the hut —I found sitting in the snow, leaning against the side of the doorway, a sack of flour, to which was attached a small card upon which was written, "Merry Christmas from the Miners, in remembrance of your kind acts and cheerful words."

This proved to be but the initial kindness shown me by these men, and during the remainder of the long, severe season our home was made comfortable and our stock of provisions kept fully adequate to our needs by the money I was able to earn with my machine and their occasional presents.

Likewise a young minister in Wyoming, H. P. Roberts, learned much of the natural goodness of frontier characters when late one evening someone sent a woman's stocking to his temporary church and it was hung on the Christmas tree as a gift to Roberts. The present was mysterious. What was its purpose? Who was its sender? The donor was Jim Brown, a notorious saloonkeeper. When the preacher inspected the stocking he found a pack of cards, a box of dice, neither of which in his profession he needed any more than he did the stocking, but at the bottom were sixty silver dollars, which he greatly needed. Brown had collected the money "from members of his profession as his voluntary act and expression of good will." Not long afterwards, Jim

Holiday Shopping High in the Rockies

Brown was killed by a marshal named Ward, who in turn soon met the same fate.

The history of the frontier is filled with accounts of humble people, many of them on the edge of disaster, ingeniously producing the near-miracle of a simple but effective Christmas. Yet there were some outstanding and long-talked-of examples of magnificent, even opulent, celebrations in the early days. Many of these exceptions to the rule occurred in the Rockies. Here millions were made. Here an H. A. W. Tabor, a Midas of silver, could rise up rich overnight, become a United States Senator, build opera houses and mansions, and with a free hand entertain scores of friends in the gaudiest traditions of Eastern splendor. Even the poor of the West loved to do things in a big way, and once the long-poor became the new-rich, Christmas was destined to be sacrificed as a jewel-studded Roman holiday. In like manner the giants of Nob Hill in San Francisco, raised to godlike affluence through metals or railroad development, good fortune in banking or shipping, marked their ascent from miner's pick or grocery counter. Although she spoke for that unbelievable hill of silver, Virginia City, Nevada, Mary McNair Mathews really characterized the whole West when it was "in the chips" when she remarked, "They think nothing of giving Christmas and New Year's presents worth from $100 to $200, a nice diamond ring, pin, or a gold watch and chain. The Christmas trees are loaded with costly gifts."

Montana was another of the treasure chests from

which such gifts could come. Already by the seventies it had become a melting pot, a cross section of of the America-that-was-becoming. In Butte, Montenegrins, Albanians, Serbs, Bulgars, Ukrainians, Russians, and Jugoslavs had arrived, first to mine gold, then to turn with Butte to silver, and finally to be transformed with Montana into copper miners. In the traditions of the Eastern Orthodox Church these newcomers celebrated Christmas on January 7. Their customs were as simple and quaint as those of the new millionaires of Gold Hill and Denver were showy and sophisticated. The Slavs believed that a family's first visitor at midnight on Christmas Eve should scatter a gloveful of wheat upon the welcoming household, saying "Christ is born," while members of the family replied, "Truly, He is born," and in return sprinkled their visitor with wheat, long saved for the beloved ceremony. Then the guest would kiss one of the three logs in the fireplace and was rewarded with a gift. Norwegians were also in the copper camp, and on December 25 they went about in fantastic costumes, garbed as "Christmas fools," invading the homes of their friends and entertaining the surprised residents. Butte had also a famous chorus of Cornishmen, miners all, who had come to the new land to practice the skills their forefathers had known for centuries. With the fine natural singing voices almost all of them possessed, they were admired by everyone. The Cornish had a custom of the wassail bowl, but this good-natured taking of punch for brotherly affection and holiday celebration eventually degenerated into a mere tour of the saloons and the burning of the Yule log. Some Cornishmen took lighted bushes into the mines at Christmas. Two little wooden hoops were fastened one into the other at right angles, and the framework thus formed was decorated with evergreens, apples, oranges, and such blossoms as could be obtained on the hillsides. It was lighted at night with a candle set inside the framework. This beautiful decoration was easily and cheaply made, so it remained for a long time a simple but effective symbol of Christmas throughout the mineral-rich Rockies.

CHAPTER XI

The Mormon Saint Nick

OF ALL the states founded by Anglo-Americans in the West, the one with the most spiritual basis was unquestionably Utah. No gold and silver formed the pedestal for the proposed State of Deseret, as the Mormons at first called their new Zion. Mining and the love of gold might split the faithful band and defeat their purposes. Deseret means honeybee, and industry was the watchword for these devout people who had gone west to practice their new religion without hindrance and build up a spiritual empire in an unknown but trusted land. The pioneer group had arrived by wagon train in the Great Salt Lake Valley on July 24, 1847. Persecuted by their neighbors on the Mississippi shore of Illinois, they had set out the year before, moving slowly across Iowa and Nebraska. Their first Christmas in the Great Basin of the West was rather a bleak one, as supplies had dwindled and the faithful lived in drafty temporary buildings. Brigham Young, their resourceful leader and President of the Church of Jesus Christ of Latter-day Saints, had returned to Winter Quarters, established farther east in Iowa; there they had spent their one winter on the way west; there the Christmas of 1846 had been passed, with hope if nothing else. Now, a year later, Young issued a triumphant Christmas greeting to all the world. This document contains the epitome of the Mormons' aims, the best of their wishes. Mankind, said Young, should help the Latter-day Saints to do their work, to build a "city of rest, a habitation for the oppressed of every clime." He closed his statement with the universal motto of the creed, "peace with God, and good will to all men." Written on the shore of the Missouri, this was indeed the essence of Christmas itself.

Meanwhile, in Salt Lake City, the day was one of thanksgiving and prayer. Food was too scarce for much celebration, though the winter was relatively mild for those lodged in the settlement's little fort. Women and children suffered from privations nonetheless. All adults worked as usual that day, and in good will. Men plowed the snowy but soft earth and cleared away the sagebrush, which would be used as fuel. On the day after Christmas, a Sunday, all the Mormons gathered about the flagpole for a meeting in the center of the fort. There they sang their praises to God and prayed for help in the hard tasks ahead. Hope was the staple, as it had been the cheerless winter before in Iowa, for these people were certain in their humility that they had begun that year a great work; the future lay wondrous ahead. About them was an ample valley, bordered on the north by wooded mountains, and there was enough game in the valley to provide some meat. Hunters were busy that week getting rabbit to be boiled. Strict Sabbatarians, the Mormons kept

Christmas on this Sunday, and celebrated it with the hunters' bag and a little bread.

One of their number, Lorenzo Dow Young, wrote in his diary that the occasion was marked by social chats and religious observances. Meanwhile, his own house was dedicated to the Lord. Another Mormon, Robert S. Bliss, had more to say:

. . . the Snow is now nearly gone & the weather fine; to day we were waked by the fireing of Cannon & the day was spent in Work by some & amusement by others & at night Dances and plays by the Yong People; I visited one of my Old Neighbors who was driven out of Illinois with me & partook of a fine Christmas Dinner; but my Joys are damped by the consideration of my Family; they are more than a Thousand miles from me & no possible chance to go to them till Spring; their trials Privation and afflictions is unknown to me & were they known I could not releive them; but the Same Being who has Preserved me in all my travels I trust will be their Support in every Situation they may be placed in

The Christmas of two years later was considerably different for the Mormons. In 1848 the harvest of Salt Lake Valley had been a modest success, and that of 1849 even better. Irrigation ditches had been dug, the streets had been laid out in a wide pattern, still characteristic of Salt Lake City, and cabins and houses had increased everywhere. New settlers were arriving. Already the influx of gold seekers en route to California over the central trails had brought a promise of commercial prosperity to the fortunately situated city. Therefore, Christmas of golden '49 saw 150 Mormons assemble by the invitation of President Young at his house in Salt Lake City. There, tables were supplied with many luxuries. Eventually, all had eaten their fill, and the tables were removed so that dancing could begin. This Mormon ball lasted until late that night. These were never a dour people; they loved a few simple luxuries as long as they could control their pleasures and were not owned by them. As the settlers at first lacked sugar and honey, molasses from cane sugar was used in the making of cookies. This was an expensive undertaking even for so special an occasion as Christmas, so children got their cookies but slightly sweetened. Throughout history mothers seem to have understood the psychology of the visual and these Mormon housekeepers were no exception. They compensated for the lack of sugar for their offspring by cutting the pastries into many fancy shapes which delighted the young.

The following Yuletide, that of 1850, saw the arrival of Captain Pitt's brass band of twenty-six members who paraded the broad streets of Salt Lake on horseback and serenaded Brigham Young, now territorial governor of Utah. The next Christmas witnessed a grand ball; about 144 persons gathered at Carpenter's Hall; a mammoth structure in comparison to most buildings of the pioneer town, it was 100 feet by 32 feet in dimensions. As the Latter-day Saints were fundamentally opposed to the use of alcohol, coffee, and tea, cool, clear mountain water was the universal drink that holiday. Yet dancing could not have been much livelier in the mining camps of California, and innocent joys of tripping the light fantastic toe lasted until eleven o'clock.

In later Christmas parties it became a tradition at Young's home, the Beehive House, for his children to hang out their stockings on the mantel. At first there was no tree, but Young arranged Christmas bundles for each family of his wives; these came from John Haslam's, something of a pioneer department store. Of course there were all the toys of childhood, drums, bugles, rag dolls, but also other presents of the more "practical sort," which boys and girls on a cold frontier would need in winter. These included such things as knitted garters, mittens, warm stockings, wrist bands, and woolen scarves. In his last years, Brigham Young decorated his home with Christmas trees adorned with gold and silver paper ornaments and garlands of popcorn, much like the trees of any other mid-Victorian American family. Fearful of fire, the Mormon leader did not allow a tree to be lighted. Family prayers at seven o'clock greeted Christmas morning. Soon Indians from the nearby mountains or the Salt Lake Valley would come knocking at the door, for it was a custom among Mormons that on Christmas Day the natives should be given generously of food and clothing.

Sometimes conditions were reversed, as in the case of Thomas H. Haskell, a Mormon missionary in northern Arizona, who visited a Hopi village in 1859 to carry Christianity far to the south of Deseret. There he spent Christmas and ate dinner with three head men of the community. It was a solemn meal as all dined quietly on boiled mutton, stewed peaches, suet dumplings, pancakes, and peek. After a while redskins and paleface smoked and sang a hymn. An unexpected ceremony, however, met the missionary when fifteen or twenty young bucks, garbed only in breechcloths, went up to the second floor of an old house "while the old woman and her two girls stood by and dashed cold water over them. They went into the back part of the house and got melons and other nicknacks which they threw down to the crowd below, yelling at the same time scandilous."

Christmas could be as hectic in other parts of Mormondom. In 1857 the United States Army had been sent to enforce the obedience by Latter-day Saints to United States regulations and recognition of federal officers as having jurisdiction above the government of the church. This episode opened the way for the influx of federal representatives, "Gentile" merchants, and others who at first were not welcome. One of these newcomers to Utah was the "Zouaves," named for the elite French African troops of that era. The Zouaves made demonstrations "of a bacchanalian character" on Christmas Day, 1860, according to an irate citizen of Salt Lake. Yet the Latter-day Saints could be noisy, too, when they were in festive mood. Mrs. B. G. Ferris, herself a Gentile visitor from Missouri, wrote of Salt Lake City in 1852:

We were awakened on Christmas morning by hearing familiar airs from a brass band parading around in an open carriage. They began thus early to usher in a merry Christmas, by serenading the dignitaries of the Mormon church. Brigham first, then Kimball, and Dr. Richards, and after that the twelve apostles; and last of all, bashaws of lesser note.

Mrs. Farnham, a mother whom the Missourian had met "loaded her dinner-table with all kinds of game, brandt, canvasback duck, antelope, hare, and intended to have served up a sirloin of grisly bear, but bruin wisely managed to evade his human foe."

An ear-splitting Fourth-of-July type of celebration was still common in the 1870's when Walter C. Powell, new to Utah holidays, was suddenly awakened by loud gunfire and pistol reports, and then came to the conclusion that it must all be to honor Christmas. For him, the day so dramatically begun soon settled down to routine. He did enjoy a ball game as a participant and later acted as a spectator in a Mormon game of quoits. The homesick Gentile's only Christmas gift was an apple, the symbol of good will from a Mormon lady, but later that day he enjoyed a good dinner which made up for the lack of elaborate presents. It included ham, milk, sardines, plum pudding, coffee, and buttered bread, still luxuries, especially when well prepared, for a traveler in the West of that period. By moonlight he rode into Kanab, a little plateau village in southwestern Utah, and there he attended a Christmas-night dance.

John W. Clampitt was another "Gentile" in the southern part of Utah in December of 1867. A Westerner of long experience with winter storms, he had been selected to go with Monroe Salisbury, mail contractor for the region, to study for the federal government the problems facing the postal service on the frontier. These two men were certainly seeing the country under the worst of conditions, for their animals suffered terribly from the cold and the rugged section through which they were passing. Finally, on Christmas Eve they reached Round Valley and stopped at a Mormon colonist's farmhouse. Clampitt noted that the man had three wives and that here was a typical planned community such as Brigham Young was founding throughout the Great Basin. The house was long and rambling, a one-story adobe which formed part of a hollow circle. Around the whole little congregation of buildings was an adobe wall as protection against the Utes. But would it prove an effective fortress if trouble came? Clampitt was not at the moment concerned about this. He felt melancholy, and his melancholia verged upon cynicism. And why shouldn't it? He spent Christmas Eve lying on the floor, for his host would not provide a bed, and there on the floor he bemoaned his fate, three thousand miles from home and friends, in a land he hated and regarded as a desert. And added to all this, the Mormon farmer would only provide him beer at a price! In this mood he finally drifted off to a sullen sleep. Time passed, and then—

But the gray dawn of the morning came at last, and with it a surprise. I heard the beating of a drum, the shrill notes of a fife, the firing of guns, and the loud shouts of men and boys. What could it mean? Was it a call to arms? Had the wily

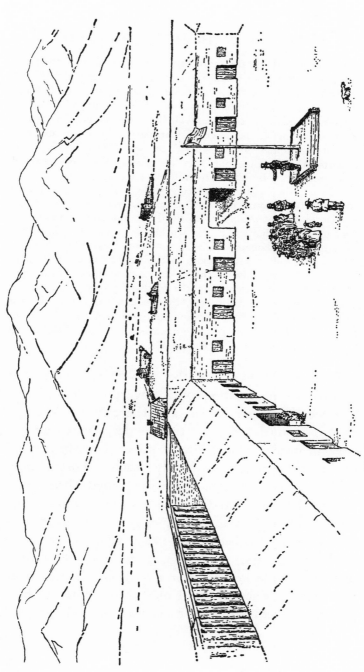

The Mormons Gather in Prayerful Thanksgiving

savage chosen that dark morning for an attack upon the sleeping town? Were we to engage in battle in Round Valley with the white man's foe? Were they already at its gates? No! What, then, means this call to arms from fife and drum? Ah, my Gentile friend, it is the sound of the Mormon boys of Round Valley ushering in the dawn of Christmas! They are marching around the hollow square with drum and fife; they are firing a salute at each household; they are singing the songs that are now being sung by Christian millions all over the world; they are ringing the bells and shouting their loud huzzas, and their notes shall be borne over the distant mountain tops on the electric chords of sympathy to swell the anthems of praise and rejoicing—the chorus of the world song that the Redeemer liveth! Three thousand miles from home, and three hundred from a base line of civilization, in the very heart of the mountains, and in the midst of the wild haunts of Indian foes, these Mormon boys are celebrating the birth of Christ. No wonder that we bought a tub of beer, the bucket was too small, and when they came to "our" house singing their Christmas carols, drank with them the early morning toast of a "Merry Christmas to all the Mormon boys of Round Valley."

Soon after breakfast the two travelers set out again, this time heading south toward Fillmore, Utah. The weather grew colder, and the cutting sleet and rain of yesterday became today's deep snow and ice. Soaked, nearly frozen, tired, and desperately in need of food and rest, they finally reached Fort Union. A Mormon in charge there welcomed them to a blazing fire and fed them to a degree which these men considered lavish. Glory of glories, he even provided them with beds—and crisp, white sheets, here in the wilderness! And then, warm and full, Clampitt and Salisbury got their first good sleep in over two days. When they awoke their Mormon host presented them with their clothes, cleaned, pressed, and dry. He and his wife refused any compensa- tion for this simple Christmas gesture, but they were repaid by the postal officials whom they had not recognized. Writes Clampitt of this happy ending:

The fort was not on the immediate line of the mail route, and letters and express packages had to be sent by special messenger from Round Valley once a week. Although it lengthened the route to some extent, we made an order changing the same so as to include Fort Union, and thereafter the hospitable Mormon received his mail and express matter three times a week as the coach rolled by. It always carried "a mail bag" for Fort Union, as a remembrance of his kindness to the half frozen strangers he let within his gates that stormy Christmas day.

In 1866, another stranger to Utah spent his Christ- mas near Utah Lake. At the time he was a twenty- five-year-old artist-photographer, but before his time ran out, William Henry Jackson would become one of the West's greatest depictors and would just miss reaching the century mark. Here, at the beginning of his career as a Western wayfarer, Jackson had hit upon a good method of getting time to do his painting. He would start off ahead of the wagon train he had joined and walk all Christmas Eve to the lake, there to set up his equipment for drawing his sketch. After the wagons had caught up with him and then gone on, he started off again to out- distance them. This strenuous activity in pursuit of a picture was postponed the following day when Jackson fraternized with a jolly ex-sailor of about fifty, almost ancient for that day and mode of life. The aging character, known as Uncle Billy, was full of forty years of sea tales; besides, he could still do a nimble sailor's hornpipe. Another acquaintance met on the trail was Fred Gibbons, a Fenian in the golden age of rampant Irish nationalism, who had mined the West from Canada to Mexico. Lastly, Jackson had made friends with a noncommissioned officer who had spent fifteen years in the regular army and was simply called Sergeant. These four men, who had knocked about the West in so many different capacities, used anecdote and tall story as other men might hors d'oeuvres and then sat down to a Christmas dinner consisting of warmed-over steak, fried potatoes, bread, and coffee. The meal might be forgotten soon, but friendships begun that day remained.

CHAPTER XII

Giving Christmas to the Indians

ALMOST all our stories about Christmas have had to do with Christians, some of them far removed from civilization, it is true, but people whose ancestors had been converted to the Way of the Prince of Peace a thousand years or more before. A few incidents have related to colored people, but, except in Texas and Louisiana, Negroes were not numerous in the trans-Mississippi West until after the frontier was gone. Long before that time the Negroes had lost almost every touch with their old ways of life and had been forced to adapt themselves to the white man's culture. The case of the Indian was different. Only the Indian was new to Christianity, the greatest achievement of Caucasian civilization. Of course it is interesting and entertaining to see how these people acted at the moment of their first encounter with the new religion and its greatest day. But it ought to be more than that, for by watching the Indian in this situation is to understand a little better his approach to Christianity and Western civilization. Like all peoples, the Indian would have to interpret the imported faith in his own terms and use its lessons to solve his own problems in his own ways.

First, let us see the Winnebagos of Wisconsin in

the 1830's. These people dwelt east of the Mississippi, but their reactions to Christmas are generally typical of those of most tribes which dealt with the fur traders in all the woodlands east of the Great Plains. Mrs. John H. Kinzie, wife of a famous Chicago pioneer, and herself an able dramatizer of fleeting scenes and even more ephemeral emotions, captured one of her dramatic encounters with the Winnebagos. She writes:

The arrival of Christmas and New Year's brought us our Indian friends again. They had learned something of the observation of these holidays from their French neighbors, and I had been forewarned that I should see the squaws kissing every white man they met. Although not crediting this to its full extent, I could readily believe that they would each expect a present, as a "compliment of the season," so I duly prepared myself with a supply of beads, ribbons, combs, and other trinkets. Knowing them to be fond of dainties, I had also a quantity of crullers and doughnuts made ready the day before, as a treat to them.

To my great surprise and annoyance, only a moderate share of cakes, the frying of which had been entrusted to Louisa, were brought up to be placed in the "Davis." "Where are the rest of the cakes, Louisa?" "That great fellow, Hancock, came in with the fatigue party to fill the water-barrels, and while I had just stepped into the store-room to get some more flour, he carried off all I had got cooked."

And Louisa made a face and whined, as if she had not herself treated every soldier who had set his foot in the premises.

At an early hour the next morning I had quite a levee of the Ho-tshung-rah matrons. They seated themselves in a circle on the floor, and I was sorry to observe that the application of a little soap and water to their blankets had formed no part of their holiday preparations. There being no one to interpret, I thought I would begin the conversation in a way intelligible to themselves, so I brought out of the sideboard a china dish, filled with the nice brown crullers, over which I had grated, according to custom, a goodly quantity of white sugar. I handed it to the first of the circle. She took the dish from my hand, and deliberately pouring all the cakes into the corner of her blanket, returned it to me empty. "She must be a most voracious person," thought I, "but I will manage better the next time." I refilled the dish, and approached the next one, taking care to keep a fast hold of it as I offered the contents, of which I supposed she would modestly take one. Not so, however. She scooped out the whole with her two hands, and, like the former, bestowed them in her blanket. My sense of politeness revolted at handing them out one by one, as we do to children, so I sat down to deliberate what was to be done, for evidently the supply would not long answer such an ample demand, and there would be more visitors anon.

While I was thus perplexed those who had received the cakes commenced a distribution, and the whole number was equitably divided among the company. But I observed they did not eat them. They passed their fingers over the grated sugar, looked in each other's faces, and muttered in low tones—there was evidently something they did not understand. Presently one more adventurous than the rest wet her fingers, and taking a few grains of the sugar put it cautiously to her mouth.

Tah-nee-zhoo-rah! (Sugar!) was her delighted exclamation, and they all broke out into a hearty laugh; it is needless to say that the cakes disappeared with all the celerity they deemed compatible with good-breeding. Never having seen any sugar but the brown or yellow maple, they had supposed the white substance to be salt, and for that reason had hesitated to taste it.

Their visit was prolonged until Shaw-nee-aw-kee made his appearance, and then, having been made happy by their various gifts, they all took their departure.

At Christmas, 1801, Alexander Henry commented on the Indians of the far Northwest, who also came for a treat of "high wine, flour, and sugar." These natives, too, were "perpetually going and coming from one house to another, getting what they asked for, without the trouble of hunting." In other words, for the Indians Christmas was at first the day of the great handout, with no genuine spiritual connotations. These deeper significances, of course, could only come through responsibility and a real religious experience.

Father Pierre Jean De Smet witnessed what he believed to be such a spiritual awakening. A Belgian Catholic missionary to the Indians of the Pacific Northwest, he spent the Christmas of 1844 near a sparkling waterfall on Clark's River. A dense forest protected the Jesuit's camp against the north winds, while there was plenty of timber for fuel. This winter headquarters was surrounded by a lofty range, inspiring to the wanderer because of its snow-clad peaks. Father De Smet would remember the site two years later and write of it:

The great festival of Christmas, the day on which the little band was to be added to the number of the true children of God, will never be effaced from the memory of our good Indians. The manner in which we celebrated midnight mass, may give you an idea of our festival. The signal for rising, which was to be given a few minutes before midnight, was the firing of a pistol, announcing to the Indians that the house of prayer would soon be open. This was followed by a general discharge of guns, in honor of the birth of the Infant Saviour, and three hundred voices rose spontaneously from the midst of the forest, and entoned in the language of the Pends d'Oreilles, the beautiful canticle "Du Dieu puissant tout annonce la gloire". . . . In a moment a multitude of adorers were seen wending their way to the humble temple of the Lord—resembling indeed, the manger in which the Messiah was born. . . . Of what was our little church of the wilderness constructed? I have already told you—of posts fresh cut in the woods, covered over with mats and bark; these were its only materials. On the eve, the church was embellished with garlands and wreaths of green boughs;

forming, as it were, a frame for the images which represent the affecting mysteries of Christmas night. The interior was ornamented with pine branches. The altar was neatly decorated, bespangled with stars of various brightness, and covered with a profusion of ribbons—things exceedingly attractive to the eye of the Indian. At midnight I celebrated a solemn Mass, the Indians sang several canticles suitable to the occasion. . . .

A grand banquet, according to Indian custom, followed the first Mass. Some choice pieces of the animals slain in the chase had been set apart for the occasion. I ordered half a sack of flour, and a large boiler of sweetened coffee to be added. The union, the contentment, the joy, and charity, which pervaded the whole assembly, might well be compared to the *agape* of the primitive Christians.

After the second High Mass had been concluded, all the adults with the chief at their head went to be baptized. Later that afternoon, De Smet united fifty couples or more in marriage. Some of these people were over eighty years old, and a Christian wedding would be the concluding rite of a long life. The happy missionary, too busy for rest, reported that "The recitation of prayers and the chanting of hymns were heard in all the lodges of the camp, till the night was far advanced." Flatheads, too, took communion that day, while the Coeur d'Alenes were given the sacrament by Fathers Point and Joset. And, according to the spiritual trail blazer, Father De Smet, "The Christmas of 1844 was, therefore, a great and glorious day in the Rocky Mountains."*

Eighteen years later, Father De Smet's spirit and

* Reprinted by permission of the publishers, The Arthur H. Clark Company, from Pierre Jean De Smet, *De Smet's Oregon Missions and Travel Over the Rocky Mountains, 1845-1846* ("Early Western Travels Series," ed. Reuben Gold Thwaites, Vol. XXIX), Cleveland, 1906, pages 297-98, 300.

the particular Christmas to which he gave meaning were reflected at Robert Vaughan's camp in the Wolfe Mountains. The stranger, wandering far from civilization, was invited by Chief Moise, a powerful man in those parts, to his Christmas dinner. Vaughan's surprise at what he beheld is evident in his account written a generation later:

He [Chief Moise] knew that it was Christmas day and respected it as such, for he had been taught what the meaning of it was by Father De Smet. His wife cooked dinner for us. She had fried doughnuts as good as any I ever ate, and excellent yeast powder bread; we had buffalo tongue and all kinds of meats. In all my life I never enjoyed a Christmas dinner better than I did that Christmas eve of 1862 in the tepee of the Flathead chief.

The Reverend Samuel Allis, visiting the Pawnee nation in eastern Nebraska in 1834, also gave himself more than any other gift to the Indians, a quality which had made De Smet's teachings successful.

Christmas came and I was spared to meet my French friends again. We got up at the chief's lodge, in which Mr. Pappan traded, a dinner of buffalo sausage meat, fried fritters, and coffee. The women of the lodge also added to our sumptuous feast by their cooking. I trust I did not forget the object of which that day should be celebrated. I shall never forget that day, separated from home, Christian friends, and associates, but I trust God was with me.

Certainly Allis did his best to teach both the Fatherhood of God and the brotherhood of man to his new friends. During the following days, without elaboration or abstraction, he quietly began to learn the

Indian Gifts for the "Grandmother Tree"

Indians' language, thereby gradually winning their respect and confidence. This rare prestige was enhanced when he went buffalo hunting with them, dried meat and dressed robes as one of them, and attended their feasts and powwows, concerts, and medicine festivities. Fortunately, the minister had with him one Pappan, an employee of Pierre Chouteau and Company, the fur-buying firm of St. Louis, whose trappers and traders were about the only whites these people had seen before. Good friend that he was, Pappan offered much sound advice to Allis on Indian lore, but the latter was able to achieve good results by himself, for every missionary, in the end result, stood always alone, a rugged testimony to Christianity.

Another missionary of the Great Plains, the Reverend John Hines, an Anglican, spent one Christmas in Saskatchewan at Sandy Lake. Even as late at 1874 when he was there, every frontiersman had to be versatile to survive, and Hines was a good pioneer. This particular man of God, as the holiday neared, set his heart on a good old-fashioned Christmas pudding, dear to his British soul and stomach. Yet he had none of the raisins or currants which he had known at home, neither did Hines own an ounce of suet or a crumb of bread. Not a hen's egg was to be found. Undaunted, he followed the Indian ways which had already spared his life. Substituting roe for eggs and using baking powder instead of crumbs, he made a beginning. Then a flour sack served nicely for the pudding bag. Turning solemnly

to his London-printed and London-intended cook-
book, he found that it specified many other ingredients which he completely lacked and never mentioned a thing that he had! Now, American dried
apples, stand-by of many a pioneer household, were
available in quantity, and these he soon had cut into
small pieces and christened "raisins." Using some
allspice which by a small wonder he did possess, and
a cup of treacle, the pudding's fixings began to take
shape. By the seventies canned milk was an innovation enjoyed by many frontiersmen, and this evaporated godsend was to make the skypilot's pudding
a reality. Hines and his Indian friends took turns
watching the kettle boil its four suspenseful hours.
Then when the pudding was taken out, it fell to
the floor with an unforgettable thud! Whether his
knife had been very dull or the pudding extremely
hard, Hines could not decide, but he had his sus-
picions. Yet, "in spite of all our failings," he concluded, "we got a pudding, and one which lasted
us a good long time!"

Gus and Jessie McGaa Craven were resolute settlers of the stuff of which Allis, Hines, and De Smet
were made, and their Christian charity was full to
overflowing. Perhaps their dogma stated that the
only good Indian was a happy Indian, for they did
their best to make the Plains' first inhabitants a little
bit merrier. In 1891 this couple planned the biggest
Christmas tree in their section of South Dakota and
also the first holiday party in those parts. To begin
with they and their friends decorated the school-

house at Kyle with cedar festoons. Flowers made of several layers of bright flannel cut into the form of petals and carefully stitched became the tree ornaments. All the children thereabout received sacks full of candy, and there was a big basket of apples and oranges. Craven himself played Santa Claus, wearing a mask and stuffing his light brown fur coat with pillows. Never before had the little Indians seen Saint Nick, and they had hardly even heard of Christmas. Craven sensed immediately that they were puzzled and shy, so he went up to each one and spoke a few words in Sioux, at the same time handing the child a new pair of shoes. One of the squaws, more fainthearted than her offspring, upon seeing Father Christmas approaching, wailed "Oh my God, what is this coming!" and fell over in a deep swoon!

During Custer's last Christmas before the Little Big Horn, his Seventh Cavalry was stationed at Bismarck, North Dakota, and as was usual, the officers and men and their families were celebrating the holidays as best they could considering the limitations of a military outpost. Katherine Gibson and her husband, Captain Francis M. Gibson, had decided to give a "Christmas tree party" at their quarters on Christmas Eve. The trader's store offered them a poor assortment of articles, and the commissary had only such staples as sugar, coffee, flour, and the like. Soldiers sent out to find a tree returned from their scrounging with forlorn bunches of sage and cedar brush. Not discouraged, Mrs. Gibson and her friends hung the plants from the ceiling down to within a few feet of the floor and placed beneath them a washtub decorated with painted paper and filled with sand and the crude presents which they could get from Bismarck. Her idea was for a "Christmas pie," that is, a tub filled with presents and placed in the middle of the floor where friends could pluck their surprise gifts buried in the sand. Paint buckets appeared and paper was brightly colored, then cut into yards of strips to festoon the room or to be turned into cornucopias and filled with homemade candy. A few nuts were covered with silver foil from cigars and hung from the tree along with aged Christmas cards which had been dug out of many a family trunk and tied with faded ribbon ironed out by the army wives.

Several young officers, gay with youthful enthusiasm, set to work like little boys, displaying considerable artistic talent as they colored candles bright red and placed them on the green branches. Huge paper bells were soon created, and on their edges the amateur decorators pasted pictures of Santa Claus. Finally refreshments were rounded up, and these included sandwiches, cake, candy, and lemonade made from citric acid crystals. There was also ice cream from condensed milk, a whipped-up gelatin, and the whites of eggs. These eggs, by the way, had quite a history. They had been brought from Bismarck by the mailman, who, to keep them from freezing, carried them inside his buckskin shirt next to his bare chest.

Christmas Eve was the culmination of the military

preparations. There were bound to be some men with musical ability among so many soldiers, and so they were "discovered." A banjo, a guitar, and a jew's-harp helped out as the Virginia reel and various square dances were called. About midnight the party at last broke up when all retired, worn out but happy.

After the guests had gone, Mrs. Gibson looked into the dark kitchen, candle in hand, to see if all was well. Suddenly she was startled to observe, very faintly in the poor light, some little Indian children staring through the cold window pane, fascinated by the marvelous tree. Cautiously she opened the kitchen door and motioned them in. At first they all cowered and shrank away, as any frightened child would do, but finally a straight-backed boy in buckskin, dragging a four-year-old girl by the hand, slowly entered. Then, this foothold of courage established, the others pushed in warily after him, single file, like miniature braves. Mrs. Gibson remembered a small hole in the stockade wall which would just be big enough for a small child. Horn Toad, a good-natured Indian scout who loved the garrison's white children, had helped these young redskins to invade the premises, after he had told them of the tree. The little girl had waited for hours in the snow, dressed only in a calico gown, a gunny-sack shawl, and moccasins and leggings of buckskin. Discovering this, Mrs. Gibson took them all into her living room, dug into the sand of the would-be Christmas pie, and fished out a jack-in-the-box for the girl, who tremblingly clutched it. The surprised hostess then busied herself preparing cocoa for her callers, who by this time had lost the last remnants of fright and were digging like happy puppies in the sand and coming up with pistols, dolls, and the like. Besides cocoa, all soon were enjoying nuts, popcorn, ice cream, and cake, and the cold of the ice cream surprised them as much as white sugar had the Winnebagos whom Mrs. Kinzie had entertained in Wisconsin so long before. Not satisfied with the extent of her Christmas giving, Mrs. Gibson went upstairs to get her little guests some warmer clothing, and when she came down she saw them dancing, the bigger boy leading the others, the smaller ones at the side clapping their hands and chanting. Swinging in perfect rhythm, the young braves stamped upon the carpet and let out whoops of joy. Louder and louder they shouted, faster and faster they circled the stove, until at last their pocket-sized "chief" called a halt and they all collapsed on the floor to catch their breath. Finally, the girl, now in oversized mittens, and the boys garbed in blankets, mufflers, and galoshes, loaded down with bags of candy, cake, and gifts, left the scene of their wonderment. Christmas had arrived, for it was one o'clock in the morning. The children looked back just once as they trekked through the snow and then gave the traditional farewell call of their tribe. A few seconds later this was succeeded by the sentinel's routine cry of "All's well." This was a perfect Christmas carol on the snowy plains. The

Holy Night had been served in those hours to a group of little children; a white woman had learned to admire Indian grace, but, much more important, she had realized the universality of childhood. Would that there had been more adults to remember it half a year later on the Little Big Horn!

A story similar to this, only in reverse, took place a decade later in northeastern Wyoming. A wounded Sioux staggered into the home of a pioneer lady, left alone with her two small children. She was too frightened to turn him away when he said that he wanted to stay the night. Quietly, lest she show her fear of one of the formidable warriors of the plains, the mother prepared him a warm meal and then fixed a bed near the fire. Puzzled by the little tree that she had been decorating, he asked her about it, and by signs she tried to explain its meaning. That was to be a sleepless night for the pioneer woman, who stayed beside her children through the long hours, not letting them know the danger which threatened. Next morning, the mother gave breakfast to her Sioux guest and then drove him by team to his camp ten miles away. She had been too wary of Indian marauders to leave the children behind, so they were in the wagon, too. Silently the brave got out, then stopped for a moment to mark a strange sign on the side of the wagon. After that he swiftly disappeared. Suddenly, before the little family could start back home, Indians began coming toward them in all directions. What should she do? Fortunately she did not have to make any decision, for the redskins started to load her wagon with presents for the children. Among them were warm beaver and bison skins, brightly colored beads, porcupine quill embroidery, feather headdresses, and a quiver of arrows. The little tree and the mother's awkward sign language had won converts for the spirit of Christmas!

After 1876 and Custer's fall, Indian wars on the northern plains were soon virtually over. For another decade the Apaches were a menace to the southern regions of the arid Southwest, but before 1890 the Indians had been defeated everywhere. Reservations and rations replaced the open hunting grounds, herds of roaming buffalo, and the warpath. Although Christmas on a reservation lacked much of the wild freedom the Indians had known, there was beauty in it, for the Indian's spirit usually remained free. At the turn of the century the few pitiful remnants of the Mission Indians of southern California might still be found surviving on a bare subsistence level. One group of California Indians lived near the Salton Sea, and there the adventurer and author, George Palmer Putnam, visited them at their domiciles on the flanks of San Jacinto, steep, snow-clad mountain rising sheer from the desert sands. It was mild weather in this country, like July in the East, and, as if the tribesmen were preparing for a summer picnic, they arranged a grand barbecue to celebrate the Nativity. Just the day before they had ridden into the hills to get the tenderest steer they could find. This task was easy work, but since a barbecue in the stark land of leanness and hunger was a rarity, to be cherished, its pleasures hoarded and its memory preserved, twenty men went out merrily to do the job that a single cowhand could have managed with ease. Having chosen the best yearling on the tablelands, they drove the prize "beef" down to their reservation where it was slaughtered. Next, the Indians dug a hole and partly filled it with rocks, on top of which they built a fire. Quickly the stones grew hot and then the fire was removed and the beef placed on the glowing rocks. This meat had first been wrapped in damp bagging, and now over it earth was packed. Then another fire was built on top of the ground. In the evening the cooking had begun, and it continued all night, a night of pageantry, when old men tended the blaze and recited with pride the glowing tales of their bygone youth. Thus passed the Holy Night under the stars of the California desert. Next morning, as the chill of dawn was evaporated by a bright sun, tables were put together under shady trees which stood by an irrigation ditch. The setting could have been more picturesque and the washtub containers might easily have been more glamorous, but nobody could have complained about the aromatic beans within the tubs or the savory coffee, the rich cakes, and the newly baked bread which awaited the diners.

From every corner of this vast region, mountain and desert, came the guests. They were whites and Indians, riding in or walking, dressed in the practical garb of the range, sombreros, buckskin, chaps, and gaudy neckerchiefs. To the natives this was "Joy Day," and the rickety wagons which carried them forth were as exciting vehicles as Santa's sleigh. Every color imaginable was on display, and to this general scene of happiness and rainbow hues was added the odor of roasting beef. Everyone got his huge share from one of the boilers in which large chunks had been placed. We will all agree with Putnam that the best of all sauces is "appreciation," and these people, observing the prime festival of Christendom in their own way, were deeply grateful for their meager blessings and shared them to the utmost. Of such material is all happiness essentially constructed.

By the latter part of the nineteenth century most Western Indians had had some contact with numerous Christians, and inevitably they had encountered Christmas. Missions and schools were now among them. Thousands were converted. Each culture, accepting a religion brought by another, always interprets it in its own manner, and so we shall find the Indians observing unique customs at the holy season.

Among the Flatheads of Montana, New Year's Day was more important than Christmas, for at that time gifts had been presented to them by the Hudson's Bay Company in the days when its fur traders had dominated their country. With one year's end, the Company balanced its accounts and gave good-will presents to prove good measure. To the surprise, but not always to the displeasure of visiting Anglo-Saxons, the Chippewas of Wisconsin called Christmas "Kissing Day" because the French *voyageurs,* or trappers, always kissed and exchanged gifts on the day. To the Pimas of far-off Arizona, however, it was known as "Eating Day," in the same spirit (but with different ingredients), as Putnam's Indians observed. For the Shoshones of the north, gustatory pursuits were appreciated perhaps even better, since they recalled the holiday, denoting it "The Big Eating."

Some Indians, of course, were influenced by something more than their stomachs, and so to the northern Cheyenne Christmas became "Big Sunday," and those Arapahoes of a spiritual inclination called it "The Birthday of the Son of the Stranger on High." Whether their main interest was festive or moralistic, all Indians enjoyed the gay Yuletide celebrations held in local school, mission church, or trading post. On this one day Indians were the honored guests and received presents as well as a fine dinner. Often, the old men and women who had never learned to sit at table or use knife and fork, huddled about the wall of the dining room, on the floor, and were served by teachers or missionaries.

The Christmas tree, as it does every child, greatly impressed the Indians, old as well as young. They were struck by its simple beauty, radiance, and mystery. It is said that Chief Ring Thunder of the Rosebud Reservation of South Dakota, a hater of whites and all their works, was won over to keeping Christmas when he saw a trader's tree set up for the Indians. The taciturn chief remarked that this fete had made the adults glad and all the children happy, and therefore it was good, and that he, too, from now on, would decorate a tree.

Pantheistic in their primitive faith, various tribes had for ages worshipped trees, and most especially evergreens, which were for them the "ever-living trees" and thus particularly sacred. To the southern Cheyennes the Christmas tree became the "giving tree." Yet, even before Columbus founded his Caribbean town of Navidad in honor of the Nativity, a tribe in North Dakota had long observed a custom similar to that surrounding the European's Christmas tree. Each spring the tribesmen would plant a cedar near the big medicine lodge and would call it the "Grandmother." Respectfully, children brought gifts to put on the little tree, and they were expected to be blessed for their actions, while adults would be absolved of all guilt through the "big medicine" of this special shrub. The tree must have been a strange sight standing there, covered with finely woven shawls, moccasins, and the best of robes. When at last fall arrived on the Great Plains, the little tree was finally dug up and, with great ceremony, set afloat on its long journey down the Missouri.

Also important in the mind of the Indian was present giving. Although in most tribes few adults began giving each other Christmas presents, children were always treated. At Indian schools these youngsters were encouraged to make each other small gifts. The lower Brule Sioux introduced the custom of

226 CHRISTMAS ON THE AMERICAN FRONTIER

choosing an old man as a "grandfather," or redskin Santa, to pass out the children's Christmas presents.

The Indians of the Pacific Northwest had, since their concept of time began, observed a famous custom, that of the potlatch. The potlatch was a ceremonial form of gift giving, the wealthier the man and the greater gifts he could present, the higher his prestige soared. Up in Alaska, along the Klawak Passage, lived a tribe which had turned the potlatch to Christian purposes, in the same manner, after all, that Teutonic pagans had turned the Yule log into a Christmas custom. Wrote Charles Wentworth Sarel, familiar with the beautiful country of trout streams, waterfalls, and pine-framed lakes:

At Christmas the Annual "potlatch" is held here. All those who have lost children or near relatives have to "Potlatch"—or give away—their goods to certain others, who, according to their laws, are entitled to them. This is all carried out with a great deal of ceremony, dancing and dressing up in various guises to imitate different animals. Very often a man will give away blankets and flour and provisions, and even money to the extent of £400 or £500; the man who gives the biggest potlatch being held in most esteem.

At some Indian missions, beautiful religious services developed. For example, at St. Joseph's, a Roman Catholic mission, the Nez Perce camped for several days before Christmas and attended services twice a day, reciting their prayers in their own tongue in perfect rhythm. Confession followed within the church on Christmas Eve. A bonfire was built before the church and the Indians formed a wide circle about it while their chiefs spoke of the significance of Christmas. Their oratory, simple but moving, was an effective lay sermon and as indigenous as the Rockies. At the high Midnight Mass within the church, the Indians sang beautifully, this time in Latin, and then at intervals, they sang hymns in English, followed by songs in their own language. Not until two o'clock the next morning did the congregation finally retire.

In these ways did Christmas reach the American Indian, first only superficially and materially, but gradually the Word of the Prince of Peace came to have meaning. The universality of Christmas became evidence of the unity of all men's deepest hopes and purposes.

CHAPTER XIII

A Merry Military Christmas

OFTEN it is a soldier who understands best the blessings of peace. This being so, it is not unusual that military posts in the Old West were headquarters of some of the most remarkable of pioneer Christmases. It is not strange that warriors should have led others in observing the birthday of the Prince of Peace.

In peacetime, soldiers were always given Christmas and New Year's as holidays. During the Mexican War, however, such a pleasant tradition could not be carried out. For example, the wartime holiday season of 1846 witnessed the battle of Bracito, or Temascalitos, on the east side of the Rio Grande near El Paso. Colonel A. W. Doniphan had marched southward from New Mexico in the autumn to occupy Chihuahua and had met no serious resistance until he reached the Rio Grande. On Christmas Day, his men had just arrived in camp, and six hundred of them had unsaddled their animals for a long-awaited Yuletide respite. Some of the soldiers were already beginning to carry wood and water for the coming meal. Then suddenly news arrived that the Mexicans had been sighted. They were advancing. Thus at two o'clock on a sunny December day, peace on earth was shattered for these men. Coming from the east, the enemy charged directly on the United States left flank. The Mexicans had one howitzer, which was used in attacking the Americans' right flank, but soon they were forced to flee. Flight led to rout when Howard Company took advantage of the Mexicans' break and seized their cannon. Provisions, arms, and baggage were hastily left behind as the Mexicans raced for the mountains. This gave the gringo invaders an unplanned Christmas "gift," won after only forty minutes of actual fighting, less than three-quarters of an hour which had brought a loss of sixty-three Mexican dead and about one hundred and fifty wounded, while the Americans had lost no dead and but seven wounded. That Christmas night, Doniphan's troops feasted on captured meat and wine and ate Mexican bread, completing their victory celebration and Christmas party with some long Mexican *cigarillos*.

The United States had acquired a vast territory with her final defeat of Mexico, and during the 1850's new military establishments were founded there as guardians of the frontier and as protection against the Indians. In the Southwest, tribes which had checked Spanish and Mexican settlement for three centuries now confronted the Americans. Fort Pueblo had been built in 1842 at the junction of Fountain Creek with the Arkansas River. It was an adobe building, rectangular, and composed of several low rooms against the outside wall and facing an interior court. Traders might pause at this bastion, but by the 1850's it was chiefly a stronghold against

Plains warfare. On Christmas Day of 1854, the fort contained only seventeen people, all of them preparing for the day's festivities. Mrs. Sandoval, a Mexican, was the fort's only woman, and of course, her time was filled that afternoon. In expectation that their labors would contribute to Christmas feasting, her two young sons fed the fire, dipped flour from a sack, and dutifully fetched water from the river. Just the day before one of the Old West's most interesting trail blazers, "Uncle Dick" Wootton, a Mountain Man whose college had been the rendezvous, his campus the Great Plains and Rockies, had noticed Indians' signs in the neighborhood. He offered his expert advice to Bento Sandoval, husband of the post's only housewife. Wooton warned him that he should not let anyone enter the fort for any reason whatsoever. Yet, when Tierra Blanca, chief of the Mohuache Utes, showed friendly signs that Christmas Day, Sandoval welcomed him in. He was not alone; other Indians were permitted to enter at the same time. All went well, and the redskins began to engage in neighborly games of skill. Then Blanca disarmingly suggested that all hands adjourn to an interior room for a congenial holiday smoke. Suddenly, at a prearranged signal, all the Indians seized the guns and began a slaughter. What had caused this massacre? "Taos lightning," that potent drink of trapper and Indian alike, may have been the immediate reason for the outbreak, or it may have been entirely unpremeditated. We can never know, but we do know that the calamity was nearly complete. Only Romaldo, a herder, temporarily escaped, but even he was fatally wounded. By sign language he told some ranchers living two miles away what had happened. Mrs. Sandoval and her two boys had been captured. Eventually she was killed, but the children were later recovered.

A similar tragedy nearly occurred at Fort Berthold in the Yellowstone country. On Christmas Eve in 1862, while most of the friendly Indians were at their winter quarters, the fort was attacked by a party of Sioux who reduced it and most of the adjacent village to ashes and almost captured the inside stockade. That was no "silent night" for the defenders at the garrison who defended themselves bravely and in the nick of time were saved by the arrival of some friendly redskins who drove off the Sioux.

Perhaps only a relatively few settlers throughout the West had heard the details of these bloody Christmases, but all frontier soldiers, whether they knew of the incidents or not, were prepared at every holiday for such occurrences. Even in the midst of merrymaking, there was always a serious note. Arms were never far away. Death might not want to take a holiday.

Yet, for all the occupation with warmaking, a series of tasks which became only a preoccupation at Christmas, Yuletide could be and usually was a merry season, for the routine of camp life needed a break, a period of recreation as its counterbalance. This was especially so during the bleakness of winter in the isolated sections. An example of persistence in keeping Christmas at almost any cost is found in what Major John Owen wrote from the Northwest in 1854: "Mince Pies & Cakes that would have done Credit to a table in a More Civilized part of the World" were enjoyed. The next year, too, he dined on mince pie and drank punch. In following years the whole population of Hell's Gate (strange name for a scene of Christmas festivals!) came to Fort Owen for a dinner and a spree. Physical barriers and bad weather could no more prevent their arrival than it could have checked a rush for gold.

Far to the southwest, Camp Arbuckle, in Indian Territory, boasted an even greater bill of fare at Christmas time in 1852: bear meat, buffalo, prairie hen or grouse, venison, wild turkey, duck, goose, quail, and pigeon. At most holiday meals soldiers ate only one or two kinds of game, but at Yuletide the menu was expanded to the natural limits of the frontier's resources. Wrote a celebrant at Camp Arbuckle in his journal that day:

> Christmas in garrison is celebrated by all the demonstrations of joy and good cheer, so far as available, customary in other places. We are generally invited to the quarters of one of the married officers to partake of such refreshments as are suitable to the occasion. At this post we are denied all those delightfully pleasant church festivities common to all civilized and christian communities, for the simple reason that we have no Chaplain. Let all young ladies who are dazzled with the glare of gilt buttons at some of the fashionable parties on East, bear these, and other deprivations, in mind, before saying "yes" to the fascinating sons of Mars.

Rodney Glisan had previously bragged jubilantly of the fine Christmas dinners of 1850 and 1851 at Fort Arbuckle, but things were not so good this later year, and he had to admit that even dietary luxury could become humdrum monotony, and how he loathed wild duck, goose, turkey, grouse, and the like, for he had consumed unnumbered pounds of these delicacies. What Glisan really wanted now was the simple, democratic diet of the civilized and sedentary East, fresh fruit and luscious vegetables, but except for a few apples brought in from Arkansas, he never saw cultivated fruits, and with the small pay of the Western soldier and no rapid transportation system available, for him and his companions fresh items were out of the question. Some enterprising troopers had set out vegetable patches near the fort, but fruit trees would take too long to bear for even the most patient of soldiers to bother with their cultivation.

Those pioneers of the covered-wagon era who were sheltered and nourished by the army posts and protected by their arms from the usually invisible redskin menace, certainly were not so ungrateful as to complain about the lack of vegetables. Although few traveled long distances in the dead of winter, occasionally there were some emigrants, like a party which arrived half frozen near Fort Leavenworth, Kansas, at Christmas, 1849. The menfolk kept the fire burning all night while the hungry wanderers were served a meal made more welcome by its warmth than through any particular culinary skill. Yet it was considered a fine meal, so memorable, in fact, that one member of the group reminisced more than half a century later, "To this day I remember how delicious the biscuits were, and then we had honey with them; and the venison, ham, and coffee!"

Near the Great Falls of the Missouri, far up in the empty wilderness of Montana, stood an adobe post, completed just before Christmas in 1850. The problems of construction had not been unusual, but now the builders were puzzled as to what to name their new fort. Lieutenant James H. Bradley wrote of the situation in his journal:

On Christmas night it was dedicated by a big ball; and until a late hour the light-headed voyageurs and their squaw wives, sweethearts and friends, danced and whirled to the music of several fiddles. In the midst of the festivities Maj. Culbertson proposed that in consideration of the warm friendship of Thomas H. Benton for the partners of the American Fur Company, and his services in saving the Company from ruin in 1844 by effecting a compromise of the suit brought against it, that the post should be re-named in his honor.

Thus Senator Benton, of Missouri, champion of the West and its first American inhabitants and father-in-law of John C. Fremont, received an unexpected Christmas honor.

Most Christmases of the fifties were dismal affairs for the army. From the far-off Northwest in what it now the state of Washington, Christmas came in 1852 accompanied by a thermometer registering of 8° F. It has been colder in those parts before and since, but to an early-day army wife, the spouse of

Here the Season Combined Joy and Vigilance

Colonel I. N. Ebey, this unfamiliar locale was a personal challenge which she both described and met:

This is Christmass day but it is so cold we cannot enjoy ourselves and it seems but little like Christmass though it makes me think of years gone by, and friends who are in their graves. Mr. Ebey is gone and this is another lonely Christmass to me. Our friends who have crossed the plains do not come. I have almost given out seeing them this winter. I can hear nothing direct from them if they knew of my uneasiness concerning them they would have writen Dr Lansdale and Mr Alexander were here today they brought me a jar of pickles and a box of mincemeat as a Christmass present. I made some mince pies for dinner and they were excellent.

Most officers of the pre-Civil War period did not share Ebey's good fortune in having a wife awaiting them at a pioneer army post. In their cases, wives or sweethearts were not within a thousand miles or more of their lonely stations. Captain Albert Tracy, who found himself on duty in Utah during the so-called Mormon War of the late fifties, was grateful for the roast rabbit and peach pie that Yuletide brought him, but his chief emotion that day was surprise mixed with considerable respect for the strong individuality and unknown and untapped abilities of what today's phrase-coiners call the "common man." He explained that "buried in among the rank and file of men about us. Here were men at this little entertainment, worthy of a place on any boards. Some of the [Christmas] pantomime was seemingly perfect, both as to the rendering of the actors, and the music. But a dream of the past, and of the hearts that were, closes in more sadly my night of Christmas." With the eyes of sentimentality, he was hardly an able critic of homespun cultural attainments, though his final remark was certainly in keeping with the day and not out of character for an army officer in the Great Basin, "Over all rises to mind the utterance, that 'Except ye be as little children, ye shall not see the kingdom of Heaven.' "

Such entertainments by enlisted men were common. At Fort Rice in Dakota Territory, 1868, a number of soldiers of German ancestry formed a club at the post, and the first group endeavor they attempted was a show for Christmas Eve. It consisted of some native songs and a fine supper. Their stimulant was only a weak, homemade beer, and for political reasons, perhaps, or maybe in the genuine spirit of the season, all officers were invited to attend. The next day was not nearly so mild. According to Surgeon Washington Matthews, it was a Christmas "celebrated chiefly by the amount of whiskey drank at the post, Soldiers having filed away whiskey orders and stored away the article itself for some time past in view of the approaching festival." Due to the boredom of ordinary times, it was natural that such a rugged and restless group would turn to alcoholic excesses.

A somewhat cynical but very knowing cavalryman of the Texas frontier, H. H. McConnell, was familiar with this old story. "During the Christmas holidays drunkenness was prevalent," he said, "and desertions very numerous, and I began to have insight into the thousand and one ways and means that a soldier will indulge in to get whiskey."

Christmas on the Great Plains could be a particularly unpleasant time, if Nature was not on the side of the celebrants. Stationed at Fort Stevenson in Dakota Territory, a region noted for its record-making blizzards, Philippe Régis de Trobriand found nothing at all which would denote the passing of Christmas. He surmised that, however, everyone stationed in his miserable little hut "probably [was] dreaming of past memories that this date recalls," while outside the storm subsided for a little while, giving way to a Holy Night with twinkling stars and clear skies such as later ballad writers would vaunt. As for Christmas Day itself, Trobriand and his friends must have been without imagination to make it better, for the best they could say of the holiday was "food plentiful, conversation banal and uninteresting."

Yet Christmas need not have been only the twenty-fifth day of a cold December. Colonel Homer W. Wheeler, stationed near Fort Washakie in the northern plains, made one frontier holiday unforgettable by thinking of someone besides himself, and by loving those whom many might then have called his potential enemies. Wheeler describes his actions:

I gave the Indians at my post their first Christmas tree. I asked the scouts to subscribe to the fund, which they did very liberally, so that every woman and child received a suitable present. I gave each child a bag of nuts, candy, cakes and some kind of fruit. Moreover, I had Santa Claus come into camp with a sled loaded down with gifts. I then explained to them in simple words about the day and how Christmas originated. They never forgot the day and very often referred to it.

During the lively times when other soldiers were fighting other Indians of the northern plains, Christmas changed but little. By the seventies and eighties, of course, rail transportation had become a reality. Now better gifts could be purchased with a minimum of difficulty. Far wider selections were possible, while the mail and telegraph systems had put army men in contact with most of the outside world. Mrs. Elizabeth B. Custer mentions in her memoirs several "lovely Christmases" that she and her Indian-fighter husband enjoyed in Kansas, Texas, and the upper Missouri Valley. Usually, just before Christmas, members of the staff went to the nearest large town to buy gifts, and the selections were quite good, even if the soldiers' tastes ran toward the big and the gaudy.

The Texas frontier of the sixties and seventies was a critical area, both because of Comanche and other Indian depredations on the one hand and the problem of Mexican marauders from across the border on the other. Pioneer conditions prevailed in this country. Yet, for all that, Christmas, at least psychologically, placed the frontier's defenders back again in the heart of civilization. Every man who had enjoyed a happy and normal childhood was filled with memories of Christmas. Some, as those we have met elsewhere, had hidden musical talent and enough wind developed on march or cavalry charge to sustain a long-lived baritone ballad. The Sixth United States Cavalry, to which H. H. McConnell was attached, had three or four good musicians to make melodious the holidays of 1867 spent near Jacksboro. These, plus some other enlisted men, formed a minstrel troupe, and with two violins, a guitar, a flute, and a banjo, some really good music resulted. Even had it not been up to professional standards, the entertainment-hungry men would not have noticed. As McConnell tells us:

A vacant forage room was fitted up with a stage and seats, and on Christmas eve they gave an entertainment which was patronized by the whole garrison, from commanding officer to camp cook. One Myers, a bugler in my company, and the life of the camp, brought down the house by singing the following ode, written for him by myself and set to the then popular air "Captain Jinks."

I'm Private Blow of the U.S.A.
At first Bull Run I ran away;
If I'd been killed that fatal day,
I wouldn't be now in the army.
Of course I don't expect to fight,
Want to fight, have to fight;
Of course I neither drill nor fight,
While I'm in the regular army.

Spoken: No, my friends, you see I have so many other things to do such as elevating the condition of the Negro, building officers' quarters, etc.; that I shall do but mighty little fighting.

Chorus:
For I'm Private Blow of the U.S.A.
Of course I live beyond my pay,
For high and low that is the way,
We do in the regular army.

> At first they sent me to Carlisle,
> They kept me there a little while,
> Since then I've footed many a mile,
> A recruit in this regular army.
> I thought, of course, I'd have a horse,
> Ride a horse, an army horse;
> I thought a trooper had a horse,
> To carry him through the army.

Spoken: But then, you see, I suppose they thought I couldn't ride; at any rate, I've had to walk so far in my cavalry service, for

Chorus:
> I'm Private Blow of the U.S.A.
> You ought to see the coat I wear,
> And then, the trousers, such a pair!
> There's no such uniform, I swear,
> In any decent army.
> I'll quit the "wearing of the blue"
> Army blue, or any blue;
> I'll quit the "wearing of the blue,"
> When I get out of the army.

Now, not all Plains soldiers spent the holiday standing up and singing their blues away. A volunteer cavalryman with Custer in the Washita region of Indian Territory tells us of Christmas Eve and Day in 1868 when the festivities were observed horizontally:

Our fireplace is a good idea so we spend much of our time inside lying on our beds. We cook our meals inside now and use a wide box lid for a table. . . . Our chimney draws nicely and we are not troubled with smoke. While out grazing our horses today we pulled enough dead grass to make a much softer bed than the one we had last night.

Their light was bright enough for reading, but

since the men had nothing to read, a member of the squad brought forth a deck of cards so the brightness would not be wasted. But thoughts of home interfered with concentration on the game, and the volunteer told his chums that if he were back East he would likely be at "some church's Christmas tree and have a good time." Hardly an army man of the plains ever existed who did not have a "white Christmas"—and curse it. And this was the case on the Washita, where Christmas Day brought a chilling blow from the north, and inevitably the trusty fireplace welcomed many a visitor to the soldier's tent.

Ben Arnold complained, as all soldiers would, of the short winter days and long, cold nights which dragged wearily on about Christmas time. He was stationed in a dugout on the North Platte, which he made as snug as his army experience allowed, and had for his only equipment the pioneer's old standbys, a Dutch oven, frying pan, camp kettle, and coffee pot, and such supplies as sugar, tobacco, flour, and salt to prepare in them—but no meat. Boredom soon abolished calendars, and Arnold lost track of weeks and months and never knew just when Christmas or New Year's had arrived.

The soldier on campaign during the historic Plains Indian wars of the seventies and eighties may have been the pivot of our Western development at the time, but he was not to be envied, and especially not on December 25. Yet Frederic Remington, who knew these men and painted their life in the last days of the frontier, explains the attitude of the average fighting man, domiciled in a Sibley tent: "He holds it [life] in no strong grip, and the Merry Christmas evening is liable to be spent in the saddle in fierce contact with the blizzard as in his cosey tepee with his comrades and his scant cheer. The jug containing the spirits of the occasion may have been gotten from a town fifty miles away on the railroad." Such liquor, the rugged artist declared, was "certainly not the distillation of summer sunlight." Yet it fitted in with the campaigner's idea of interior decoration for a Yuletide at fifteen below.

If excessive drinking was the soldier's weakness, its twin liability of gluttony did not necessarily follow in the Indian country, for overeating was virtually an impossibility when the forward camp offered only beans, coffee and bacon, and then bacon, coffee, and beans. In a sense symbolic of the young United States, these soldiers were from all sections of the country, a true cross section of a vigorous people, individualistic and democratic, and yet, buttoned up to the chin in big canvas overcoats and topped by muskrat caps which were almost never removed indoors, they seemed the disillusioning proof that human beings can be made uniform. The cold weather which forced this uniformity of appearance upon them around about Christmas time, also minimized differences of rank, for even the "shoulderstraps," of their day, or "brass," as officers are called in ours, would creep in under the tent flaps "like a Turk at prayer," so as not to let the Dakota chill follow

them and make the shivering men howl. Thus passed
a Christmas Day. The evening was not one to be
marked by prolonged cheer, but rather shortened to
a few stolen moments from the ordinary grind,
livened by toasts all around, before welcome sleep
prepared them for more hardships and the expectancy
of Indian combat.

Sometimes the ever-present "ardent spirits" made
the ruthlessness of nature in the Dakotas seem less
than total. Ferdinand A. Van Ostrand, who visited
Fort Berthold in 1871, said that too much of the
stuff circulated to make the day pass off happily,
though "we had a very good dinner—all things considered." The Indians, too, got handouts from the
military that day, gifts mostly of the liquid sort.
Somewhat of the same mind as Fremont, who, we
remember, had turned to Blackstone for Christmas
cheer, Van Ostrand spent his holiday reading Mark
Twain's *Innocents Abroad*. Every bit of reading
matter, from best to worst, was eagerly scanned and
reread by the troopers, who at this time had probably never even heard of a Christmas card.

Sometimes Christmas was announced by a salute
from a howitzer of four pounds or so. In long-
established posts, far from the immediate danger of
attack, booming cannon would delight the children
and thrill the soldiers' wives. If there was a number
of families present, of course there would be dances
which lasted until well after midnight, and between
the polkas, waltzes, and reels traditional eggnog was
served, accompanied by rounds of greetings. Dur-

ing this holiday season the busiest man at an army post where petticoats held forth was usually the trader. A true hero of the festivities, he was kept occupied for at least a week before Christmas preparing decorations and supplying fowl, fruit, and presents for the officers and their families as well as the enlisted men. Although enlisted men were usually excused from all but urgent activities at this time, such tasks as guard duty and police assignments had to be attended to. The post trader did his job well, serving as a department store for the soldiers, who had him send off for special gifts, or order them for wives and sweethearts in "the States." By the late days of the century, the older forts had a chaplain and a chapel where the year's most important services were conducted at Christmas. Almost the entire garrison attended, for the soldier needed his faith for a rugged life. As there were no atheists in the foxholes of their great-grandsons, in the same sense, there were few Ebenezer Scrooges in the barracks of the Great Plains.

CHAPTER XIV

Sentimental Cowboys

IN THE middle of the last century the Great Plains was an ocean of grass, known as the Great American Desert to white men too shortsighted to predict its future. In this vast realm of little rain but much fertile soil grazed the bison, shaggy king of the prairies, and nearby lurked centaur-like Indians who hunted the buffalo. The life of the plains was a mobile existence, for the bison constantly moved in herds of hundreds of thousands, seeking water and grass, and the Indian followed close behind to secure his own living. After the Civil War the situation changed. Into the vast unfenced acres of mid-America came white ranchers, driving their herds of longhorn cattle to feed on the rich grasses which had fattened the buffalo for ages. The railroad lines were pushing westward at this time, and to their railheads came the cattlemen, Texans for the most part, seeking a money crop to recoup their small fortunes, lost in the war years. These men struggled against a merciless nature and Nature's logical ally, the unpredictable redskin. Prairie fire and drought, and later on cattle diseases, checked their progress, but not for long. Before the sixties were out they had founded a new era, they had forged the golden age of the open range. Their cattle drives pointed toward the North Star and the Kansas railheads, and these treks became epics of American history and literature. The role of characters had changed in a few years; the bison was slaughtered, giving place to the steer; the Indian retreated to reservations, charging a bloody fee for his defeat, and the cattleman reigned triumphant, but still the Great Plains made a mobile life inevitable for all its residents.

This new American cowman became what he was because of his natural environment and his Mexican neighbors. He borrowed much of his equipment, a large per cent of his "lingo," and many of his most effective techniques directly from the Mexican *vaquero,* who was his companion and in a few cases his kinsman. Then a series of natural catastrophes and the settlement of sections of the plains by farmers forced the fencing in of ranches and meant the end of open-range days. Yet before this took place late in the eighties, cattle ranching had spread throughout the Plains and Mountain states and territories. This lonely life on the range, requiring almost total self-reliance, molded a special character for the American cowboy. He might be easygoing in nonessential matters, but he was relentless in doing his job; he could turn wild and sometimes murderous when drunk, but he respected fair play, honesty, and courage. The typical cowhand was hardly a churchgoer, although, as it has to all wilderness dwellers, his life urged him to meditate on the nature of things, and he was usually on talking terms with his Maker. Most cowboys were aware of the

Yuletide's deeper meaning, and, loving color and celebrations, both so rare to them on the ranch or trail, they eagerly welcomed the sentiment as well as the glitter and tinsel of Christmastide.

In the early days cattlemen found one universal way to celebrate every great event—a dance. A roundup's close, Christmas, New Year's, or some purely personal achievement of local interest, all were valid excuses for going to town to visit the dance hall. Of course, lady partners were scarce in pioneer days; even the proverbial cowhand's idol, the schoolmarm, had yet to arrive in most areas before the frontier was gone. Philip Ashton Rollins, expert on the culture of the cowboy, says that it was not unusual for ranchers to go two hundred miles to fetch a female for a dance. If, however, one was not within toting distance, then the "heifer-brand" was used. This was accepted dance procedure, whereby one man, who was never thought the less of for his part in the strange undertaking, tied a handkerchief around his arm and served as the "lady" partner of another dancer. More vigorous than graceful, the movements were evidence of good spirits, and at least in part satisfied a craving for fun. One of the most famous bits of cowboy literature commemorating a holiday is "The Cowboys' Christmas Ball," which reveals the Yuletide mood in the cattle country of which it has become a part of the poetic folklore.

Whether they were cowboys or sheepmen, Texans knew how to celebrate Christmas in many an un-

The "Heifer Brand" at a Cowboys' Ball

forgettable manner. Let us follow the fortunes and the holidays of a family of tenderfeet who spent their pioneer Christmases as herders down by the Rio Grande. These were the Hughes boys, British-born and anathema to true cowmen because they raised sheep. One of them, William, who inevitably found his name shortened to "Willy," dated his letter at Christmas, 1878 "Guinagato Ranche, 20 miles from Anywhere, Texas." Eavesdropping on his correspondence to Merry England, we can almost touch the soul of a ranchland newcomer and feel his homesickness and undisguised ineptitude:

By the by, I hope you had a merrier Christmas than we had. It was most amusing. We had an awful day, and were out of provisions, and corn, and everything, and nearly got frozen. I will give you a list of that day's proceedings: 5 a.m., got up from under wagon and found icicles all about. It was raining, everything was wet, sheep had stampeded and were at last found in three different places some miles off, and brought back by three of the others nearly at night. X—and I started in the middle of the day on horseback for the nearest ranche to get corn for the horses. It was awful cold and raining, and we thought we had lost our way, but at last we heard the roosters crowing and got to the ranche, where we thawed and had coffee and "muscal," or brandy made from cactus. Then we started back and dried the blankets and things as well as possible in a rain, before a fire enough to roast an ox. We had killed a wild pig, and had intended to have boar's head for Christmas dinner (only, as some one would remark, it was a sow), but unfortunately a dog ran off with the head. That day was the worst we have had, and no one is a bit the worse for it. It is now warm again, though it rains pretty often; but we got some more sheeting and have a tent fixed from the wagon, and so keep everything dry. P. S.—I hope my Christmas Day description don't frighten you; it exaggerates itself on paper, and taking all in all, we are having bully weather, and are as healthy and jolly as pot-boys.

Willy had not yet become a typical Texan by the Christmas of 1879, but by then he was considerably less a tenderfoot. At that time he wrote home that one of his friends had made a plum pudding for the occasion, and "it was a great success, and we bought some whiskey [let not the reader jump to conclusions here!] and set the pudding alight in good old style. We didn't do any decorating, as we hadn't any holly, and mistletoe would have been out of place among such a lot of old bachelors as we are." By Christmas of 1882 they were all Texans to the core, though still sheepherders. Their Yuletide observance seems to have taken on a good bit of the broad Western exuberance, too, as British reserve had vanished on the frontier for, said Willy, of a Christmas songfest: "I thumped the wall by way of accompaniment, and we had enough noise to fill the Albert Hall. The wall of a wooden house, which is double, and has a space between, makes a first-rate drum." After four years in the Southwest, he had even hung the mistletoe, though this transplanted Briton had to admit "it's beginning to look bilious. I expect it's rather indignant at the very small amount of slobbering that was gone through under it."

Willy's countrymen had come to the plains in considerable numbers during the seventies, as Britishers sought new opportunities in a fresh region where land was cheap, abundant, and fertile. A good percentage of them turned to cattle ranching. Apparently along with reserve, the well-known British traits of cleanliness and tidiness suffered some radical modifications on the trail. One English-bred cowman tells us that:

On the 22nd, [of December] I washed all my clothes, a very great undertaking, as I had a large collection—in fact, every stitch I possessed—not having washed my clothes since we left the Canadian [River]. On the 23rd and 24th it snowed. We all shaved and "greased up" with bear-oil for Christmas,—the only thing we could think of doing, as we had run out of all grub except flour; but then flour, bear, buffalo, and turkey is pretty good lining.

On their part, Texas cowboys enjoyed the traditional Western "turkey shoots," and were for the most part well armed and dead shots, perfectly suited for an undertaking such as James B. Gillett relates. In the late seventies when Gillett and a friend visited a big turkey roost on Elm Creek they killed seven wild fowl and on their return got a buck deer, while an acquaintance on the San Saba brought down six or eight wild geese and a dozen mallards. The local baker made them all pies, while a ranch lady furnished fruitcake and some of the boys concocted eggnog, producing one of the finest Christmas dinners of any range camp. A dance at nearby Menardsville supplied all the holiday-week dancing that any of them wanted.

One such Christmas Eve get-together on the Purgatoire got a little out of hand. A cowboy decided to tie his horse on the host's Christmas tree. Needless to say, he had had too much eggnog or its bigger and stronger brother. One of his friends lighted a fire-cracker, and the untrusty steed, thinking the explosion that of a six-shooter, raced out, dragging the tree after it. Cowboys had to chase after tree and horse for a mile before an end was brought to the unusual race, but it took a week to gather up the scattered gifts. The girl who was given the horse accepted it all right, but she married someone else!

Whenever possible cowmen ate well at Christmas. This took some large-scale planning, which occasionally went far awry. Oliver Nelson, a rancher near the Cheyenne country during the eighties, roasted two turkeys and baked a couple of cakes—sixteen inches across and four inches high—for he knew a cowboy's capacity. The Dutch oven worked over-time that day, but a severe storm occurred on Christmas Eve, and all hands went to the south line to keep the cattle from drifting away. Five days after the holiday, Nelson sent a sack filled with holiday grub to the camps, so his efforts were not completely wasted. Yet bad luck was sometimes serious enough to bring tragedy at Christmas. One holiday that Nelson would never forget was that of 1887 when the cowhands went to a dance in a snug sod house. Momentarily a well-liked married couple was ex-pected to join them in the merrymaking, and as the "shindig" progressed everyone wondered why the pair never appeared. Later they found the husband and wife frozen to death and nearly covered with the snow that had drifted over the trail.

A blizzard almost as bad occurred in the Medicine Range of Wyoming in 1874, but for the cowmen caught in it, their snowed-in Christmas dinner turned out to be by far the best that they had ever eaten. It included marrowbone soup, beef stew, hamburger steak, corn bread, wheat bread, English plum pudding, raisins, cake, coffee, and tea. The ranchmen had no butter or milk but plenty of salt and pepper. Their tasty meal was prepared by an enthusiastic twenty-year-old cook, who, with all the vigor, self-assurance, and optimism of his age, would listen to no ominous predictions of awaiting gustatory defeats. True, he had pretty poor material with which to work. The boys had killed "Old Tex," a veteran of their herd, a longhorn bull who had achieved local fame, and like all longhorns of those days, was rangy and tough. Yet the youthful chef was undaunted. He bragged that his companions would soon be eating a meal such as they had never tasted before. No better plum duff and pudding could be found anywhere outside London or Liverpool than the one that he was about to make for them. And his motive power was not hot air, for he proved his point and bettered his word by baking corn bread from meal milled from shelled corn he found in the cargo. The "plums" for his pudding were really raisins, which he had saved, along with a small hoarding of baking powder, wheat flour, and grease, the latter obtained from the final ration of bacon which had given out a week before. Sauce there was, too, made from sugar and some flavoring extract. Two miles away the resourceful cowhands, who by now had begun to respect their cook's talents, found some water cress at a spring; it was fresh and green, having been protected by the water which never froze.

Even more than it is today, Wyoming was then a hunter's paradise, but at that particular moment of winter there were no mountain grouse, sage hens, deer, antelope, or elk to be had, because all the game had drifted with the terrific storm. Thus the menu was not enriched by the usual Western selections of meat, but ingenious flavoring and careful preparation had made up the difference. Later there would be plenty of wild meat, but this Christmas dinner was more significant than any feast which followed, since it reminded all the cowboys who were lucky enough to partake of it that "in the midst of greatest hardships and sufferings we often find something to be thankful for, something to bring us to our senses when we grumble or complain of our ill-luck or misfortunes." William F. Hooker, who was one of the diners that day, observed tardily in 1918, that "therefore I take this opportunity to say grace more than forty years late! Thank God for that snowbound Christmas dinner."

Even sheepmen had to eat, and at Christmas time, among true Christians, the bitterness between herders of cattle and tenders of sheep sometimes was forgotten. A Wyoming cattleman's wife, Elinore Pruitt Stewart, perhaps remembering who were the Christ Child's first visitors, was one of these. Just before

Christmas she saved all the butter that she could spare for the shepherds, her neighbors, for they never had any otherwise, but she did not dare tell the cowboys about her hoard. She also prepared jars of gooseberry jam. A man was sent out to see how many camps there were and where they were located. He found twelve of them, with two men to a camp, and for these lucky twenty-four sheepherders, Elinore Stewart and her women friends roasted six geese, boiled three small hams, and three hens. Meat loaves were readied, links of fine sausage stuffed, and twelve large loaves of rye bread and a small tub of dough-nuts prepared to go forth. Coffee cakes, too, were decorated with seeds, nuts, and fruit. Bright and early the day before Christmas, the Samaritans went out with a dozen baskets, touring the camps and de-lighting the shepherds, whose charges were said to destroy the grazing lands of the cattle. For one day in 365, at least, their dull diet, prepared by lonely novice cooks, was renounced.

With others, the feud did not even die on Christ-mas Day. For example, "Old Scotty," a picturesque cowboy in the Dakota country, was offered a buf-falo robe to cover his bunk if he would dress up as Santa Claus for a school program. This was in 1886 when the cowboy-sheepman feud was at its peak. Scotty, a loyal cowpuncher, balked at the odor of sheep in the raw wool whiskers that the well-meaning ladies had made for him, but his heart was tender for youngsters, so he went through with the masquerade, though the discomforts and discom-

fits of the occasion prompted his profanity. Fortunately for the type of audience he attracted, his
words were drowned out by sleighbells. Mothers
were shocked that Scotty smelled of alcohol, but
their children recognized only the other sort of spirits
which his holiday temperament so obviously revealed.

Most cowboys were not driving cattle at Christmas
time, except those in certain parts of the Southwest.
One of these was Thomas Hunter, who arrived in
Tucson in 1867 just in time for his holiday dinner,
which consisted solely of a can of jelly and a piece
or two of Mexican sugar *panoche*. After a long
drive, this was a cowboy's luxury, for on the trail
Hunter and his buddies had dined only on beef
broiled on a stick, and not even much of that.

Tales of Christmas privations and the heroism and
humor of ranch life are filled with human interest.
Joseph Schmedding, a cowboy returning to the home
ranch two days before Christmas, got caught in a
Rocky Mountain blizzard. Forcing his horse into
the storm, he hoped to reach his destination before
Christmas was done and they had both frozen. Swift
and lashing snow blinded man and animal. They
lost their way. As Schmedding had no watch, time
and space now had no measurement. Stopping in
a clump of piñon trees, he tried to eat snow, but
the attempt only made his growing thirst tantalizing.
He had drifted forty miles out of his way and could
see familiar ranges to the left. To the right, about
two miles away, was a curling puff of smoke. Like
a reversal of the shepherds' following of Bethlehem's

Star of Light, he trailed the somber column and finally reached a Navajo's camp site where he found only two young girls in a hogan. The frightened children were slow in understanding that Schmedding wanted a good meal, but at last they became calm enough to give him coffee and biscuits and his horse some corn. A little earlier their parents had gone to get the customary Christmas food distribution and presents at the mission. The children had remained home to care for the animals. After giving each girl a quarter, Schmedding left, and in the late afternoon of Christmas Eve he reached a trading post and the trader's crude but very welcome hospitality —a comfortable bunk in his storeroom.

Next day Schmedding overtook some Indians en route to the big free meal which his bosses, the Wetherills, gave to all neighboring Indians. Meanwhile, the Wetherills had become worried about him, and Mrs. Wetherill had delayed the holiday feast until that evening, hoping for his quick return. The young cowhand broke down and cried over this kindness when he finally reached the ranch house. Everything turned out well for everybody. At dusk the Indian visitors had their baked bread and gallons of coffee, as well as a fat yearling steer. Motherly Mrs. Wetherill kissed the stray cowboy, and the other hands kidded him about this gesture as well as for his being lost, but he forgot the embarrassing moments as soon as he was at table, eating the standard Christmas dinner we all know so well. Later, the boss and his wife distributed presents from the

treeside. First the children received their gifts, then
the two Navajo girls who served as housemaids, and
finally the grinning cowboys. The last-mentioned got
spurs, hand-braided rawhide quirts, imported Mexican *reatas,* bandanas, gauntlets, socks, and other gear
dear to cowhand hearts. Bull Durham tobacco, boxes
of matches, plug tobacco, and cigarette paper pleased
the smokers among them.

Though he had arrived somewhat tardy, Schmedding had come in time for a good meal, but deep
snows did not always time events so well. During
one bad winter in the seventies, William Francis
Hooker lived in a dugout on La Bonte Creek in
Wyoming. Far removed from civilization, Hooker
and his fellow bullwhacker, "Nick," had only one
contact with the outside world, Fort Fetterman,
which was forty miles away. Yet the pair did not
often mind the solitude. This unspoiled wilderness
was beautiful country. In December it was covered
with snow, and one could view the magnificence
of Laramie Peak through the clear atmosphere. The
peak had evergreen trees, such as those which had
made other cowboy Yuletides green, but the height
was sixty miles off. One might think that Hooker
would have had little spirit for Christmas in his
crude dugout, a shanty with gunny sacks for a door
and with no one to celebrate with him but his taciturn old partner, but William F. Hooker was touched
by the solemnity and beauty of the season. Maybe
it was the mysticism of the wilderness which many
another pioneer had claimed to have sensed, for one

day as the winter deepened, Hooker suggested to Nick that the two of them get a Christmas tree. Nick thought that his friend had gone slightly crazy, but he did not say so. He was not exactly a Scrooge himself, but he had his full share of earthy common sense. Quietly he marshalled for Hooker all the reasons against such an undertaking. In the first place, neither of them had seen a calendar in a year, and with no communication with the outside, they did not know the date. Why, Christmas might already be over. Still, Hooker was not fazed; he was sure that it was December, though he had no notion of the exact date. The idea of Christmas keeping held him. Next morning he told Nick that he was going to Fort Fetterman to find out what day it was. Apparently Nick knew that it was no use to talk any further, so without hindrance Hooker set out right after breakfast to walk through the bitter cold day. Trotting like an Indian, he kept a steady pace of five miles an hour and reached the fort at eight o'clock that night.

First Hooker got the supplies for the practical life of two old hermits. These included thread, needles, green coffee berries, but then he added something else he had not bought before—a present for Nick. It was a skinning knife such as he'd wanted. Hooker's sentimental mood was shaken soon after that when the post trader revealed the stunning truth—this was Christmas Day! Hooker said nothing, for he did not want to let on that he was ignorant of the date. That night he slept as best he could huddled in a blanket among the box elders at the creek, for the soldiers would not let him inside the fort, since civilians were not popular at that post even at Christmas. The trip back was slower, since now Hooker carried sixty pounds of supplies. He had left the fort early on December 27 and reached La Bonte late on December 28. When he arrived, Nick was waiting for him, and excitedly showed off a small pine tree. It was decorated with paper flowers made from white, brown, and red soap wrappers, so we know that he, too, had been traveling. With his jackknife, the busy old fellow had fashioned a jumping jack and a whistle, reasoning that even the biggest of men is part little boy, especially at Christmas, and he gave both of these to his friend, presenting them with a broad, proud smile. Nick Huber was a Bavarian who had worked in his father's toy factory in Nürnberg before coming to America and he had not forgotten his trade. Of course, Hooker did not have the heart to disappoint Nick, especially when he had told Hooker that not only was this Christmas, but also his sixty-fifth birthday. Thus Nick never learned that his Christmas and his birthday were three days late, though for both men tardiness proved to be just as good as promptness.

Barricaded by snow, the narrow confines of a ranch house in the northern plains was the bizarre scene of Christmas grief for a group of cattlemen one winter during the seventies. To keep from freezing to death in their beds, as many other men would be that night, the ranchers built a shelter of boxes around their fireplace. This kept out the constant drafts. For yet another reason was that Christmas unusual. The men were spending their Christmas Eve with a corpse! A Catholic missionary, the Reverend W. B. Youngman, was in the region, and his reminiscence is well put, with the skill of a man of letters:

A strange Christmas for Willie Woodhouse, who, had Kirwan been by, would have had some one to talk with—some one to console. But with these rough Ranche-men, what could he do? The Christmas morning broke once again upon the world. Slowly did the gray light gleam upon the prairie world, white with the driven snow; and now the men with spades dug a path out into the day, and down to the creek, and hurried after their cattle, who were sheltered under the trees in places built for them; they had to be fed, although Brown Kirwan lay stiff and cold in the Ranche, on the snow-white prairie. The storm began again after a few hours' respite and then came the knowledge that no one would venture from the Mission with a coffin that day; and also that none of them could assist at any offices at the Mission church, on Christmas Day.

Tom had been unwell, so he was about the Ranche in the morning, and with energy was trying to learn some Catechism when his work was done. "Seven Gods, and three Sacraments." "Eh? No, Tom, no." "Three persons in God, and seven Sacraments," and in this style the wall of Tom's ignorance was being broken down.

And then came the preparation for the Christmas dinner. Roast quail, pork, and chicken; gently, reverently, and with whispered conversation were the preparations made. None forgot that silent, white-robed figure, and the rough wooden cross, with the light burning before it. True, there were no bright flowers to make wreaths to lay near the dead; but they had collected some slight branches of a tree, with long thorns two inches in length, and with these they had plaited a crown of thorns—a wreath, if you will, and it lay upon the breast of the corpse, the dark shade contrasting strangely against the whiteness of the linen sheet.

Almost in silence was the dinner eaten, and then again began the watch, barricaded near the fire. And so the Christmas Day died upon the Prairies.

Another missionary on the Great Plains of about that time, the Protestant, Reverend Cyrus Townsend Brady, witnessed more than one Christmas, the outline of which was traced by deep snow, though the warming details were purely of human achievement. One bitter cold Christmas he left his own family at one in the morning to go to conduct religious services in a little church where none had been held before. Driving a two-horse sleigh, he arrived at the little brick church and found there a smoldering fire in a dilapidated stove which smoked but did not warm. The wind entered the building freely through the ill-fitting window and door frames. Only a dozen people attended the service which Brady conducted, dressed in a rough buffalo overcoat, fur cap, and gloves. After the sermon, his temporary parishioners drove him to the nearest ranch house where the holiday dinner consisted of corn bread, ham, and pot roast. It was a poor supper for Christmas, but to liven it a bit the minister gave his hostess a small mince pie that he had received from his own wife. "The pie makes it seem like Christmas after all," said the rancher's little girl through her full mouth. The year before their mother had made the children "potato men" from "spuds," matches, and buttons; these were the only things in their stockings.

Hearing this pathetic confidence from a child, Brady excused himself and hurried back to the cold little church, took the collection basket, and with the speedy and reliable needlework that marked him a former sailor, he added ribbons to the basket. This he gave to the daughter of his hostess, and his penknife, nearly new, to her small brother. The girl also received his sewing equipment, while a small box of candy went to all the children. Indirectly this last was a gift from children to children, since his own youngsters had presented Brady with it before he had left home. Later he remarked that these "were the cheapest and most effective Christmas presents it was ever my pleasure to bestow."

In his memoirs of pioneer life, Brady recalled another celebration of the Christ Child's birthday in the cattle country. This occasion came on a snowbound train, stalled somewhere in Kansas. Brady did not mention the participants by name, and so the tale is written in a somewhat allegorical, semifictional manner, but it is probably based on an anecdote he had heard from participants. When snows had proved too much for the locomotive, he says, the trainmen left to get a snowplow. Now the passengers were in for a long wait around a stove in the front car. This was a motley little group, all strangers to one another, and perfect material for a novelist, as Brady later became. Here were a drummer, a cowboy, a wealthy cattleman, and quietly sitting beside them a young widow with two threadbare children hoping to reach Grandmother's for Christmas. The children were sobbing, not as spoiled youngsters who wanted their way would, but as one might expect of children who were tired, cold, and disappointed in a strange environment. Apparently wasting no time on embarrassment or ceremony, the menfolk hurried to improve the situation and soon had made beds for the boy and girl from the plush seats of the car and were using their overcoats for blankets. This was not enough for them to do, they felt, especially on Christmas Eve. The men decided to give the little ones a real Christmas, even without Grandma. First, the cattleman donated his two new pair of woolen socks. As he watched the children say their Christmas prayers and soon fall off to sleep, the cowboy offered all he had to give, his gun and spurs, and the cattleman showed a bottle of whiskey. Of course, all these were inappropriate. What, then, would they do? "Never mind," said the cheerful traveling salesman. He had a whole trunkful of trinkets. The other men, not so fortunately equipped, insisted on paying him for some of the geegaws as their share in the giving, and the salesman donated the rest. Even the trainmen still aboard the motionless cars caught the spirit of the occasion and collected more presents. Watching all this kindliness, the mother was dazed by the goodness of complete strangers. Bigger and bigger bulged the sacks for her children. Then two of these Western Samaritans went out on the range to get a tree. They found no cedar or spruce, but did come back with a large sagebrush, which the mother covered with tissue paper from the notion stock of the salesman, and some clean waste from the engine completed the ornaments. That night, everyone was excited and sleepless, except the objects of all the activity. Needless to say, when they awoke the next morning they were the most thrilled young people in that part of the plains. Their mother had not been forgotten either. The cattleman, the cowboy, and the drummer presented her with a red plush album, decorated in high Victorian taste and autographed by all aboard that Christmas train. Between the pages the cattle owner had placed a one-hundred-dollar bill. Later that morning the Reverend Mr. Brady held a happy Christmas service in the car while the radiant mother sang "Jesus, Lover of My Soul" and the cow-country residents joined in. With the coming of afternoon, the train crew returned with a snowplow—and a whole cooked turkey.

Beside this incident, beautiful and simple as "Silent Night," is weighed another which Brady knew of, the tale of another ranchman, caught in a Christmas blizzard and found near town where he had been shopping, frozen on Christmas morning, "his poor little packages of petty Christmas presents tightly clasped in his cold hands lying by his side. On the horn of his frozen horse's saddle was a little piece of evergreen tree. It was so puny, an Easterner would have thrown it away." Yet, like most other cowboys, he had kept Christmas in his heart, and, as Brady concludes, "that is the place above all others where it should be."

CHAPTER XV

Christmas-Tree Country

ONE OF the last regions within the contiguous forty-eight states to be explored by Europeans was the Pacific Northwest. The first white men who labored in that country were fur hunters from Britain, Canada, Russia, and the United States. It was the sea otter and the beaver which set the pattern of the Oregon country from the 1780's until the 1830's. Next came American missionaries who built their bases for converting the native, bringing Christianity to the Willamette Valley of Oregon and a few scattered posts in Washington. With the 1840's the first ox-drawn covered wagons struggled along the Oregon Trail, bringing their farming families to break the sod of Oregon and make the Northwest Coast American in custom and sentiment. Until this time both Britain and the United States disputed ownership of the Pacific Northwest, but in 1846 the Oregon treaty was signed by which the land was divided at 49°N; the territory to the south became American soil; that to the north eventually was renamed British Columbia.

For a time the gold rush to California drained off some of the influx of American settlers. Three-quarters of Oregon's people raced to the diggings, but Willamette Valley, fertile in soil, well watered, and mild in climate, inevitably came into its own in the fifties. A little later the commercially important Puget Sound area of present-day Washington also became a focus of newcomers interested in agriculture, fishing, commerce, and timber.

Here in the Northwest was real Christmas-tree country. A land abundant in rainfall, it was characterized by the mighty Douglas fir, the spruce and true fir in the north, and, in southern Oregon, by large stands of sugar pine, Port Orford cedar, and a few redwood. Even in the early 1850's Oregon had its decorated trees, which at that time were an innovation even on the Atlantic coast. These trees were embellished with homemade ornaments of the same materials as frontier families used in Iowa or California, Dakota or Colorado. As Ezra Meeker, a colorful old pioneer who lived a full life even into the automobile age, tells us, everybody was happy at a pioneer Oregon Christmas because everyone had some say in what should be done and also something important to do. Since each person was indispensable to the success of the festivities, it was in a real sense everybody's Christmas or it was nobody's Christmas.

One little girl who shared in such a holiday remembered best of all the rarity of sweet, pure sugar in the shapes of fruits and animals. These edible gifts were hollow. Her mother had added a splash of color to the front of each sugar animal she prepared for her offspring. Our ten-year-old heroine once got a small sugar dog, but un-Christmaslike, she tried to hoard her candy, only to find that her little sister found its hiding place and each day licked away part of its sugary deliciousness. One day the secret visitor licked once too often and the dog collapsed, becoming but a Christmas memory.

Adults shared in the receiving as well as the giving, and their presents in the pre-commercialized era were usually as simple as those given children. Charles Stevens, of Astoria, found in 1857 that his stockings had been filled with a piece of an old pipe, some tobacco, an old penknife, and the remains of a paper of tacks. His wife got a dress pattern with trimmings, and thus she could make her own Christmas in the days to follow. These sound poor enough items to us today, but each one of them was an out-of-the-ordinary remembrance on a frontier cut off from the civilized world for months at a time and only spasmodically supplied by sailing ships or an occasional steamer which had rounded the Horn, or a wagon train or freight team via the perilous Oregon Trail.

Usually there was plenty of game, and it at least could be procured nearby. The same day that the Stevenses were exchanging their simple gifts, Jacob Meek, James Stuart, and several other Oregon pioneers of Blacktail Creek dined on buffalo meat and a preserve made of chokeberries. As had the Mountain Men, these first settlers lived largely on a meat diet.

Speaking of meat, James Swan, a pioneer in the Shoalwater Bay area of southern Washington, knew some men who cared little for their viands during the Christmas of 1854. Due to the cold weather, game had decreased, though there were plenty of salt salmon and potatoes to be had. Still, the settlers wanted a traditional goose or duck to make it seem more like the merry season that their Eastern homes had always given them. So it was a fowl they wanted? Well, they had among their number a sea captain who had strong opinions on just about every subject, and food seems to have been one of his favorite topics of conversation. When he heard of his neighbors' desires, he told them that he was sure that crow would make good eating, and for that matter, so would eagle or owl. Reasoning that the crow would be especially tasty because it had a crop like that of a chicken and eagles and owls were good even without a crop, since they did not feed on carrion, he had the original narrator of this true story, James G. Swan, shoot a couple of crows. Swan had his doubts about the whole scheme, but he was willing to experiment and waste a few shots. Now, let Swan the crow-killer relate his exploits and their results:

They were very ancient, entirely devoid of fat, and altogether presented to my mind a sorry picture of a feast. But the captain was delighted. "I will make a sea-pie of them," he said, "and then you can judge what crow-meat is." The birds were cleaned and cut up, and a fine sea-pie made with dumplings, salt pork, potatoes, and a couple of onions. And precisely at meridian on Christmas-day (for the old captain liked to keep up sea-hours), the contents of the iron pot were emptied into a tin pan, and set before us smoking hot.

   I tried my best to eat crow, but it was too tough for me.

"How do you like it?" said the old man, as, with a desperate effort, he wrenched off a mouthful from a leg.

Few present, even for the sake of conviviality, could agree with the old seadog, but as cocksure as ever, he insisted that they should all eat some soup and dumplings and not condemn crow meat on their first trial, for Swan had "shot the grandfather and grandmother of the flock." Far from convinced, Swan ended his Christmas dinner with a slim helping of dumplings and potatoes.

Most early Christmases in the Northwest did not boast such unconventional fare as this. Usually the church and the home alternated as headquarters for the celebrations, each having its own tree. These trees stayed up until New Year's. Where there was no regular church or mission, private citizens held prayer meetings on Christmas Day, such as the one recorded by Basil N. Longworth, who attended services shortly after his arrival in Oregon late in 1853.

If we listen to William V. Wells's convincing words, then even the most inaccessible of backwoods communities enjoyed about as many thrills and as much genuine romance as our jet-propelled generation, especially at Yuletide. He explains the circumstances, as of 1855:

Now, in Oregon, where people reside ten miles apart, and call a man neighbor who lives half a day's journey away, it is not so easy to make up a fashionable party, for sundry reasons, as in Fifth Avenue, or any other of the "close settlements" of New York. If a hop is to take place, weeks must be given to prepare in; the "store clothes" taken out, aired and brushed, old bonnets furbished up, horses driven in from distant pasture, and saddles made ready. Then the nearest settlement must be applied to for a proper amount of whisky and sugar, raisins and flour. But on the occasion above alluded to [Christmas], great efforts were made to have matters go off with *éclat*. Deacon L——, residing on the ocean beach, about twenty miles to the southward of Coos Bay, and known as the most liberal, warmhearted old gentleman of Southern Oregon, had appropriated, some time in advance, the right to give the Christmas ball. It was to last two days and two nights. Oceans of whisky, hills of venison and beef, no end of pies and "sech like." The ladies of all Coos County were to be there, and a fiddler from the distant point of Port Orford itself engaged. To this feast did all hands look forward with secret longing and hope.

. . . And on Christmas-eve the ball commenced. There were gay roystering blades from Port Orford, gallants from Coos Bay, select men and distinguished individuals from all over the country, and belles from every where. Such a *recherché* affair had not occurred since the settlement of the Territory. For two nights and days the festivities continued; and after all the dancing, riding, drinking, singing, and laughing—and all this without sleeping, and with a determination to "never give up" —there were buxom forms and brilliant eyes that dared us to another breakdown!

I snap my fingers at all civilized Miss Nancys henceforth and forever. Give me, for the essence of fun and the physical ability to carry it out, a corn-fed, rosy-cheeked, bouncing Oregon lass, with eyes bright as the rivers that sparkle merrily on their way to the sea from those snow-clad mountains, and hearts light as the fresh breezes of that northern climate!

Obviously, an Oregon Christmas was primarily a triumph of group participation. Of course, that was true everywhere, and everywhere in Christendom the season was not merely an opportunity for sweethearts to meet. Though the first bloom of romance was often experienced among the garlands and beneath the Northwestern mistletoe, Oregon children,

The Perils of an Oregon Schoolmaster!

too, as children always will, helped make Christmas. They took part in tableaux and carol singing and even participated in loud and vigorous declamatory exercises, for which they practiced several hours every evening for weeks before Christmas Eve. Although the words of these hard-learned pieces were quickly forgotten, their parents surely must have remembered longer the youngsters' comments on Christmas morning. Children a little older decorated the church and their homes with strands of popcorn, cranberries, and gilded walnut shells. Boys would save up the sea shells that they had found on a rare excursion to the Oregon beaches and make boxes for their mothers, sisters, or sweethearts and glue the colored shells on their tops and sides. Grown men, too, had their sources of simple pride. They congratulated each other upon the symmetry of the tree that they had cut for the church. Usually it was a cedar, brought to town by horse and wagon or by ox team. Anyone, boy or girl, man or woman, might be a carol singer, even if his voice were not of the best, and on Christmas Eve he could go forth to visit dozens of neighbor houses.

For the schoolboys of the early Pacific Northwest, this was an especially good time for horseplay, and the pranks that they played now they could get away with—just this once. No one dared go against tradition and punish them. Their favorite custom, in Lane County, for example, was to rush to the schoolhouse ahead of the teacher just before Christmas vacation. Once inside they would bar his entrance, or they might catch him before he got in. Then, with roars of glee, such as only the generation between eight and fourteen can emit, they would carry him protesting to a convenient pond. Either the master, now ·thoroughly devoid of false dignity, treated them all, or else——!

But for Louis Banks, one pioneer Christmas was a boyhood tragedy, and it was all due to a circuit rider named Kenoyer. Years later, still with a little of the sadness that happier holidays had not completely removed, Banks described his nemesis:

He was a tall, cadaverous brother, with an awfully solemn mien, and was considered a powerful exhorter. I shall never forget my first memory of him. It was at Christmas time, and he had come home with us from preaching at the school-house for Christmas dinner. We had been fattening a big turkey gobbler for that happy occasion, and he was a monster. He had turned the scales after he was dressed at over eighteen pounds. It was a settled thing in the family that I being the eldest son, always had the gizzard of any fowl that appeared on our table. I had lotted on that old gobbler's gizzard every time I had seen him strut for the last three months, and a good many times that morning had looked forward with happy anticipation to seeing it on my plate while listening to a very long and, to me, dull sermon. The fashion at our table was to carve up the meat, and then pass it around, and let each guest select what he desired. Never a thought of danger entered my head as father passed the turkey to Parson Kenoyer as the guest of honor, and so what happened came as a flash of lightning out of a clear sky. The old man deliberately lifted his fork and set it into that gobbler's gizzard, and laid it on his own plate. If that fork had gone into my own heart, it couldn't have hurt me worse. That my father was biting his lips to keep from laughing, my mother peering out of the corners of her eyes to see how I took it, and my sister pinching my leg under the table, did not help to make it a more pleasing situation. I could not help a big tear rolling down my cheek, though I gulped down my sorrow and did the best I could in silence; but the charm of that Christmas dinner had fled.

Whether bright with surprise or marred by childhood tragedies, Oregon Christmases were seldom white with snow, as in the East, but rather marked by rain. Yet this was a forested country which the settlers could understand; it was a much more beautiful land than the plains that they had crossed, and a friendlier, less dangerous frontier than the formidable Rockies they had encountered coming west. For the most part, they were glad to be here, especially during the holidays. Somewhat facetiously, but by no means incorrectly, one might conclude that Christmas in this Christmas-tree land was like the holiday back on the Atlantic seaboard, only more so.

CHAPTER XVI

On Santa's Doorstep

ACCORDING to the Bureau of the Census, the American frontier officially ended in 1890. At that time no substantial area existed in the United States which contained less than two inhabitants per square mile. Within the year just past, six new territories had become states, and the "Battle" of Wounded Knee, noted as the last organized Indian battle (if such this massacre of the Sioux could have been called) had occurred. By 1890 railroads crossed the continent by central, northern, and southern routes.

No date, of course, can be fixed for the psychological termination of the American frontier. The Western spirit continued; the optimism did not die, and many people still hoped to do better beyond the Mississippi. In fact, late in the nineties Americans turned to the so-called "last frontier," Alaska, which had been purchased from Russia in 1867. East of Alaska gold had been discovered in Canada's Yukon Territory. Inevitably, the gold hidden in the sands of Nome Beach was soon uncovered, and the rush now broadened to include Alaska. By 1900 the great age of the sourdough was well under way.

Christmas in pioneer Alaska was very much different from that holiday on earlier American frontiers. At Sitka in the south, Christmas waits, musical watchmen whose privilege and joy it was to welcome Yuletide, went about town all the long evening, from sunset at three in the afternoon, singing their Christmas carols and carrying on a long pole a revolving star to represent that of Bethlehem. Masking parties also went out to make calls on their acquaintances. They were garbed in strange dress, disguised as animals, Eskimos, or Indians. They could enter any home, much as did the shepherds in California's *Pastorela*. Yet unlike the shepherds so far to the south, these fur-enveloped visitors remained silent and solemnly seated themselves while they dined on the best of cakes and wines. Meanwhile, their hosts were trying to guess their identity. If by some wile the former were successful, a merry shout went up, but if they were not, then the masked callers left just as they had come, the mystery intact.

Alaska's few settlements before the gold rush were still Russian in culture. As early as 1793 the Czar had sent out missionaries to Kodiak Island. The Slavic Eastern Orthodox churches, though of crude board or log on the outside, sheltered a wealth of embroidered and jeweled vestments which were displayed on this holiest of days. There were also ikons of fine Byzantine art work, covered with gold, and candles blazing in massive holders. Incense and special chants added to the nearly Oriental magnificence of the celebration. Since Czarist Russia still counted by the Julian calendar, uncorrected by improvements introduced in 1582 into Western Europe, the Rus-

Awaiting the Holy Night at Sitka

sian Christmas was eleven days after the American.

Undismayed by calendars and chronicles they could not understand, the Alaska Indians feasted on smoke-dried salmon, venison, and the greatest delicacy that they had yet discovered—strawberries preserved in seal oil and kept in old kerosene cans. We can only imagine the rare flavor! Around the Protestant and Catholic missions which were established after American occupation, the Indians took part in the Christmas ceremonies, although their pagan customs were oddly mixed with the symbolism and sound of the rites of the Nativity.

Few Americans had visited Russian America, but Frederick Whymper was there with an exploring party at Christmas, 1866, the last year before the purchase of Alaska. At Nulato on the Yukon River, about 250 miles east of Nome, Whymper's group, strangers to Arctic ways, attempted rather pathetically to be merry. Maybe this was Santa Claus's doorstep, but there were no reindeer, no "jolly old elf" dressed in red. The best they could do was:

We decorated our room with flags and Indian trading goods, and spruce-fir brush, in place of holly; got out the newest and brightest of our tin plates and pewter spoons, raised a big fire of logs—in the oven! and Dall set to work vigorously in the manufacture of gingerbread and pies, but it could not quite put out of mind the dear ones at home. . . .

At five o'clock that Alaskan evening the table was set and the following bill of fare served:

Soupe à la Yukon.
Arctic Grouse-roast.
Alaska reindeer meat.
Nulato cranberry sauce.
California (preserved) peas and tomatoes.
Dried-apple pudding.
Pies. Gingerbread à la Dall. Iced cheese.
Coffee. Tea.
Iced water.

Among the most notable of the missionary groups arriving in the seventies was that of the Presbyterians who founded a school at Fort Wrangell. In 1877, A. R. McFarland wrote of Christmas there among his Indian converts, and by doing so, showed how the holiday was celebrated and also the extent of his success:

Between twelve and one o'clock Christmas morning I was awakened by hearing persons coming up to my house. I arose, and from my window saw about sixty of my Indians standing in a double row in front of my house, with their lanterns and umbrellas, for it was raining heavily. Just as I looked out they commenced singing, "While shepherds watched their flocks by night." They sung that and another hymn, and then went quietly away. It seemed to me that nothing ever aroused my gratitude as that did. I did not know that there was anything more to come. But about nine o'clock in the morning I saw a large procession filing into my yard. First came the son of one of our prominent men, a boy about thirteen, carrying a large British flag. Perhaps some Sabbath-school class of boys would be willing to present our mission with an American flag, the Stars and Stripes. Next came the Christian chief, Toy-a-att. Then came all the leading men; then their wives, then my school. They walked in single file. I stood in my door, and as they walked past each one shook hands with me and wished me "A Merry Christmas." The old chief took my hand and said, "A Merry Christmas," and "God bless you, dear teacher," and, much

to my surprise, leaned forward and kissed me on the cheek.
He had evidently learned his speech for the occasion, as he does
not speak English. I wish I could describe their costumes. But
as I have not time I will only say that the boy who carried the
flag was dressed in light blue cashmere, covered over with gilt
stars. He had also on a head-dress made of flowers and stars.
There were about two hundred in the procession.

Another report of this Christmas at Wrangell was
carried in the *Puget Sound Argus,* January 25, 1878.
According to the observer,

Christmas was ushered in by a grand raffle for Christmas cakes,
after which came a magnificent display of eatables and drinkables, which, being free to all, everybody partook thereof and
became happy. Hootzenoo and all other brands of liquor flowed
in abundance, and in honor to the residents of Wrangel [*sic*],
be it said, that on this occasion no white man erected any dis-
turbance. The only commotion was by an Indian, and he, I
regret to say, is a native of Washington Territory. As midnight approached our attention was attracted towards the Indian
village. The school and church-going portion of the Indians
had . . . collected in numbers near two hundred, and were on
the march towards town, singing as they came. Arriving at
the residence of their teacher, Mrs. McFarland, they halted and
serenaded her by singing several hymns. Their singing was admirable, considering the length of time they have been under
tuition. As I listened to these natives, who are seeking to become enlightened and benefitted by the teaching of Christianity,
I could not but admire their seeming sincerity, and reflect that
they were showing a good example to many of us who claim
to be their superiors in all things.

That evening the anonymous writer attended a white
man's dance of about twenty couples, but although
it was unusually gay for that outpost of civilization, it seemed almost humdrum compared to the

Indian scenes. Finally he strolled to the residence
of Toy-ah-att, a chief of the Stikines:

The church and school people were giving an entertainment at
his house, and he having given me to understand that the presence of myself and friends at the feast would be considered an
honor greatly appreciated by all, therefore, together with my
friend Vanderbilt, I went forth. Arrived at the place of attrac-
tion, a building in size 30 by 40, we beheld congregated together
about 200 Indians, old and young, of all sizes and all shades of
color. The room was well lighted by lamps, candles, and a huge
fire of dry wood in the center of the building. The walls were
gracefully decorated with evergreens, flags, and pictures. In the
room were four large tables on which were placed in abundance
"Boston muck-a-muck" of every description, and around which
were seated youth and age doing justice to all before them. As
the tables were finished, a fresh lot would be seated, and before
anything was eaten grace was said by Mrs. Dickinson. In a small
room near the tables was an organ at which was seated Mrs.
Constantine (an Indian woman), who regaled the throng with
several pieces of music. After all had eaten, Toy-ah-att entertained us with tableaux, which were very laughable.

In these strange surroundings, peopled with sturdy
dark Indians of the north country, Christmas was
being celebrated, surprisingly enough, much as it
was in the East or Middle West. The churchgoing
Indians, says our chronicler, opposed the introduc-
tion of *hootzenoo,* which was livening other celebrations. Although Wrangell was a quiet place and
had had no repairs in many a year, its log buildings,
covered with lichen and bleached by summer suns,
became the scene of elaborately planned merriment
when Christmas came. The samaritanism of Westerners who had known frontier life themselves was
the moving spirit. Fort Wrangell's little mission was

supported by Christians who lived in the far-off Colorado Rockies and had sent food and clothing for the Indians they would never meet. Some of these supplies and funds provided presents for the Alaskan children. The little mission there had Alaska's first Christmas tree, and the strange new decoration proved "a perfect success," according to the delighted clergy. It was the magnet which lured a pilgrimage of hundreds of curious, well-bundled Indians to the post. There was no compulsory education in early Alaska, and so at Sitka the Greek Orthodox clergy noted the same phenomenon once presents were traditional. Children flocked into town in expectation of some wonderful gift from the fair-skinned Magi from farther south.

As the years advanced, more and more missionaries came to the isolated North. Far up on the Koyukuk River in north central Alaska, the Reverend Hudson Stuck, traveling by the universal conveyance, dogsled, arrived at Christmas time at St. John's-in-the-Wilderness Mission and marvelled at the efforts made by the natives to reach the post for the festival. He did not know which to admire more, their "simple, earnest piety or the whole-hearted enthusiasm for their sports and pastimes," for like the whites who taught them, these Indians loved both the religious and social aspects of the holiday. Few Christians of longer standing would have followed their worship with as strenuous activity as did these people:

Right out of church they go to the frozen river, old men and maidens, young men and matrons, mothers with babies on their backs and their skirts tucked up, and they quickly line up and are kicking the football stuffed with moose hair and covered with moose hide in the native game that their fore-fathers played ages before "Rugby" was invented. When the church-bell rings, back they all troop again, to take their places and listen patiently and reverently to the long, double-interpreted service, the babies still on their mothers' backs, sometimes asleep, sometimes waking up and crying, comforted by slinging them around and applying their lips to the foun-tain of nourishment and solace.

At Chilcat Mission manse located at Haines, late December arrived with more than one delightful sur-prise that Americans could have found in no other part of their expanding nation! Listen to a lady missionary's report:

On last Friday evening a little rowboat arrived from Juneau with two naturalists from Berlin—Dr. Aurel and Dr. Arthur Krause—who intend to study here until spring, boarding at the trader's. The gentlemen brought a package of mail, which they offered with evident pleasure for our Christmas gift. It proved to be the Sitka mail from San Francisco, whither ours may have been sent by mistake; so we had no letters, but we had a very pleasant Christmas, with many thoughts of the loved ones at home. I had work enough, you may be sure, in pro-viding, from my brain, my wardrobe and my scrap-bag, presents for sixty-nine schoolboys and girls and women. We graded them all by the number of days they had been in attendance, and had something for each one. . . . The gentlemen brought some cotton-jeans for pants for the boys; the little fellows came to school through the snow with nothing on but cotton shirts, the snow sometimes stained by their bleeding feet. . . .

Then I think you would like to hear about our Christmas. Oh how I did wish for some of your deft fingers then! Just think! sixty-nine children, besides some grown folks, to provide for! I'm sure it's a good thing I have a long scrap-bag. I had to use many a bit and all the wit I had. Many of the children were very irregular in attendance at school; so about two months before Christmas I told them about it and that the presents would be graded according to their good works. So I had to grade every child and every present. Mrs. Dickinson, the teacher, knit several little collars of yarn and two small scarfs, and gave me about a dozen tiny dolls out of the store, which helped a good deal. Then my little Indian girl, Kittie, dressed the dolls, and she and Mr. Willard trimmed the house with evergreens and flags, and we had a splendid tree, a crowded house and a good time. For one of our head-girls I made a charming little hood out of an old red-flannel drawer-leg and a little bit of black-velvet; for a good many others I made little bags out of an old blue-silk ruffle I had, and filled them according to works with buttons, needles, thread and thimbles. For some—the lowest—I made only little red-flannel needle-leaves; for others, little handkerchiefs with the Turkey-red initial of their English name.

Different was the holiday brought to Nome and other camps by the miners at the end of the century. Nome was a tent city five miles long and a single block wide. Like miners' towns on every other American frontier, it had been born overnight, preordained to suffer all the social turmoil of a community without roots. Few pioneers, roughing it for the first time in this wild country, had brought wives with them, and fewer still had young children. At Christmas time Nome was a camp of snowdrifts which literally covered the place. Some miners' shacks were buried a dozen feet or more beneath the inundation of white, and the only sign of many a cabin was a smokestack which peeped through the snow. As this snow piled higher and higher the residents had to add extra lengths of pipe. Those who forgot might be suffocated. Six feet of snow was an average depth for "home sweet home," but often tunnels twenty-five or more feet long were dug through the white blanketing.

This was the real-life Christmas-card picture of gold-rush Alaska. And what might one do, rising cheerily on a typical Yuletide morning? Well, he might look out on the Bering Sea, frozen for miles, or view the perfect whiteness of thousands of acres of cold land. Everywhere the snow was a very fine, flourlike stuff. Yet, buried in a "white Christmas," Nome was destitute of trees to decorate. Unlike Oregon and Washington, through which most of these latter-day gold seekers had passed, this northern land was treeless. Those who could not do without their evergreen gay with lights would really have to work hard to get it. Trips had to be made of seventy-five miles or more over ice and snow by dogsled to a promising forest, and it was a heroic journey indeed. Pioneers with enough stamina to make such a sentimental trip had to start about December 10 in order to be back a day or so before Christmas. The spruces they sought were five to ten feet high. At Nome in 1900 they sold for $5.00 to $25.00 each, a tidy sum even by the inflated values of a gold camp.

As elsewhere on the edge of civilization, stores were few and Nome had no toys to sell. Mothers, who were even rarer than Christmas trees, made rag dolls for their even scarcer little girls.

The few children of gold-rush Nome were not forgotten, however. Many of these were little Eskimos who came to town for the occasion. At the church they attended a festival in their honor, saw their first tree, as mission visitors had done a few years earlier in other outposts, and wondered at the decorations in the forms of paper flowers. Like the Indians at Wrangell, they received their first gifts from white men. Eskimo children on the Kowak River in 1898 got for their Christmas some dolls turned out on the lathe of an enterprising gold hunter. While this young fellow was cutting dolls, another goodhearted lad from California was painting on the faces. He was even considerate enough to make the eyes almond-shaped and the noses flat, just like those of the little boys and girls for whom they were meant.

Keepers of diaries, if they had little imagination, might record a typical Nome Christmas Eve temperature of twenty-eight degrees below zero. But others would remember that, even so, the local church was crowded. A Jesuit brother left us, not a monotony of weather reports, but a vignette of a Nativity commemoration in a gathering made warm by about equal parts of physical activity and simple kindliness:

The Sisters of Providence had decorated the sanctuary with green boughs, brought from the nearest forest, seventy-five miles away, and for the first time in this extreme end of the western world, the Infant Saviour, lying in His manger of Arctic moss, stretched out His tiny arms to bless all who knelt before Him. . . .

Santa Claus, stout and hearty as usual, with kindness in his eyes and snowdrifts on his eyebrows, came tripping over the Arctic hills, carrying his bundles of good things. But he did not come alone. Three lively, kicking reindeer, with their merry bells jingling in the frosty air, brought the old gentle-man in his poulkeh across the hardened snow crust, to spread joy and sweet meats among the astonished school-children. The reindeer feature had been kept quite secret, and never did I witness such enthusiasm as lighted up the expectant and de-lighted little sea of faces when the cry, "Here he comes! here he comes!" was heard, and jolly old Santa and his reindeer drove up to our door. Reindeer are quite gentle, I am told, and not at all demonstrative, but the shouting and enthusiasm of the Nome children were too much for their nerves. They skipped and jumped about, turned to the right and then to the left. They raised their noble antlers, sniffed the air, wondering, no doubt, whether all this Christmas excitement meant peace or war, and finally, they made a desperate effort to get away. It took the united efforts of Santa Claus and his Lapland driver to hold them back.

This unforgettable Yuletide "premiere" of the reindeer occurred only five years after the United States government had introduced these animals into Alaska as an experiment. At the time they were rare, unique to most Eskimo eyes, as indeed was their theoretical neighbor, Santa.

Wherever one lived, Christmas dinner was a real problem in frontier Alaska. Strange as it may seem, with powdered water all around them, Northland cooks had a problem that only settlers in the deserts and the driest of the plains had encountered—lack of water! This valuable commodity cost twenty-five cents a can and was delivered to the cabin door almost solidly frozen. Then came the task of thaw-ing, and this took time and became one of the big-gest—and most regular—of domestic tasks. It was the inevitable headache for anyone planning a big meal, such as Christmas dinner, since eggs, butter, potatoes, onions, and apples also came frozen, and the main job of making a plum pudding was the thawing out of the ingredients. Eggs were not only frozen, but they were expensive. A dollar a dozen was average, a notoriously high price for eggs anywhere else under Old Glory at the century's turn. Butter was seventy-five cents a pound, while coal cost $100 a ton, or more. Turkey at Nome, was, of course, the traditional *piece de resistance,* and brought seventy-five cents to a dollar a pound, and for cold-storage meat at that. The thawing of this noble American bird required ten hours. Fortunately, the blessings of the American canning industry had developed far enough by that time to enable the perplexed housewife on the last frontier to serve vegetables and some common fruits.

Farsighted homemakers in gold-rush Alaska could decorate their cabins with the ferns and vines that they had thoughtfully gathered and pressed in the autumn. The most glorious ornamentation for Christmas, however, was provided by Nature, and unlike everything else, cost not a cent. Only three hours after noon the sun set and Christmas night had come. Now one needed only to step outside his door and behold. More beautiful than the hard-got tree, more splendid yet than the presents, and probably much more satisfying than even the rare and expensive dinner was the majesty of the northern lights, like the glory of the angels of the first Noel, praising their Creator.

CHAPTER XVII

Holiday Gift from the Pioneers

IT IS impossible to conceive of a pioneer without vision, of a frontiersman without his store of hopes, plans, and good works for the future. The wilderness of the American West was conquered only by those who lived partly in tomorrow. In keeping with this philosophy, the pioneers' great day, Christmas, was not observed merely for the moment. We have seen that as an amalgam of the happy and the holy it was often a storehouse of morale for the hard winter ahead.

Strange indeed would it have been if such an important asset to Western society and development had not survived the short future of the pioneer generations and flourished in the larger future of today's America. Fortunately, it has survived, and it has flourished. The modern West retains many gifts from the pioneer Christmas keepers.

First of all, Christmas itself became a legal holiday through their efforts. Westerners were early in proclaiming it officially. Alabama had been the first state to do this, in 1836, and only two years later Louisiana and Arkansas followed the example, as did California the year after its statehood, 1851. Nevada, Colorado, Minnesota, Montana, Nebraska, the Dakotas, Arizona, Utah, Wyoming, Washington, and Oklahoma did not even wait for the end of territorial government to legalize Christmas.

Even earlier, the glory of Yuletide had been written, perhaps imperishably, on the maps of the West. Lately, a growing group of historians has attempted to trace the past of a given area through its place names. If this can be done thoroughly and with significant results, then the importance of Christmas in Western history will be even better appreciated. There are many dramatic examples of how Christmas got on the map, and almost all of them carry a warm, human anecdote, a capsule-size story of man's achievements against Nature's barricade of handicaps. Christmas was not written on the face of the American West by a soft white hand guiding a gilded plume, but was scrawled by the rough paw of the scarred seeker of knowledge and treasure. For instance, let us look into the history of Christmas Lake in today's Lake County, Oregon. This small body of water east of Fort Rock is known to many in the Pacific Northwest, but it was on the edge of nowhere little more than a century ago. In 1838 Christmas River had been named in that country, probably by the Hudson's Bay fur men. Their brigades were scouting out central Oregon as early as 1825. Another pioneer, this one seeking to solve the mysteries of Western geography, reached that section on Christmas Eve of 1843. This was John C. Fremont, on his second exploring expedition. He arrived in Warner Valley and named the body of water he found there Christmas Lake. In this case, the name did not stick, for it is today's Hart Lake.

There are other places named for Christmas by discoverers who happened to reach them on the holiday. One may note the Christmas Mountains in the lower Rio Grande Valley of Texas. Christmas also gave its honorable name to a number of mining strikes. The expedition of Dr. Samuel Gregg George, of Visalia, California, visited Death Valley in 1860. On Christmas Day George's party crossed into Wild Rose Canyon near the Death Valley National Monument summer headquarters of today. There the explorers discovered a deposit of antimony ore which they thereupon christened the "Christmas Gift Lode." It became a profitable holiday present, the first mining claim to be located in the Panamints, a range also named during the expedition by George for the Indian tribe inhabiting the valley to the west.

The famous Christmas Mine of Arizona, a copper strike in the Gila Valley, earned more for its stockholders than had been expected. The town of Christmas, Arizona, now no longer in existence, was christened in December, 1902, when news that the San Carlos Indian Reservation's bounds had been changed was wired to George Crittenden and N. H. Mellor, two prospectors who rushed to the copper claims in this area and named the townsite for the day of their arrival.

Still, words in old atlases and gazetteers are only a means of passing entertainment for most Westerners busy with their twentieth-century chores. The old-time Christmas would hardly be worth remembering if that is all it bequeathed us. A good story never really dies, and the frontier West was full of good stories. It was a "natural" that when the rugged regionalism of frontier themes was combined with the ancient Christmas story, good listening and good reading often would result. All that was needed was a good storyteller, and the early West produced more than its share of these. The Western Christmas in American literature deserves a volume of its own, for it covered the field of the written word—poetry and prose, truth and fiction, and that borderland of both, novelized history. Among those who made such letters live were the fiction writers Marshall Graham, H. Elton Smith, J. Torrey Connor, and others who wrote of Christmas as they had experienced it. Their chief outlet was the *Overland Monthly,* the best literary journal of the early Pacific Coast. One of the *Overland's* editors and its greatest contributor, Bret Harte, also touched on pioneer Christmases in several of his short stories. His contemporary and fellow prospector in the treasure hills of mining-camp literature was Mark Twain. Twain, too, could not resist the urge to exploit the dramatic possibilities of Christmas. Edward Rowland Sill, California poet of the late nineteenth century, wrote "Christmas in California," one of his better works.

There have not been many illustrations made on the spot of early Christmases beyond the Mississippi, but there is one outstanding exception, the work of Remington. Frederic Remington was probably the

West's greatest depicter. Almost annually during the nineties he sketched or painted a typical Western Christmas celebration in camp, on the range, or high in the mountains. Seeing his pictures in magazine or gallery, Easterners had a graphic view of the mythical, magical West, and perhaps some of them longed for the strange ways holidays were observed a thousand miles from where the sidewalks ended.

Slowly, subtly, the twentieth century has dissolved, or at the least greatly minimized, American regionalism. Of course, the West still has a flavor of its own, but perhaps that savor has become more a state of mind than it has remained clear-cut evidence of a genuine type. Certainly Americans have grown increasingly more standardized, more uniform in their ways of living and working, and even thinking, at about the same rate that consumer goods in this industrialized age have become more standardized. Still, the West has retained some aspects of noncomformity, if not of downright uniqueness. There are still a few regional Christmas festivals. Most of these are not based upon any particular Western beliefs about Christmas, or dietary differences, but rather take advantage of the West's eternal asset, the great outdoors, dressed by its Maker on a grander scale than most other areas of the continent can boast. At Yosemite, and among the redwoods of the Russian River, special ceremonies have been held. It is appropriate that the West, where outdoor living was once a necessity and now is a pleasant adjunct to workaday existence, should sponsor a back-to-nature sort of Yuletide. This is especially apropos since the first Christmas was more or less observed in the open.

The modern West contributes to Christmas in still another way. It gives America most of its Christmas trees. At Kalispell in the Flathead National Forest the little town of Eureka, Montana, became in the 1950's the "Christmas tree capital of the world." As it is on the main line of the Great Northern Railway, the community has been able late each fall to ship more holiday trees than come from any other state. For the most part, these are hemlock and fir, and they are grown on Christmas-tree "ranches" where seedlings are set out. These may seem strange ranches indeed. At first thought we might conclude that it is far from the wildest dreams of the pioneers of a century ago, but then, remembering their own ingenuity for observing Yuletide, we might easily agree that, given time and a few modern tools, they would have hit upon the same idea. Other modern Westerners, true heirs of the old-timers who liked to make the most of their opportunities, especially at Christmas time, are today making a lot more than just pocket money by gathering and preserving ferns and other greenery which are shipped all over the country for holiday use. Here is a new big business, spurred by those who are not afraid of the future.

Almost everywhere we discovered that early Christmases were noted for an abundance of valuable natural resources—plenty of game, often limitless

The Modern West as the Pioneers Never Saw It

supplies of wood and water. Being common, these treasures were extravagantly and dramatically used. What was not eaten was wasted. The strangeness of new surroundings added to the excitement of the holiday, and the awed accounts of the participants even inspire like sentiments in readers today. Yet though it could be lavishly supplied with savage splendor in fur man's camp or Plains Indian village, the pioneer Christmas in a settler's cabin could be as barren as the former was abundant. Pared down to the simple necessities of survival, the frontier family saved to make their Christmas special, and they came to appreciate the little things that we take for granted.

Yet all these characteristics—the newness of surroundings, the extravagance with raw resources, and the careful, ingenious preparing for the holiday—all disappeared with the frontier. Buffalo meat and bear flesh are no longer served; the white man's holy day is no longer observed with ignorant curiosity by the Indian first encountering a new culture and a strange race. Neither does the foreigner, just arrived from Europe to wield the miner's pick, lift the railroad tie, or guide the plow, add his quaint Old World customs. Long since he has been amalgamated in America's efficient and inevitable melting pot. All these elements, which at first appeared eternally incompatible, but which made Western Christmases so different from those to the East, have at last passed away. They have left a folklore and the permanent memory that written records keep accurate after human remembrance begins to play tricks. Christmas in the West, at least on the surface, is today little different from the holly-wreathed celebration in Boston or Birmingham. Yet it is not the material side of the holiday, though that helped, that the pioneers would have had us remember best.

Today, we seem farther removed from the gold seekers and fur trappers than they were from Columbus. But like Columbus they were bearers of a heritage which could only be kept alive by being added to. In basic situations, we are actually very close to both Columbus and the Western pioneers, for we are the trail blazers on the frontiers of the Atomic and the Space ages. Therefore it is good to remember that Christianity is a frontier, too. It must ever be a new challenge or it no longer will serve its Founder's purpose.

Long after we have forgotten the quaintness and humor of our predecessors' wonderful, irretrievable holidays we will be able to find ways to profit by their lesson. Their ingenuity, patience, and optimism shine brighter than the tallow candles which they molded so skillfully. Pioneer faces that could smile on Christmas when that day was only a slice of light between two periods of privation and danger are the lasting gifts the first Western Christmas makers have left for us. And, after all, what better presents have there ever been on Christmas than those from heart to heart?

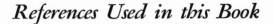

References Used in this Book

The sources used in this work are listed below under the chapter to which they refer. The order in which they appear is the same as that in which the material is discussed in the particular chapter. The pages noted are those which contained information pertinent to the Christmas celebrations discussed above.

NOTES FOR CHAPTER I

Edward Everett Hale. "The Same Christmas in Old England and New," *Galaxy* (New York), V (January, 1868), 47-59.

Abram English Brown. "The Ups and Downs of Christmas in New England," *New England Magazine* (Boston), N.S. XXIX (December, 1903), 479-84.

Martha J. Lamb. "Christmas Season in Dutch New York," *Magazine of American History* (New York), X (December, 1883), 471-74.

J. H. Dubbs. "Christmas Among the Pennsylvania Germans," *Pennsylvania German* (Lancaster), XII (December, 1911), 705-7.

George W. Ranck. *Boonesborough: Its Founding.* Louisville: The Filson Club, 1901, pp. 46 and 125.

Richard Flower. *Letters from Lexington and the Illinois, 1819.* ("Early Western Travels Series," ed. Reuben Gold Thwaites, Vol. X.) Cleveland: The Arthur H. Clark Co., 1904, pp. 123-24.

William Faux. *Faux's Journal, 1818-1820.* ("Early Western Travels Series," ed. Reuben Gold Thwaites, Vol. XI.) Cleveland: The Arthur H. Clark Co., 1905, p. 300.

NOTES FOR CHAPTER II

Elizabeth Thérése Baird. "Reminiscences of Early Days on Mackinac Island." (*Wisconsin Historical Collections,* ed. Lyman Copeland Draper, Vol. XIV.) Madison: Wisconsin Historical Society, 1908, pp. 20-21.

Albert G. Ellis. "Fifty-four Years' Recollections of Men and Events in Wisconsin." (*Wisconsin Historical Collections,* ed. Lyman Copeland Draper, Vol. VII.) Madison: Wisconsin Historical Society, 1908, pp. 263-64.

Walter Prescott Webb. "Christmas and New Year in Texas," *Southwestern Historical Quarterly* (Austin, Texas), XLIV (January, 1941), 357-58.

Norman McF. Walker. "The Holidays in Early Louisiana," *Magazine of American History* (New York), X (December, 1883), 460-66.
Mary S. Helm. *Scraps of Early Texas History.* Austin, Texas: Privately printed, 1884, pp. 27 and 33.

NOTES FOR CHAPTER III

Ina Sizer Cassidy. "Christmas in New Mexico," *El Palacio* (Santa Fe, New Mexico), LVII (December, 1950), 402-6.
Lillian H. Wistrand. "Strange Christmas Celebrations," *Pony Express Courier* (Placerville, California), XIX, No. 7 (December, 1952), 7.
Elsie Clews Parsons. "Isleta, New Mexico," *Bureau of American Ethnology 47th Annual Report, 1929-1930* (Washington, D.C., 1932), pp. 303-6.
Leslie A. White. "The Acoma Indians," *ibid.,* p. 106.
George C. Sibley. *The Road to Santa Fe: The Journal and Diaries of George Champlin Sibley,* ed. Kate L. Gregg. Albuquerque: University of New Mexico Press, 1952, p. 134.
William H. Emory. "Notes of a Military Reconnoissance, from Fort Leavenworth, in Missouri, to San Diego, in California, including Part of the Arkansas, Del Norte, and Gila Rivers," *House Executive Document 41* (serial 517), 30th Cong., 1st sess., 1847-1848, p. 512.
Randolph B. Marcy. *Thirty Years of Army Life on the Border.* New York: Harper & Bros., 1866, p. 103. P. G. S. Ten Broeck is quoted herein.
John Udell. *John Udell Journal: Kept during a Trip across the Plains, Containing an Account of the Massacre of a Portion of His Party by the Mojave Indians in 1859,* ed. Lyle H. Wright. Los Angeles: N. A. Kovach, 1946, pp. 62-63.
"Notes and Documents: Letters of Rev. Jacob Mills Ashley, 1887-1888," *New Mexico Historical Review* (Albuquerque), XXIV (April, 1949), 158.
Mrs. I. H. Rapp. "Los Pastores Is Gem of Miracle Plays," *El Palacio* (Santa Fe), XI (December, 1921), 151-63.
Cleve Hallenbeck and Juanita H. Williams. *Legends of the Spanish Southwest.* Glendale, California: The Arthur H. Clark Co., 1938, pp. 119-26.
George W. Kendall. *Narrative of an Expedition across the Great South-Western Prairies, from Texas to Santa Fe.* 2 vols. London: David Bogue, 1845, II, 133.
Bernice Cosulich. "Christmas Eve at San Xavier," *Arizona Highways* (Phoenix), XVII (December, 1941), 12-15.
Edward H. Spicer. *Pascua: A Yaqui Village in Arizona.* Chicago: University of Chicago Press, 1940, p. 215.

NOTES FOR CHAPTER IV

Herbert Eugene Bolton. *Fray Juan Crespí, Missionary Explorer on the Pacific*

Coast, 1769-1774. Berkeley: University of California Press, 1927, pp. 258-59.

Pedro Font. *Font's Complete Diary: A Chronicle of the Founding of San Francisco,* trans. and ed. Herbert Eugene Bolton. Berkeley: University of California Press, 1933, pp. 149-50.

James Culleton. *Indians and Pioneers of Old Monterey.* Fresno: Academy of California Church History, 1950, pp. 10-11, 60, and 67.

(Zephyrin) Charles Anthony Engelhardt. *The Missions and Missionaries of California.* 4 vols. San Francisco: The James H. Barry Co., 1908-16, II, 256.

Nellie Van de Grift Sánchez. *Spanish Arcadia.* (Series "California," ed. John Russell McCarthy.) Los Angeles: Powell Publishing Co., 1929, p. 308.

William E. Smythe. *History of San Diego, 1542-1908.* 2 vols. San Diego: The History Co., 1908, I, 152-53.

Chester S. Lyman. *Around the Horn to the Sandwich Islands and California, 1845-1850,* ed. Frederick J. Teggart. New Haven: Yale University Press, 1924, p. 246.

Maymie R. Krythe. "Daily Life in Early Los Angeles, Part II, Holiday Celebrations," *Historical Society of Southern California Quarterly* (Los Angeles), XXXVI (June, 1954), 125-27.

NOTES FOR CHAPTER V

John Boit. *A New Log of the Columbia,* ed. Edmond S. Meany. Seattle: University of Washington Press, 1921, p. 20.

Meriwether Lewis and William Clark. *The Journals of Lewis and Clark,* ed. Bernard De Voto. Boston: Houghton Mifflin Co., 1953, pp. 74 and 294-95.

Zebulon Montgomery Pike. *Zebulon Pike's Arkansaw Journal,* eds. Stephen Harding Hart and Archer Butler Hulbert. 2 vols. Denver: Denver Public Library, 1932, I, 146-49.

Herbert Bashford and Harr Wagner. *A Man Unafraid: The Story of John C. Frémont.* San Francisco: Harr Wagner Co., 1927, p. 102.

Effie Mona Mack. *Nevada: A History of the State from the Earliest Times through the Civil War.* Glendale, California: The Arthur H. Clark Co., 1936, p. 83.

James H. Simpson. *Report of Explorations across the Great Basin of the Territory of Utah for a Direct Wagon-Route from Camp Floyd to Genoa, in Carson Valley in 1859.* Washington: Government Printing Office, 1876. Appendix Q contains "Journal of Mr. Edward M. Kern of an Exploration of the Mary's or Humboldt River, Carson Lake, and Owens River and Lake, in 1845," pp. 483-84.

Amiel Weeks Whipple. *A Pathfinder in the Southwest: The Itinerary of Lieutenant A. W. Whipple during His Explorations for a Railway Route from Fort Smith to Los Angeles in the Years 1853 and 1854,* ed. Grant

Foreman. Norman, Oklahoma: University of Oklahoma Press, 1941, pp. 170-72.

Balduin Möllhausen. *Diary of a Journey from the Mississippi to the Coasts of the Pacific with a United States Government Expedition*, trans. by Mrs. Percy Sinnett. 2 vols. London: Longman, Brown, Green, Longmans & Roberts, 1858, II, 148-53.

NOTES FOR CHAPTER VI

James B. Marsh. *Four Years in the Rockies; or, the Adventures of Isaac P. Rose*. New Castle, Pennsylvania: W. B. Thomas, 1884, pp. 214-15.

Edwin James. *Account of Stephen H. Long's Expedition, 1819-1820*. Part I. ("Early Western Travels Series," ed. Reuben Gold Thwaites, Vol. XIV.) Cleveland: The Arthur H. Clark Co., 1905, p. 274.

Maximilian, Prince of Wied. *Travels in the Interior of North America in the Years 1832-1834*. ("Early Western Travels Series," ed. Reuben Gold Thwaites, Vol. XXIV.) Cleveland: The Arthur H. Clark Co., 1906, p. 48.

Charles Larpenteur. *Forty Years a Fur Trader on the Upper Missouri*, ed. Milo Milton Quaife. Chicago: The Lakeside Press, 1933, pp. 134-35.

Ross Cox. *The Columbia River: or, Scenes and Adventures during a Residence of Six Years on the Western Side of the Rocky Mountains*. 2 vols. London: Henry Colburn and Richard Bentley, 1832, I, 178.

Peter Skene Ogden. *Peter Skene Ogden's Snake Country Journals, 1824-25 and 1825-26*, ed. E. E. Rich. London: HBC Record Society, 1950, pp. 7 and 108.

Rufus B. Sage. *Rocky Mountain Life; or, Startling Scenes and Perilous Adventures in the Far West*. New York: R. Worthington Co., 1884, p. 113.

George Bird Grinnell. *Beyond the Old Frontier: Adventures of Indian-Fighters, Hunters, and Fur-Traders*. New York: Charles Scribner's Sons, 1926, p. 293.

William S. Brackett. "Bonneville and Bridger," *Contributions to the Historical Society of Montana* (Helena), III (1900), 192.

Warren Angus Ferris. *Life in the Rocky Mountains*, ed. Paul C. Phillips. Denver: The Old West Publishing Co., 1940, pp. 189-91, and 238.

Rudolph Friederich Kurz. *Journal of Rudolph Friederich Kurz: An Account of His Experiences among Fur Traders and American Indians on the Mississippi and the Upper Missouri Rivers during the Years 1846 to 1852*, trans. by Myrtis Jarrell and ed. by J. N. B. Hewitt. ("Bureau of American Ethnology Publications," Bulletin 115.) Washington, D.C.: Smithsonian Institution, 1937, p. 250.

Frederick Gerstaecker. *Wild Sports in the Far West*. Boston: Crosby, Nichols & Co., 1859, pp. 282-83.

Gabriel Franchère. *Narrative of a Voyage to the Northwest Coast of America in the Years 1811, 1812, 1813, and 1814*. New York: Redfield, 1854, p. 143.

Balduin Möllhausen. *Diary of a Journey from the Mississippi to the Coasts of the Pacific with a United States Government Expedition*, trans. by

Mrs. Percy Sinnett. 2 vols. London: Longman, Brown, Green, Longmans & Roberts, 1858, I, 146-47.

David Thompson. *David Thompson's Journals Relating to Montana and Adjacent Regions, 1808-1812*, ed. M. Catherine White. Missoula: Montana State University Press, 1950, pp. 74 and 190.

"Journal of Occurrences at Nisqually House, 1833," ed. Clarence B. Bagley, *Washington Historical Quarterly* (Seattle), VI (October, 1915), 273.

"The Nisqually Journal," ed. Victor J. Farrar, *Washington Historical Quarterly*, XI (January, 1920), 140.

Hubert Howe Bancroft. *History of Oregon.* ("The Works of Hubert Howe Bancroft," Vol. XXIX.) 2 vols. San Francisco: The History Co., I, 578.

Clinton A. Snowden. *History of Washington: The Rise and Progress of an American State.* 4 vols. New York: The Century History Co., 1909, II, 406-7.

Samuel Parker. *Journal of an Exploring Tour Beyond the Rocky Mountains.* Ithaca, New York: Privately printed, 1840, pp. 189-90.

Where Rolls the Oregon: Prophet and Pessimist Look Northwest, ed. Archer Butler Hulbert. Denver: The Stewart Commission of Colorado College and the Denver Public Library, 1933, pp. 212-13.

Paul Kane. *Wanderings of an Artist Among the Indians of North America.* London: Longman, Brown, Green, Longmans & Roberts, 1859, pp. 374-78.

Osborne Russell. *Journal of a Trapper; or, Nine Years in the Rocky Mountains, 1834-1843.* Portland: Oregon Historical Society, 1950, pp. 114-15.

NOTES FOR CHAPTER VII

Alfred S. Waugh. *Travels in Search of the Elephant: The Wanderings of Alfred S. Waugh, Artist, in Louisiana, Missouri, and Santa Fe, in 1845-1846*, ed. John Francis McDermott. St. Louis: Missouri Historical Society, 1951, pp. 76-77.

Mary Alicia Owen. "Social Customs and Usages in Missouri during the Last Century," *Missouri Historical Review* (St. Louis), XV (October, 1920), 176-90.

Cora Call Whitley. "A Pioneer Christmas Tree," *The Palimpsest* (Iowa City, Iowa), XVIII (December, 1937), 381-88.

William J. Petersen. "The Pioneer Cabin," *Iowa Journal of History and Politics* (Iowa City, Iowa), XXXVI (October, 1938), 408.

O. J. Felton. "Pioneer Life in Jones County," *Iowa Journal of History and Politics*, XXIX (April, 1931), 262-63.

"Christmas in Iowa," *The Palimpsest* (Iowa City, Iowa), XVI (December, 1935), 383-86.

Bertha L. Heilbron. "Christmas and New Year's on the [Minnesota] Frontier," *Minnesota History* (St. Paul), XVI (December, 1935), 373-90.

"Kansas Chronology," *Collections* of the Kansas State Historical Society (Topeka), XII (1911-12), 424.

"A Southerner's Viewpoint of the Kansas Situation, 1856-1857; The Letters of Lt. Col. A. J. Hoole, C. S. A.," ed. William Stanley Hoole, *Kansas Historical Quarterly* (Topeka), III (May, 1934), 153.

Cyrus R. Rice. "Experiences of a Pioneer Missionary," *Collections* of the Kansas State Historical Society (Topeka), XIII (1913-14), 305.

George Douglas Brewerton. *The War in Kansas.* New York: Derley & Jackson, 1856, pp. 203-6.

C. E. Cory. "The Osage Ceded Lands," *Transactions* of the Kansas State Historical Society (Topeka), VIII (1903-4), 195.

Percy G. Ebbutt. *Emigrant Life in Kansas.* London: Swan Sonnenschein & Co., 1886, pp. 76-77.

Hezekiah Brake. *On Two Continents: A Long Life's Experience.* Topeka: Crane & Co., 1896, p. 223.

Francis S. Laing, O. M. Cap., "German-Russian Settlements in Ellis County, Kansas," *Collections* of the Kansas State Historical Society (Topeka), XI (1909-1910), 518.

Marie A. Olson. "Swedish Settlement at Stotler," *Kansas Historical Quarterly* (Topeka), IV (May, 1935), 155-56.

Everett Dick. *The Sod-House Frontier, 1854-1890.* Lincoln, Nebraska: Johnsen Publishing Co., 1954, pp. 62 and 382.

Louise Pond. "Old Nebraska Folk Customs," *Nebraska History* (Lincoln), XXVIII (January-March, 1947), 9.

S. Hermann. "Bellevue and Fort Calhoun [Nebraska]," *The Spirit of the Missions* (New York), XXX (March, 1865), 96.

Permelia Corey Thompson. *How the Coreys Went West.* San Diego, California: Frye & Smith Press, 1908, pp. 115-16.

William R. Lighton. "Christmas When the West Was Young," *Ladies' Home Journal* (Philadelphia), XXX (December, 1913), 12 and 64.

James Grassick. "One Christmas Eve," *North Dakota Historical Quarterly* (Bismarck), IX (October, 1941), 21-26.

Moses K. Armstrong. "Early Sketches of Pioneer Legislatures and Indian Wars," in *The Early Empire Builders of the Great West.* St. Paul, Minnesota: E. W. Porter, 1901, p. 92.

Ernest V. Sutton. *A Life Worth Living.* Pasadena, California: Trail's End Publishing Co., Inc., 1948, pp. 72-73.

NOTES FOR CHAPTER VIII

William Ransom Hogan. *The Texas Republic: A Social and Economic History.* Norman: University of Oklahoma Press, 1946, pp. 114-15.

Gustav Dresel. *Gustav Dresel's Houston Journal: Adventures in North America and Texas, 1837-1841,* trans. by Max Freund. Austin: University of Texas Press, 1954, pp. 41 and 90-91.

William Bollaert. *William Bollaert's Texas,* ed. W. Eugene Hollon and Ruth Lapham Butler. Norman: University of Oklahoma Press, 1956, pp. 293-95.

"Diary of Adolphus Sterne," ed. Harriet Smither, *Southwestern Historical Quarterly* (Austin, Texas), XXXV (July, 1931), 80.

William A. McClintock. "Journal of a Trip through Texas and Northern Mexico in 1846-1847," *Southwestern Historical Quarterly,* XXXIV (January, 1931), 249.

Walter Prescott Webb. "Christmas and New Year in Texas," *Southwestern Historical Quarterly,* XLIV (January, 1941), 357-79.

R. L. Biesele. "Prince Solms's Trip to Texas, 1844-1845," *Southwestern Historical Quarterly,* XL (July, 1936), 20.

Emmanuel Henri Dieudonné Domenech. *Missionary Adventures in Texas and Mexico: A Personal Narrative of Six Years' Sojourn in Those Regions.* London: Longman, Brown, Green, Longmans & Roberts, 1858, pp. 128, 186-87, and 350-51.

Cecil Roberts. *Adrift in America; or, Work and Adventure in the States.* London: Lawrence & Bullen, 1891, pp. 125-27.

James S. Hogg in "The First Christmas That I Remember," Los Angeles (California) *Times,* December 24, 1893.

Frederick Law Olmsted. *A Journey through Texas* (New York: Dix, Edwards & Co., 1857, pp. 68-69.

NOTES FOR CHAPTER IX

Chester S. Lyman. *Around the Horn to the Sandwich Islands and California, 1845-1850,* ed. Frederick J. Teggart, New Haven: Yale University Press, 1924, p. 287.

Francis D. Clark. "Christmas Night, 1848," San Jose (California) *Pioneer,* XII, January 15, 1897, p. 2.

James Clyman: American Frontiersman, 1792-1881, ed. Charles L. Camp. San Francisco: California Historical Society, 1928, p. 239.

Anson S. Blake. "An Early Day California Letter from Charles T. Blake," *Quarterly* of the Society of California Pioneers (San Francisco), VII (March, 1930), 25.

Mary Bennett Ritter. *More Than Gold in California, 1849-1933.* Berkeley: Professional Press, 1933, pp. 40-41.

William Wellington White. "An Autobiography," *Quarterly* of the Society of California Pioneers (San Francisco), IV (December, 1927), 211.

William Kelly. *An Excursion to California over the Prairie, Rocky Mountains, and Great Sierra Nevada.* 2 vols. London: Chapman & Hall, 1851, II, 153-56.

William Downie. *Hunting for Gold: Reminiscences of Personal Experience and Research in the Early Days of the Pacific Coast from Alaska to Panama.* San Francisco: California Publishing Co., 1893, pp. 66 and 69.

John W. Audubon. *Audubon's Western Journal, 1849-1850,* ed. Frank Heywood Hodder. Cleveland: The Arthur H. Clark Co., 1906, p. 193.

William S. Jewett. "Some Letters of William S. Jewett, California Artist," ed. Elliott Evans, *California Historical Society Quarterly* (San Francisco), XXIII (June, 1944), 157-58.

Samuel C. Upham. *Notes of a Voyage to California via Cape Horn.* Philadelphia: Privately printed, 1878, p. 265.

"History of San Jose," San Jose (California) *Pioneer*, I, January 27, 1877, p. 4.

Ida Pfeiffer. *A Lady's Visit to California, 1853*. Oakland: Biobooks, 1950, p. 68.

Garrett W. Low. *Gold Rush by Sea;* ed. Kenneth Haney. Philadelphia: University of Pennsylvania Press, 1941, pp. 17-20.

Enos Christman. *One Man's Gold: The Letters & Journal of a Forty-Niner;* ed. Florence Morrow Christman. New York: Whittlesey House, McGraw-Hill Book Co., 1930, pp. 66-67.

"Sea Voyage by a Forty-Niner," ed. Sylvia F. Roper, *Mississippi Valley Historical Review* (Cedar Rapids, Iowa; Lincoln, Nebraska), XXVIII (December, 1941), 415.

William Graham Johnston. *Overland to California*. Pittsburgh, Privately printed, 1892, p. 222.

Owen C. Coy. "The Last Expedition of Josiah Gregg," *Southwestern Historical Quarterly* (Austin, Texas), XX (July, 1916), 47-48.

William Lewis Manly. *Death Valley in '49*. San Jose, California: The Pacific Tree & Vine Co., 1894, p. 137.

J. Goldsborough Bruff. *Gold Rush: The Journals, Drawings, and Other Papers of J. Goldsborough Bruff;* ed. Georgia Willis Read and Ruth Gaines. 2 vols. New York: Columbia University Press, 1944, II, 673-75.

Lorenzo D. Aldrich. *A Journal of the Overland Route to California and the Gold Mines*. Los Angeles: Dawson's Book Shop, 1950, p. 71.

David Rohrer Leeper. *The Argonauts of 'Forty-Nine: Some Recollections of the Plains and the Diggings*. South Bend, Indiana: J. B. Stoll & Co., 1894, p. 135.

Nelson Kingsley. *Diary of Nelson Kingsley, a California Argonaut of 1849;* ed. Frederick J. Teggart. ("Publications of the Academy of Pacific Coast History," Vol. III, No. 3.) Berkeley: University of California Press, 1914, p. 163.

Walter Griffith Pigman. *The Journal of Walter Griffith Pigman;* ed. Ulla Staley Fawkes. Mexico, Missouri: Walter G. Staley, 1942, p. 49.

Chauncey L. Canfield. *The Diary of a Forty-Niner* [Alfred T. Jackson]; ed. Chauncey L. Canfield. New York and San Francisco: Morgan Shepard, 1906, pp. 127-28.

John Carr. *Pioneer Days in California*. Eureka, California: Times Publishing Co., 1891, pp. 224-25.

Louise Amelia Knapp Smith Clappe. *The Shirley Letters from the California Mines, 1851-1852;* ed. Carl I. Wheat. New York: Alfred A. Knopf, 1949, pp. 51-52 and 103-4.

Lemuel Clarke McKeeby. "The Memoirs of Lemuel Clarke McKeeby," *California Historical Society Quarterly* (San Francisco), III (June, 1924), 128-29.

Rosena A. Giles. *Shasta County, California: A History*. Oakland: Biobooks, 1949, p. 223.

San Francisco *Daily Evening Bulletin*, December 27, 1855, and December 27, 1857.

308   REFERENCES USED

George Tisdale Bromley. *The Long Ago and the Later On; or, Recollections of Eighty Years.* San Francisco: A. M. Robertson, 1904, pp. 34-35.

James F. Rusling. *The Great West and Pacific Coast.* New York: Sheldon & Co., 1877, p. 292.

San Francisco *Daily Evening Bulletin,* December 24, 1859, and December 26, 1856.

William H. Brewer. *Up and Down California in 1860-1864: The Journal of William H. Brewer;* ed. Francis P. Farquhar. Berkeley and Los Angeles: University of California Press, 1949, pp. 20 and 359.

Edwin R. Bingham. *Charles F. Lummis: Editor of the Southwest.* San Marino, California: Henry E. Huntington Library, 1955, p. 82.

Franklin A. Buck. *A Yankee Trader in the Gold Rush: The Letters of Franklin A. Buck;* comp. by Katherine A. White. Boston and New York: Houghton Mifflin Co., 1930, pp. 186 and 210.

Marcia Rittenhouse Wynn. *Pioneer Family of Whiskey Flat.* Los Angeles: Haynes Corporation, 1945, p. 70.

Catherine Coffin Phillips. *Coulterville Chronicle: The Annals of a Mother Lode Mining Town.* San Francisco: The Grabhorn Press, 1942, p. 124.

Bess Adams Garner. *Windows in an Old Adobe.* Pomona, California: Saunders Press & Progress-Bulletin, 1939, p. 117.

William H. Workman. "Olden Time Holiday Festivities," *Publications* of the Historical Society of Southern California (Los Angeles), V, Part I (1900), 23-24.

Harris Newmark. *Sixty Years in Southern California, 1853-1913;* ed. Maurice H. Newmark and Marco R. Newmark. New York: The Knickerbocker Press, 1916, p. 102.

NOTES FOR CHAPTER X

Colorado Gold Rush: Contemporary Letters and Reports, 1858-1859; ed. LeRoy R. Hafen. ("Southwest Historical Series. Vol. X.) Glendale, California: The Arthur H. Clark Co., 1941, pp. 189-98.

Rose Georgina Kingsley. *South by West; or, Winter in the Rocky Mountains and Spring in Mexico;* ed. Charles Kingsley. London: W. Isbister & Co., 1874, pp. 99-101.

Emily Faithfull. *Three Visits to America.* New York: Fowler and Wells Co., 1884, pp. 143-44.

E. Shelton. "The Religious Side of Pioneering in Routt County," *Colorado Magazine* (Denver), VII (November, 1930), 235-41.

Sister Blandina Segale. *At the End of the Santa Fe Trail.* Milwaukee, Wisconsin: Bruce Publishing Co., 1948, pp. 35 and 54-55.

J. S. Campion. *On the Frontier.* London: Chapman & Hall, 1878, p. 146.

Granville Stuart. *Forty Years on the Frontier, as Seen in the Journals and Reminiscences of Granville Stuart;* ed. Paul C. Phillips. 2 vols. Cleveland: The Arthur H. Clark Co.; 1925, I, 192.

Alexander K. McClure. *Three Thousand Miles through the Rocky Mountains.* Philadelphia: J. B. Lippincott Co., 1869, pp. 418-19.

Mrs. Nat Collins. *The Cattle Queen of Montana,* comp. by Charles Wallace. St. James, Minnesota: C. W. Foote, 1894, pp. 170-71.

Julius C. Birge. *The Awakening of the Desert.* Boston: The Gorham Press, 1912, pp. 172-73.

H. G. Merriam. "Ethnic Settlement of Montana," *Pacific Historical Review* (Berkeley and Los Angeles), XII (June, 1943), 161-63.

Caroline Bancroft. "Folklore of the Central City District," *California Folklore Quarterly* (Berkeley and Los Angeles), IV (November, 1945), 339-40.

Mary McNair Mathews. *Ten Years in Nevada; or, Life on the Pacific Coast.* Buffalo, New York: Baker, Jones & Co., 1880, p. 222.

NOTES FOR CHAPTER XI

"Pioneer Celebrations," ed. Kate B. Carter, in *Heart Throbs of the West.* Salt Lake City, Utah, II (1940), 1-16.

Lorenzo Dow Young. "The Diary of Lorenzo Dow Young," *Utah Historical Quarterly* (Salt Lake City), XIV (1946), 164.

Robert S. Bliss. "The Journal of Robert S. Bliss," ed. Mary J. Clawson, *Utah Historical Quarterly,* IV (October, 1931), 127-28.

Thomas H. Haskell. "Journal of Thomas H. Haskell," ed. Juanita Brooks, *Utah Historical Quarterly,* XII (January, 1944), 88.

Elias Smith. "Elias Smith: Journal of a Pioneer Editor," ed. A. R. Mortensen, *Utah Historical Quarterly,* XXI (1953), 242.

Mrs. Benjamin G. Ferris. *The Mormons at Home: With Some Incidents of Travel from Missouri to California, 1852-3, in a Series of Letters.* New York: Dix & Edwards, 1856, p. 131.

Walter Clement Powell. "Journal of Walter Clement Powell," ed. Charles Kelly, *Utah Historical Quarterly,* XVII (1949), 381-82.

John Wesley Clampitt. *Echoes from the Rocky Mountains.* Chicago and New York: Bedford, Clarke & Co., 1889, pp. 353-58.

William Henry Jackson. *Time Exposure: The Autobiography of William Henry Jackson.* New York: G. P. Putnam's Sons, 1940, pp. 146-47.

Kate B. Carter. *Treasures of Pioneer History.* 5 vols. Salt Lake City, Utah: Daughters of Utah Pioneers, 1952, I, 101-29.

Leonard E. Harrington. "Journal of Leonard E. Harrington," *Utah Historical Quarterly,* VIII (January, 1940), 30 and 34.

NOTES FOR CHAPTER XII

Mrs. [Juliette Augusta Magill] John H. Kinzie. *Wau-Bun: The "Early Day" in the Northwest.* Chicago: D. B. Cooke & Co., 1857, pp. 116-18.

New Light on the Early History of the Greater Northwest, ed. Elliott Coues. 3 vols. New York: Francis P. Harper, 1897, I, 192.

Pierre Jean De Smet. *De Smet's Oregon Missions and Travels over the Rocky Mountains, 1845-1846.* ("Early Western Travels Series," ed. Reuben

Gold Thwaites, Vol. XXIX.)   Cleveland: The Arthur H. Clark Co.,
1906, pp. 297-300.

Robert Vaughan. *Then and Now: Thirty-Six Years in the Rockies.* Minne-
apolis: Tribune Printing Co., 1900, p. 211.

Samuel Allis. "Forty Years among the Indians and on the Eastern Borders
of Nebraska," *Transactions and Reports* of the Nebraska State Historical
Society (Lincoln), II (1887), 138.

John Hines. *The Red Indians of the Plains: Thirty Years' Missionary Experience in the Saskatchewan.* London: Society for the Promotion of
Christian Knowledge, 1915, pp. 84-86.

Joy Keve Hauk. "The Story of Gus and Jessie McGaa Craven," *South Dakota
Historical Collections* (Pierre), XXVII (1954), 539.

Katherine Gibson Fougera. *With Custer's Cavalry.* Caldwell, Idaho: The
Caxton Printers, Ltd., 1940, pp. 237-44.

William R. Lighton. "Christmas When the West Was Young," *Ladies' Home
Journal* (Philadelphia), XXX (December, 1913), 64.

George Palmer Putnam. "Christmas on an Indian Reservation," *Travel* (New
York), XV (December, 1909), 135-37.

Francis E. Leupp. "How the Indians Spend Christmas," *Ladies' Home Journal*
(Philadelphia), XXIV (December, 1906), 18.

Charles Wentworth Sarel. "Alaska and Its People," *Westminster Review*
(London), CXXXIX (June, 1893), 621.

NOTES FOR CHAPTER XIII

George Rutledge Gibson. *Journal of a Soldier under Kearny and Doniphan,
1846-1847;* ed. Ralph P. Bieber. ("Southwest Historical Series," Vol.
III.) Glendale, California: The Arthur H. Clark Co., 1935, p. 303.

James G. McCurdy. *By Juan de Fuca's Strait: Pioneering Along the Northwestern Edge of the Continent.* Portland, Oregon: Binfords & Mort,
1937, p. 106.

LeRoy R. Hafen. "The Fort Pueblo Massacre and the Punitive Expedition
against the Utes," *Colorado Magazine* (Denver), IV (March, 1927), 49-58.

Jessamine Slaughter Burgum. *Zezula; or Pioneer Days in the Smoky Water
Country.* Valley City, North Dakota: Gettchell & Nielsen, 1937, p. 31.

John Owen. *The Journals and Letters of Major John Owen, Pioneer of the
Northwest, 1850-1871;* ed. Seymour Dunbar and Paul C. Phillips. 2
vols. New York: Edward Eberstadt, 1927, I, 90, 187, and 228.

Rodney Glisan. *Journal of Army Life.* San Francisco: A. L. Bancroft & Co.,
1874, pp. 64 and 100-101.

Percival G. Lowe. *Five Years a Dragoon, and Other Adventures on the Great
Plains.* Kansas City, Missouri: Franklin Hudson Publishing Co., 1906,
pp. 15-16.

James H. Bradley. "Affairs at Fort Benton, from 1831 to 1869, from Lieutenant [James H.] Bradley's Journal," *Contributions to the Historical
Society of Montana* (Helena), III (1900), 264.

Colonel and Mrs. I. N. Ebey. "Diary of Colonel and Mrs. I. N. Ebey," ed.

Victor J. Farrar, *Washington Historical Quarterly* (Seattle), VIII (1917), 58.

Albert Tracy. "Journal of Captain Albert Tracy, 1858-1860," *Utah Historical Quarterly* (Salt Lake City), XIII (1945), 79-80.

Washington Matthews. "The Diary of Surgeon Washington Matthews, Fort Rice, D. T.," ed. Ray H. Mattison, *North Dakota History* (Bismarck), XXI (January, 1954), 28-29.

H. H. McConnell. *Five Years a Cavalryman; or, Sketches of Regular Army Life on the Texas Frontier, Twenty Odd Years Ago.* Jacksboro, Texas: J. N. Rogers & Co., 1889, p. 42.

Philippe Régis de Trobriand. *Military Life in Dakota: The Journal of Philippe Régis de Trobriand;* ed. and trans. by Lucile M. Kane. St. Paul, Minnesota: Alvord Memorial Commission, 1951, p. 194.

Homer W. Wheeler. *Buffalo Days: Forty Years in the Old West.* Indianapolis, Indiana: Bobbs-Merrill, 1925, p. 326.

Elizabeth B. Custer. *Tenting on the Plains; or, General Custer in Kansas and Texas.* New York: Harper & Bros., 1915, p. 155.

David L. Spotts. *Campaigning with Custer and the Nineteenth Kansas Volunteer Cavalry on the Washita Campaign, 1868-1869;* ed. E. A. Brininstool. Los Angeles: Wetzel Publishing Co., 1928, pp. 87-88.

Ben Arnold. *Rekindling Camp Fires;* ed. Lewis F. Crawford. Bismarck, North Dakota: Capital Book Co., 1926, pp. 64 and 202.

Frederic Remington. *Pony Tracks.* New York: Harper & Bros., 1895, pp. 240-43.

Ferdinand A. Van Ostrand. "Diary of Ferdinand A. Van Ostrand," ed. Russell Reid, *North Dakota Historical Quarterly* (Bismarck), X (April, 1943), 97-98.

F. Stanley [Stanley Francis Louis Crocchiola]. *Fort Union, New Mexico.* Canadian, Texas: The World Press, 1953, pp. 209-11.

NOTES FOR CHAPTER XIV

Philip Ashton Rollins. *The Cowboy: An Unconventional History of Civilization on the Old-Time Cattle Range.* New York: Charles Scribner's Sons, 1936, p. 189.

William Lawrence Chittenden. *Ranch Verses.* New York: G. P. Putnam's Sons, 1895, *passim.*

G. T. T.: *Gone to Texas: Letters from Our Boys;* ed. Thomas Hughes. New York: Macmillan & Co., 1884, pp. 37-38 and 196-97.

"Cattle-Herding in the Great West," *Littell's Living Age* (Boston), XVIII (April, 1877), 127.

James B. Gillett. *Six Years with the Texas Rangers, 1875-1881;* ed. Milo Milton Quaife. New Haven: Yale University Press, 1925, p. 57.

J. Frank Dobie. *A Vaquero of the Brush Country.* Dallas, Texas: The Southwest Press, 1929, p. 162.

Oliver Nelson. *The Cowman's Southwest;* ed. Angie Debo. Glendale, California: The Arthur H. Clark Co., 1953, pp. 188 and 323-24.

William Francis Hooker. *The Prairie Schooner*. Chicago: Saul Bros., 1918, pp. 79-84.

Elinore Pruitt Stewart. *Letters of a Woman Homesteader*. Boston and New York: Houghton Mifflin Co., pp. 64-76.

Joe Koller. "Minnesela Days," *South Dakota Historical Collections* (Pierre), XXIV (1949), 65.

Thomas Thompson Hunter. "Early Days in Arizona," *Arizona Historical Review* (Phoenix), III (April, 1930), 108.

Joseph Schmedding. *Cowboy and Indian Trader*. Caldwell, Idaho: The Caxton Printers, Ltd., 1951, pp. 191-205.

William Francis Hooker. *The Bullwhacker: Adventures of a Frontier Freighter;* ed. Howard R. Driggs. Yonkers-on-Hudson, New York: World Book Co., 1924, pp. 111-18.

William Ernest Youngman. *Gleanings from Western Prairies*. Cambridge, England: Jones and Piggott, 1882, pp. 122-23.

Cyrus Townsend Brady. *Recollections of a Missionary in the Great West* New York: Charles Scribner's Sons, 1900, pp. 163-81.

NOTES FOR CHAPTER XV

Ezra Meeker. *Ox-Team Days on the Oregon Trail*. Yonkers-on-Hudson, New York: World Book Co., 1925, p. 151.

Harriet Nesmith McArthur. "Recollections of the Rickreall," *Oregon Historical Quarterly* (Salem), XXX (December, 1929), 376.

Charles Stevens. "Letters of Charles Stevens. Part V," ed. E. Ruth Rockwood, *Oregon Historical Quarterly*, XXXVI (June, 1937), 186.

T. C. Elliott. "Richard ('Captain Johnny') Grant," *Oregon Historical Quarterly*, XXXIV (March, 1935), 7.

James G. Swan. *The Northwest Coast; or, Three Years' Residence in Washington Territory*. New York: Harper & Bros., 1857, pp. 325-26.

John E. Simon. "William Keil and Communist Colonies," *Oregon Historical Quarterly* (Salem), XXXIV (June, 1935), 127.

George N. Belknap. "McMurtrie's Oregon Imprints: A Supplement," *Oregon Historical Quarterly*, LI (December, 1950), 247. See also, Ruth King, "How Christmas Came to the Klamaths," Klamath Falls *Herald and News*, Klamath Falls, Oregon, December 3, 1947.

Wallis Nash. *Two Years in Oregon*. New York: D. Appleton & Co., 1882, pp. 211-12.

Basil N. Longworth. *The Diary of Basil N. Longworth, Oregon Pioneer*. Portland, Oregon: Historical Records Survey, W.P.A., 1938, p. 65.

Polly McKean Bell. "A Pioneer Woman's Reminiscences of Christmas in the Eighties," *Oregon Historical Quarterly* (Portland), XLIX (December, 1948), 284-96.

Joseph H. Sharp. "Early Schools in Lane County," *Oregon Historical Quarterly*, IV (September, 1903), 268.

Frank C. Lockwood. *Pioneer Days in Arizona: From the Spanish Occupation to Statehood*. New York: The Macmillan Co., 1932, pp. 336-37.

William Curry Holden. *Alkali Trails; or, Social and Economic Movements of the Texas Frontier, 1846-1900.* Dallas: Southwest Press, 1930, p. 179.

William R. Lighton. "Christmas When the West Was Young," *Ladies' Home Journal* (Philadelphia), XXX (December, 1913), 12.

William V. Wells. "Wild Life in Oregon," *Harper's New Monthly Magazine* (New York), XIII (October, 1856), 604.

Louis Albert Banks. *An Oregon Boyhood.* Boston: Lee & Sheppard, 1898, 135-36.

NOTES FOR CHAPTER XVI

Philip Weaver, Jr., "Christmases and Christmases," *Overland Monthly* (San Francisco), Second Ser., XXI (January, 1893), 32-44.

Frederick Whymper. *Travel and Adventure in the Territory of Alaska.* New York: Harper & Bros., 1869, pp. 199-200.

Sheldon Jackson. *Alaska, and Missions on the North Pacific Coast.* New York, Dodd, Mead & Co., 1880, pp. 164-65 and 224.

Anna M. Bugbee. "The Thlinkets of Alaska," *Overland Monthly* (San Francisco), Second Ser., XXII (August, 1893), 193.

Mrs. Eugene S. Willard. *Life in Alaska: Letters of Mrs. Eugene S. Willard;* ed. Eva McLintock. Philadelphia: Presbyterian Board of Education, 1884, pp. 135-36 and 158-59.

Edward James Devine, S.J. *Across Widest America: Newfoundland to Alaska.* New York: Benziger Bros., 1906, pp. 190-91.

Hudson Stuck. *Ten Thousand Miles with a Dog Sled.* New York: Charles Scribner's Sons, 1914, p. 189.

Genevieve Wheeler. "A Christmas Under the Snow," *Ladies' Home Journal* (Philadelphia), XXVI (December, 1908), 19.

Joseph Grinnell. *Gold Hunting in Alaska, as Told by Joseph Grinnell;* ed. Elizabeth Grinnell. Elgin, Illinois: David C. Cook Publishing Co., 1901, p. 44.

Lulu Alice Craig. *Glimpses of Sunshine and Shade in the Far North.* Cincinnati, Ohio: The Editor Publishing Co., 1900, p. 72.

NOTES FOR CHAPTER XVII

James H. Barnett. *The American Christmas: A Study in National Culture.* New York: The Macmillan Co., 1954, pp. 11 and 20.

Lewis A. McArthur. *Oregon Geographic Names.* Portland: Oregon Historical Society, 1952, p. 128.

Carl I. Wheat. "Pioneer Visitors to Death Valley after the Forty-niners," *California Historical Society Quarterly* (San Francisco), XVIII (September, 1939), 201.

Marshall Graham. "A Christmas on the Arkansaw," *Overland Monthly* (San Francisco), Second Ser., XIII (January, 1889), 26-40.

J. Torrey Connor. "Christmas at the Diggins," *Overland Monthly,* Second Ser., XIII (January, 1889), 64-67.

H. Elton Smith. "A Christmas Eve on Hangman's Bar," *Overland Monthly,* Second Ser., XVII (January, 1891), 63-72.

Paul G. Clark. "Christmas Under the Redwoods of California," *Overland Monthly,* Second Ser., XLVI (December, 1905), 534-38.

Eric Thane [Ralph Chester Henry]. *The Majestic Land.* Indianapolis, Indiana: Bobbs-Merrill Co., Inc., 1950, p. 283.

Index